SHAH RUKH
KHAN

SHAH RUKH KHAN

LEGEND ★ ICON ★ STAR

MOHAR BASU

Photographs by
Pradeep Bandekar

HarperCollins *Publishers* India

First published in India by HarperCollins *Publishers* 2024
4th Floor, Tower A, Building No. 10, DLF Cyber City,
DLF Phase II, Gurugram, Haryana – 122002
www.harpercollins.co.in

2 4 6 8 10 9 7 5 3

Copyright © Mohar Basu 2024
Images copyright © Pradeep Bandekar 2024

P-ISBN: 978-93-6569-812-1
E-ISBN: 978-93-6569-033-0

The views and opinions expressed in this book are the author's own and the facts are as reported by her, and the publishers are not in any way liable for the same.

Mohar Basu asserts the moral right
to be identified as the author of this work.

All rights reserved. No part of this publication may be reproduced, stored in a retrieval system, or transmitted, in any form or by any means, electronic, mechanical, photocopying, recording or otherwise, without the prior permission of the publishers.

Typeset in 11/15 Adobe Caslon Pro at
HarperCollins *Publishers* India

Printed and bound at
Thomson Press (India) Ltd

This book is produced from independently certified FSC® paper
to ensure responsible forest management.

To

Everyone who has stopped believing in good things. Here's a modern-day fairy tale about love, hard work, hope and, as Om from Om Shanti Om said, 'happys endings' …

The detailed notes pertaining to this book are available on the HarperCollins *Publishers* India website. Scan this QR code to access the same.

CONTENTS

Prologue ix

1. The Return of the King 3
2. It Takes a Village, Even for a Badshah 25
3. The Big Bombay Dream 43
4. A Love Story for the Ages 65
5. The Anti-Hero 83
6. Everyone Wants a Raj 109
7. The World Is His Oyster 133
8. Shah Rukh Khan: The Man Everyone Loves, and Wants 155
9. Doom of Y2K 187
10. Risk Hai Toh Ishq Hai, Baby 205
11. The Khan Stood Tall 227
12. Picture Abhi Baaki Hai, Mere Dost … 255

Epilogue 281
A Tribute 285
Acknowledgements 287
Notes 291

PROLOGUE

Wednesday, 24 January 2023. 6.17 p.m.

A tweet went up from a handle to its more than 43 million followers: '*Bachpan mein saare filmein single screens par hi dekhi hain. Uska apna hi maza hai. Duas, prarthna aur prayers karta hoon… aap sabko aur mujhe kaamyaabi mile* [We used to watch all films on single-screen theatres when we were young. That is a different kind of fun. I hope and pray that all of us win today].'

Whenever @iamsrk tweets it goes viral, but this one was special. It came with a list of film theatres across the country that had had to shut down during the pandemic. It instantly got 3.4 million views and 72,000 likes. It's almost as if everyone understood that their favourite hero was calling.

That evening, single-screen theatres across India flung open their shutters, taking a gamble on their fortunes once again. There was a sizzle in the air; everyone could feel it.

Just like many other theatres in the country battered by the pandemic, there was one in Kolkata. In the past four years, the lanes leading to one of the city's most frequented single-screens theatres, Menoka, had been eerily quiet. The beloved establishment stood at Kalighat, in the southern part of the city, since 1949, and even as multiplex chains invaded Kolkata, it had miraculously managed to hold out, right through the Covid-19 lockdown. India's 70-mm big-screen experience had been standing on a shaky foundation ever since the advent of OTT streaming platforms such as

Netflix, Amazon and Hotstar, and the lockdown pushed it further on to the path of doom. This fate was reflected in the country's entertainment pages, which were wistfully carrying obituaries of previously popular cinemas.

***The Sunday Guardian*[1]**

17 July 2021

'Pandemic Forces Many Theatres to Shut Shop'

***Mumbai Mirror*[2]**

29 August 2020

'SoBo Single-Screen Theatre Central Plaza Shuts Its Doors'

***The Quint*[3]**

15 September 2020

'100 Single Screens across India May Shut after COVID-19 Lockdown'

The Ormax Box Office Report 2020 & 2021[4]

8 February 2022

'Indian Box Office Lost More Than ₹15,000 Crore to the Pandemic in 2020 and 2021'

There was little hope.

On 25 January 2023, a procession made its way through a bustling Kolkata street, headed towards Menoka. It was grander than anything

seen before. A golden carriage. Two shiny white horses. A massive film poster carefully bound to the seat. The catchy title track of the film—*Jhoome Jo Pathaan*'—blasted on the screechy music system. A pipe band joined in as accompaniment. Though off-key, the tunes played were music to everyone's ears. The members of All the King's Men, as the Kolkata chapter of the fan club SRK Universe calls itself, filled the air with euphoric chants of '*Bachche, buddhe aur jawan, sab dekhenge* Pathaan'.

When the procession reached the gates of Menoka, more fans joined in. With an hour to go before the 'first day first show', the drums, the music, the dancing continued. Shah Rukh Khan's poster from the film, adorned with marigold garlands, was placed outside the hall for fans to pour milk on. This didn't feel like a regular Friday at the movies. But it was a common sighting in every city, every theatre, every multiplex.

In Kashmir, where cinema screens once went dark for decades, *Pathaan* ignited a fervour unseen in thirty-three years. The film didn't just open, it exploded, filling theatres that had long been ghosted and shut by fear. Vikas Dhar's multiplex, the only one in the Valley, witnessed something unusual—every show sold out, every seat was occupied. The crowd, unyielding to past threats, reclaimed their right to joy and flooded into the cinema hall with the kind of passion that made the air electric. The Valley roared back with the magic of the movies, proving that the allure of Shah Rukh Khan and the power of cinema could outshine even the darkest shadows.[5] Similarly, Indore's Jyoti Cinema, a single-screen theatre that was on the brink of collapse, got a new lease of life with *Pathaan*. Manager Adarsh Yadav was gleeful when he said, '*Pathaan* has helped us bring in new faces and a whole new lot of viewers to our theatres. For the first time 9 p.m. shows have been added back to the schedule.'[6]

It was nothing short of Eid, Diwali, Christmas or any other festival anywhere in the world. Millions of Shah Rukh Khan fans across the world made sure of it.

After all, it was Pathaan Day.

The Badshah was back.

> *A*B *P*ATHAAN KE VANVAS KA TIME KHATAM HUA ...
>
> *Pathaan, 2023*

1

THE RETURN OF THE KING

How 'Pathaan Day' came about, no one knows for sure. Something like this perhaps happened last when Rajinikanth released his much-awaited *Robot 2* on 29 November 2018 or when Amitabh Bachchan's films were released in his heyday. It is said that once, during the screening of *The Great Gambler*, a mischief-maker set off a firework in the cinema hall. Despite the obvious hazard, only a few people rushed to the exit. But they promptly returned to their seats within minutes; most of the audience remained focused on the film. And when the authorities paused the screening to investigate the incident, the audience protested vehemently, demanding that the theatre resume the film and investigate later![1]

But that is the pull of a superstar—the audience waits with bated breath to see their hero on the big screen. Even when the films don't set the cash registers at the box office ringing, the fans know that their hero will come back, bigger than before.

Shah Rukh's last hit was *Chennai Express*, but that was a decade ago, in 2013. After a string of underwhelming films—there were six consecutive releases—an unceremonious obituary for the superstar was written. It was assumed that Shah Rukh's reign was over. *Zero* was the final blow that pushed him into a shell—he stopped talking to the press, giving interviews or even signing new projects.

After a superstar has done television, reality shows and films of every kind, shape and size, and of every scale, with every promising film-maker there is in India, 'What next?' becomes an uncomfortable yet inevitable question. After three decades of a glorious career, maybe reinvention is the name of the game. And Shah Rukh did just that. He kept giving himself new challenges, pushing himself creatively. The lover-boy image was slowly dwindling. Romance was no longer a genre that ensured footfall. It was a natural progression for him to find roles that were out of the box: a complex film about a superstar and his troubled fan in Maneesh Sharma's *Fan*, a vagabond in Imtiaz Ali's *Jab Harry Met Sejal*, a gangster in Rahul Dholakia's *Raees* and eventually a dwarf in Aanand L. Rai's ambitious *Zero*. There was merit in the choices made, but none of them landed. *Zero* was arguably the biggest bomb of Shah Rukh's career. He had never fallen that hard, that low. For the budget it was made on, the film struggled to make respectable box-office numbers.

The film's failure hurt him on a personal level. It was probably the fact that his peers Salman Khan and Aamir Khan were delivering blockbusters such as *Tiger Zinda Hai* and *Dangal* around the same time. A trade analyst and exhibitor I frequently talk to for my stories said, '*Zero* was the biggest film after *Thugs of Hindostan*, which was released on Diwali. It had a sharp trailer. But within the first week, it was clear that the film would not connect with the audience. It was too ambitious, too convoluted. It's never about personal likings. The eccentricity of the plot landed with many, but that number was few and far between. Largely, the film didn't resonate with the people. And this was coming on the back of several underwhelming movies from Shah Rukh—be it *Fan* or *Jab Harry Met Sejal*. *Zero* was a sign that Shah Rukh needed to look from a macro perspective at what was not working.'

Or maybe Shah Rukh felt he was losing the pulse of what people wanted from him. He needed to weave people's expectations into his reinvention process. This wasn't about one failure. He needed an overhaul, and for that to happen, he needed to cut out the noise. Much to the surprise of everyone in the industry, Shah Rukh retreated into a sabbatical.

Much after the success of *Pathaan*, Shah Rukh mustered the courage to put his emotions of that time into words. In an interview with Robin Uthapa, he said, 'I was actually taking a break for just one year. I thought, "*Thoda rukta hoon, physically fit hota hoon* [Let me stop a while, get physically fit]." *Zero* required a lot of hard work, and then it didn't work as well and nobody liked it. I felt bad. But then I thought I will do something which people like, *bohot karli apne dil ki* [I've done enough of what my heart wants]. I have been working for the last 32 years and I never thought there will be a time when I will not work.'[2]

Lockdown altered everything in everyone's lives. Holed up at home, even one as big as Shah Rukh's, can be scary. Being left alone with your darkest thoughts, not knowing if you'll ever get the chance to go back to work again—in his case to a film set, in front of the camera—can be daunting. But stars like him burn too bright to fade on a low note. A resurgence was inevitable.

Shah Rukh's career, and his life, have been like that of a cosmic, mythological hero—one whose life is full of obstacles but who always has the gods smiling down on him (even if sometimes he has to fight the gods himself). Add to this epic tale a sprinkle of magic, the blessings of his deceased parents, an epic, enduring love and the prayers of a million fans across the globe, and you have a much-loved man who is fallible, yet invincible. The love Shah Rukh enjoys isn't ordinary. By design of this industry, superstars are loved and adored. They are pampered, they have fans screaming their names, an army of women swooning over them. But Shah Rukh is different. He gets blessings from our mothers. Our fathers tell us, '*Shah Rukh Khan jaisi shiddat se mehnat karo, saari kaynat tumhe tumhare manzil tak le jaane ki saazish karegi* [Work as hard as Shah Rukh Khan, and the whole universe will conspire to take you to your destiny].'

Shah Rukh himself believes it is the duas that have brought him back from the dead. 'When I started working again, there was this strange hunger and newness to work [in me]. Ever since I have returned, I feel bigger, better, faster and happier.'[3]

On 20 November 2020, Shah Rukh returned to his turf, Yash Raj Films, where he once shot the biggest movies of his career, to kick off the shoot for *Pathaan*. In some ways, the film was the realization of his lifelong dream—to be an action hero. Everyone, including his mentor Yash Chopra, had felt there was something too deep about Shah Rukh's eyes to waste on action. It is possible they were simply being polite. Shah Rukh didn't have the gait, physique or technique to be an action star. He was neither a martial arts aficionado like Akshay Kumar, nor a stunt expert like Ajay Devgn, and neither did he have the irreverent swagger of Salman Khan. Shah Rukh's charm was made of something else.

Since *Darr*, action had been his elusive dream. He had said in an interview, 'In *Darr*, I was doing action, running, shooting guns, and I thought—this is my path now. I am going to be an action hero. Somewhere without me realizing it, I was converted into a lover. Adi [Aditya Chopra] fooled me.'[4]

Aditya Chopra had his own reasons to keep Shah Rukh away from action. In his only interview after 1995, he addressed it. 'He is a soft, nice guy who pretends to be all macho. He says he likes action but he is not like that. While working on *Darr*, I had told him action ideas, and six months later, I took *DDLJ* [*Dilwale Dulhania Le Jayenge*] to him.'

It's not as if Shah Rukh hadn't tried his hand at action before. He knows how to throw punches and look suave doing it, but the world has always been too busy sinking into his dimples and intense eyes. *Pathaan*, in every sense of the term, was a perception shift. It was Shah Rukh owning his own identity, embracing his dream and giving himself a much-deserved chance at doing something that everyone thought he wasn't cut out for.

At fifty-five, he had little to lose—and he finally stepped into the shoes of a bona fide action hero.

The path to success for *Pathaan* was mired in hate and controversy. You'd think Bollywood and cricket would unify the nation, but nothing is quite as potent as hate. *Pathaan*, in the months leading up to its release, was met with all kinds of hate under the sun. Until a few decades ago, everyone believed that all publicity was good publicity, but not any more. The power of hatred cannot be undermined, and in films preceding *Pathaan*, its effects had already been seen. Aamir Khan's beautiful adaptation of *Forrest Gump—Laal Singh Chaddha—*had fallen prey to insurmountable hate the previous year. The same could have happened with *Pathaan*. Everyone everywhere seemed upset with the film.

Since the film's song *'Besharam Rang'* dropped, it was dogged by controversy, which arose due to Deepika Padukone's attire, particularly a saffron-coloured bikini she wore in the song. This issue swiftly garnered criticism from politicians and online activists, leading to calls for boycott of the film.

Home minister of Madhya Pradesh, Dr Narottam Mishra, expressed strong disapproval of the song, labelling it highly objectionable. The minister took to Twitter (now X), criticizing the song for being 'shot with a dirty mindset'.[5] Mishra branded Padukone as a 'supporter of the "Tukde Tukde gang"' and demanded the reshooting of certain scenes with different costumes, warning that the movie would not be released in the state otherwise. This fire spread to multiple states. Numerous right-wing groups organized protests calling for a boycott of the film. In Indore, members of the Veer Shivaji Group burnt effigies of the actors. Concurrently, in Uttar Pradesh, Bharatiya Janata Party (BJP) activists staged similar demonstrations, calling for a complete ban on the film.

In January 2023, in Gujarat, members of the Bajrang Dal caused disturbance at a mall, vandalizing movie posters. The party's official Twitter account declared its intention to prevent the film from being screened anywhere.

It didn't end there. The attacks only got more personal and brutal. Jagadguru Paramhans Acharya, a prominent seer from Ayodhya, publicly issued a threat to Shah Rukh, declaring that he would burn him alive. Religious sentiments had been hurt.[6]

Like I said, hate has a strange unifying quality. Once the Hindu extremist groups had made their anger known, it seemed the All India Muslim Tehwar Committee didn't want to live with the fear of missing out. The group, based in New Delhi, voiced objections to the movie's title, asserting that it portrayed the Pathan community negatively. Peerzada Khurram Miyan Chishti, the group's leader, expressed that naming the film 'Pathaan' amounted to disrespecting the sentiments of the Pathan clan. He called for a ban on the film unless its title was changed.

The Central Board of Film Certification (CBFC), whose primary job is to certify films, decided to throw more drama into the mix. It requested ten cuts in the movie, including some words being edited and some sensual moves removed, though the title and the much-debated bikini remained unscathed.

These were uncertain times and there was a good chance that *Pathaan* would plummet, like many others did over the past few years.

But then something curious happened—and that was a phenomenon driven by Shah Rukh's fans. Arguably, no one has fans like he does. They are an army shielding their king with all their might. They sprang into action to ensure the 'Boycott *Pathaan*' trend didn't affect the film. The Twitter army of SRK Universe organized a number of events for *Pathaan*, including the first-day-first-show procession in Kolkata that drew nearly 50,000 people, a special show on 26 January for Delhi Police and NGO kids, an IMAX show and two single-screen shows. The entire auditorium of the Cinepolis TDI in Rajouri Garden in Delhi was booked for the screening. The fans raised money by selling personalized *Pathaan* merchandise, including T-shirts, bands and badges.

Another Shah Rukh fan group called Shah Rukh Warriors, which has a presence in thirty-five Indian cities and eleven countries across the globe, worked to change the narrative by selling devotion to devotees. Think about it: How does a tribe function? It's a tightly knit community

> **Shah Rukh's career, and his life, has been like that of a cosmic, mythological hero—one whose life is full of obstacles but who always has the gods smiling down on him (even if sometimes he has to fight the gods himself). Add to this epic tale a sprinkle of magic, the blessings of his deceased parents, an epic, enduring love and the prayers of a million fans across the globe, and you have a much-loved man who is fallible, yet invincible.**

that rallies around its charismatic leader. So Shah Rukh was projected as the messiah who could save the Hindi film industry at a time when it was being attacked from all sides. Through persuasive rhetoric and emotional appeal, Shah Rukh's fan clubs made sure that the negative reviews—which were plenty—phased out. The good word outnumbered the critics' opinions. Fans were no longer simply watching a film. They asked: 'Are you celebrating *Pathaan* Day?' The hate-filled trends online were combatted with #ShahRukhPrideofIndia and #ShahofHearts. Not a single Shah Rukh fan responded to the boycott hashtags, lest they add to the growing hate.

Lalita Kambhampati, a fifty-two-year-old IT professional from Michigan, who heads the US chapter of the SRK Universe fan club, said in an interview, 'Shah Rukh Khan brings so much love to everyone in this world. His presence is attached with joy. And sometimes we take this positivity for granted. His fan clubs are his community and we mobilized the tribe.' The fan clubs in Chennai activated their pan-India network in 120 cities. SRK Universe activated its network in countries such as Egypt, Australia, Nigeria and Iran, where there is a strong Shah Rukh fan base.[7]

A grand plan was hatched to make *Pathaan* the ultimate FOMO (fear of missing out) experience. From quizzes on social media and song snippets to movie discussions, the fans went at it relentlessly. Detailed content strategies that would put the communication plans of big corporations to shame were chalked out. With each hashtag, discussions on Shah Rukh's previous films began. For instance, #ShahRukhthePrideofIndia included snippets from older interviews, his old dialogues, how he had made India proud and other quotable quotes. The fact that Shah Rukh was returning to the big screen after four years was spoken about in every tweet. The fans appealed to nostalgia. Human beings have a tendency to romanticize the past and live in the sweetness of the time gone by. Shah Rukh reminds us of that time. Remember the guy who taught us how to love? Well, he is coming back, and you don't want to miss it. Through the release week, fans the world over joined to add fuel to the frenzy by posting their pictures online with the film's posters at different cinema halls, showing how excited they were.

Ordinary people, joined together in this global brotherhood, were unstoppable in their passion for their hero. There were pictures of serpentine queues at cinema halls and reports of ticket counters ringing like never before. No one was sure what the film was about, no one cared to wait until the reviews were out—everyone just flocked in.

One would think that with the hundreds of interview snippets circulating online during this time, Shah Rukh would be promoting his film. But he didn't give a single interview through the making of the film. Neither did he speak to the press after its release. It was at the film's success press conference three days after the release that he made his first promotional appearance since *Zero*. And talk about an appearance going viral online. With his director Siddharth Anand and co-stars John Abraham and Deepika Padukone by his side, he flashed his million-dollar smile to the people gathered. And just like any event that Shah Rukh graces with his presence, it took many minutes to calm the crowd down. Even the journalists who had spent hours interviewing him earlier were seeing him after many years.

The best lines of that evening came from John Abraham, who plays Shah Rukh's nemesis in the film. John, generally a man of few words, attributed the film's success quite plainly to the fact that Shah Rukh was not an actor any more—he was an emotion. When a fan from the audience screamed 'He's back!', John jumped in to make a quick correction and said, 'Just one correction—Shah Rukh Khan is not "back", he [had] just gone for a loo break!'[8]

As for Shah Rukh, he sat back, quite evidently with his heart full, humbled by all the love. His fans had spoken loud and clear—they had his back. That evening Shah Rukh let us in on a few intimate details of his life when he was away from the public glare. We found out about that bathroom in his home where he cries when he feels hurt, pain and heartache. He made us feel less lonely by acknowledging that it was okay to not be okay. 'I am very proud to say I get scared sometimes, I feel sad sometimes, I lose confidence many times in a day,' he said.[9]

He spoke about not shying away from being rescued, be it on or off screen. Shah Rukh told everyone about how Aditya Chopra put his faith in him even when Shah Rukh himself didn't entirely agree with it. 'Four years ago I was feeling a little weak. I had injuries, went through surgeries ... but I thought I should do something that I haven't done before. I should get physically very fit. I told my friend Aditya Chopra and Siddharth Anand, "*Ek action picture banao* (Make an action film)." So they told me, "*Sir, ye aap kya keh rahe ho, aap thak jaaoge* (You will get tired)." I asked them to at least try. I told them, "I might not be as good as Tiger (Shroff) or Duggu (Hrithik Roshan), but I will try my best."¹⁰

> 'To be honest, I don't think we set out to break records. We set out to make a good film. This is what Shah Rukh taught me in my first movie. He told me you should work with people who make you happy.'
> —Deepika Padukone

Shah Rukh attributed *Pathaan*'s success to the hundreds who stand outside his house every day. The numbers don't dwindle when his films don't work. On every festival his fans wait outside his home to catch a glimpse of the man who makes them believe in magic and love. They show up every time, no matter what. 'They love me absolutely ... it is selfless and beautiful. Whenever I am down, I just need to go out, and there is a sea of people. I make sure that this happiness they give me, I can give back to them.'

Deepika Padukone, who went through her own trial by fire because of the saffron-coloured bikini she wore in the film, teared up while addressing the press. She said while wiping tears of joy, relief and disbelief, 'To be honest, I don't think we set out to break records. We set out to make a good film. This is what Shah Rukh taught me in my first movie. He told me you should work with people who make you happy. It's such a lovely atmosphere to work in, and that's what the audience is taking back. It's pure love and joy, and it reflects.'

Attributing the success of her career to Shah Rukh, who launched her in *Om Shanti Om* in 2007, she said, 'Whether it's *Om Shanti Om* or *Chennai Express*, what makes it special is the relationship we share, the trust. I wouldn't be here today if it wasn't for Shah Rukh and his vision for me. To shower me with so much love and grace. He has given me confidence and even he doesn't know that. I do what I do because I know Shah Rukh will always be there for me.'[11]

And this pair did recreate success, and how. Like before, the headlines heralded victory.

> ***The Guardian***
>
> **'*Pathaan* and the King of Cinema Blast Bollywood Out of the Doldrums'**

> **Vox**
>
> **'Breaking Down *Pathaan*, the Most Popular Movie in the World'**

> ***The Conversation***
>
> **'From *Deewana* to the success of *Pathaan*: The Global Impact of Bollywood's Enduring King, Shah Rukh Khan'**

> **ThePrint**
>
> **'Everyone Wrote Bollywood Obit. Then Shah Rukh Khan Made the Miracle Happen'**

> **Film Companion**
>
> '*Pathaan*, Shah Rukh Khan and the Art of Killing with Kindness'

> ***Foreign Policy***
>
> 'Modi Is Losing His War on Bollywood'

> ***The Hindu***
>
> 'Shah Rukh's *Pathaan* Registers Record-Breaking Opening Day Collection for Any Hindi Movie'

> **WION**
>
> 'Why *Pathaan* Is a Strong Rebuke to #BoycottBollywood Gang'

On screen, Pathaan was an action hero we hadn't ever seen before. We saw Shah Rukh give the genre his own touch. But not once did we see him endorse the toxic masculinity associated with the genre itself. Pathaan pops painkillers, fixes broken pottery with gold, gets saved by both Deepika's Rubai and Salman Khan's Tiger. Even in action, Shah Rukh remains vulnerable.

The film's gross collection in India was Rs 657.50 crore ($82 million) and overseas Rs 398 crore ($50 million). In terms of global business, the film raked in Rs 1,055 crore ($130 million).[12]

Pathaan's box office triumph was a sign of rejuvenation for Bollywood itself. The arid period of underwhelming releases seemed to have come to an end. King Khan, ever the charmer, not only brought back the joy of watching him on screen but also redefined the action-hero archetype. This money-spinner of a film reminded everyone that there are heroes, there are movie stars and then there is Shah Rukh.

If one Shah Rukh Khan makes you this happy, imagine what two of them in the same film can do. Film-maker Atlee Kumar took this thought as the selling point and gave us one of recent years' most massy films—*Jawan*. There seemed to be a shift in Shah Rukh too. During a press conference in the UAE, when asked if releases made him nervous, he said, 'I don't think I need to be nervous. I think all my films are going to be superhits. That's the belief I sleep and wake up with, and which makes me at the age of fifty-seven go and do stunts and work eighteen hours a day.'[13]

Jawan was lavishly mounted. It starred Shah Rukh alongside south Indian superstar Nayanthara and had Bollywood superstar Deepika Padukone in an extended cameo. The much-loved Vijay Sethupathi played the antagonist. The film's music, by Anirudh Ravichander, was an ode to Shah Rukh's on-screen persona. They even got Raja Kumari to do a rap song on King Khan. She put all her love for the King in the following words:

'Running with King Khan
Bullets rain down like it's thunder.'

It was punchy and hit home, staying true to the essence of *Jawan* and to its evergreen hero, Shah Rukh Khan.

The film had one of the best entry sequences of a Hindi film hero. Our man, covered in bandages, lands from the sky, in a place somewhere in India's Northeast, where an entire village has been attacked by dacoits. Silhouetted against the full moon, with the wind whipping around him, Shah Rukh emerges as the messiah come to save everyone. Ravichander's music, set to the beat of drums, amped up the effect as the star slashed goons with panache. The metaphorical entry turned out to be accurate, for Bollywood at least. The film has earned a total of Rs 1,200 crore lifetime business worldwide. The arid spell for the Hindi film industry post-pandemic was finally over in 2023—and it had everything to do with Shah Rukh.

Jawan worked because of multiple reasons. The story stitched in the primary fan base of Shah Rukh—the women—while staying true to its sensibilities. In the film, Shah Rukh quite literally has an army of women by his side. The actor retained his best quality—his ability to headline a movie without dimming the shine of those around him. Something that all actors he has worked with in his career say of him—a rare trait in a movie star of his stature. For an action film, it was powered and presented by women, mirroring his own career as a superstar. For good measure, dialogue writer Sumit Arora threw in a line to this effect: '*Jail mein aadmi tere hai, par yeh jail meri aurton ka hai* [The men in jail may be yours, but this jail belongs to my women].'

But perhaps what benefited the tropey telling of this masala movie, over and above the larger-than-life presentation of India's favourite superstar, was its inherent rage. *Jawan* was an angry film. It represented the common man's rage; it gave voice to his concerns. It didn't take sides—right, left, front, centre. It spoke for the people, whose leader was Shah Rukh himself. It spoke about the pressing issues that had been conveniently sidelined by everyone. After a decade, there was a mainstream masala movie that was deeply political, and even unsubtle, in its messaging.

Shah Rukh, towards the climax, appears in a monologue and breaks the fourth wall to talk to us: '*Main kaun hoon, kaun nahi, pata nahi. Maa ko kiya wada hoon, ya adhura ek irada hoon ... Main achha hoon, bura hoon ... punya hoon ya paap hoon, ye khud se poochna ... Kyun ki main bhi aap hoon* [Who I am, who I am not, I don't know. Am I a promise made to my mother, or an unfulfilled intention? Am I good, am I bad, am I a virtue or a sin, ask yourself. Because I, too, am you].'

Over the next three minutes and eighteen seconds, Shah Rukh verbalizes everything that has been playing on our minds for the past many years. Masquerading as a potboiler, *Jawan* is really a vigilante movie in its essence.

Shah Rukh resurrected the Angry Young Man of Bollywood after four decades. *Jawan* brought all the inherent rage bubbling inside us, the people of India, on to the big screen. Early on in the film, he presents a conundrum to a minister, citing the number 10,281, leaving everyone in the hall perplexed. He then goes on to reveal that this figure represents the staggering number of Indian farmers who have succumbed to despair and taken their own lives. The silence in the cinema hall was deafening as the weight of this tragedy crashed upon the audience. *Jawan* doesn't shy away from the harsh realities plaguing India. The film confronts the heartbreaking rise in farmer suicides, a direct consequence of flawed agricultural policies. From crippling debt to the merciless whims of weather—drought, flood, you name it—*Jawan* sheds light on the factors pushing India's desperate farmers to the brink.

The film acts as a powerful indictment of the government's inaction, pushing for the urgent need for reforms that truly empower and protect the backbone of India's economy.

In the film, Sanya Malhotra plays the role of a doctor wrongly accused of being responsible for the deaths of numerous children at a hospital. The true culprit is revealed to be corruption and the lack of necessary facilities at the hospital. People could see parallels between her character and the real-life ordeal of Dr Kafeel Khan from Uttar Pradesh. Despite the doctor's fervent efforts to secure adequate oxygen supply for the hospital, sixty-three children succumbed to acute encephalitis syndrome in 2017. Subsequently, the state government imprisoned him, citing negligence in his duties. Dr Khan tweeted a heartfelt letter to Shah Rukh, saying, 'While I understand that *Jawan* is a work of fiction, the parallels it draws to the Gorakhpur tragedy serve as a powerful reminder of the systemic failures, apathy and, most importantly, the innocent lives lost. It underscores the urgent need for accountability within our health care system. The character portrayed by Sanya Malhotra (Dr Eeram Khan), although not directly referencing me, encapsulated the experiences I faced. It was heartening to witness the real culprit of "The Gorakhpur Hospital Tragedy" get caught, though, sadly, in real life the real culprits are roaming free …'[14]

Throughout its almost three-hour runtime, the movie delved into myriad national issues—from the disparity of loan waivers benefiting billionaire industrialists while debt-laden farmers resort to suicide, to the dismal conditions of government hospitals, corruption plaguing defence contracts and the repercussions of irresponsible voting. Yet, amid this vast landscape of concerns, the focus remains primarily on the protagonist, delving into his personal struggles, tragic history and driving motivations. This narrative approach often blurs the lines between the character and the actor portraying him.

The film came out of nowhere. Its promos were dubious. A trade expert explains, 'One would have expected the biggest opening from Tamil Nadu. Nayanthara as the lead, Atlee as director, Anirudh Ravichander on music. This was a massy film from the word go. But the film that people went to watch was very different from the one they expected. It became a film whose themes cut across demographics. The first-day collections were always expected to be in the range of Rs 50 crore. It made Rs 75 crore because the word spread that this was a movie that was relatable and talked about the issues people were facing!' Atlee had thrown in dialogues such as, '*Jab main villain banta hoon, tab mere samne koi hero tik nahi paata* [When I become the villain, no hero can stand before me].' It was only natural to assume that Shah Rukh would play some sort of anti-hero, going against the law. And by definition he was—only that in doing so he was standing by the people.

Azad is alternatively avenger and victim, much like the audience watching it. Shah Rukh's demeanour is one of anger, agitation and profound devastation. Despite the potentially dull impact of these moral lessons, Atlee infuses the film with the energy of an action thriller, complemented by Shah Rukh's double role. Shah Rukh portrays the father, Vikram Rathore, who retains his ability to effortlessly break bones with swagger and style, and the son who is the spitting image of his father. Both father and son have suffered injustices, and their coming together results in the formidable force of two enraged heroes united as one. Who doesn't remember the whistles, the screams and the cheers when the silver-haired father explodes on to the screen as he rescues his son, all while using a belt to bash up the bad guys!

The furore after *Jawan* was something else. Fans formed human towers outside theatres, danced inside as if the theatre floor was a nightclub and even wrapped themselves up like extras from the movie, complete with head bandages. Shah Rukh's choice to showcase five unique appearances for his character added to the frenzy surrounding the movie.

At Gaiety Galaxy cinema in Bandra, Mumbai, Shah Rukh fans weren't waiting in line, they were building a ladder—a human one. They were trying to hoist a colossal standee of the King himself, his face beaming down on the crowd below. The massive cut-out became the centrepiece of this electrifying tableau. No queue could contain the fervour. This was pure, unadulterated fandom, the epitome of Shah Rukh's enduring reign in Bollywood. Hundreds of fans gathered at the iconic theatre before an extraordinary 6 a.m. screening of *Jawan*. In Mumbai, the frenzy surrounding *Jawan* was palpable, and across India, the Shah Rukh mania reached unparalleled heights. Exhibitors scrambled to accommodate the overwhelming demand by adding early shows. In Raniganj, the anticipation peaked with a remarkable 2.15 a.m. screening of the movie as fans just couldn't contain their excitement any longer.

Even Google joined in the excitement, providing a playful Easter egg for fans. When people typed 'Jawan' into their Google search bars, they found Shah Rukh himself responding on a walkie-talkie with a cheerful 'Ready'.

Fans took their love for the superstar to new heights, turning the release of *Jawan* into an unconventional dance party of mummies. Theatres echoed with joyous beats as fans sporting head bandages danced to *'Zinda Banda'*. Crowds celebrated by throwing money at the screens. Dialogues drowned in the screams of the fans. Viewers were mad with excitement as they exited screenings. One fan told IANS, '*Movie nahi bawal hai, bawal. Aasman neeche gira dega yeh movie … Shah Rukh zindabad* [This is not a movie. This is madness. Long live Shah Rukh]!'

A fan in Bengaluru started crying, scrambling for words. His friend said, 'Don't call us just fans. He is our idol. We can go to any level to make his movies a hit … *Woh star nahi hai, duniya hai meri* [He is not just a star, he is my whole world].'

Another fan at Gaiety said, 'Shah Rukh is back, baby! Big time! *Black mein ticket bik rahi hai* [Tickets are being sold in black]. I have watched it three times at the theatre now, and I still couldn't hear the dialogues …'

A fan shrieked into the boom, '*Shah Rukh king hai, tha aur rahega* [Shah Rukh was, is and will remain the king]!' His friend joined in, *Gadar*-style, '*Shah Rukh Khan zindabad tha, zindabad hai aur zindabad rahega* [Long live Shah Rukh Khan].'

The videos and bites kept coming, and the manic frenzy went on for two months after the release.

Jawan's success was a personal one. In some ways more personal than *Pathaan*'s. It was the win of the common man. And the best man to decode what really contributed to *Jawan*'s success was Atlee. In an interview to PTI, he explained what he thought made the film work. '*Jawan* is about Indian emotion, and I think I have placed it in the right proportions. It speaks about your heart and what you feel when you read a newspaper, when you take life seriously and when you are very responsible. As a film-maker, you have to be responsible. You can't just entertain, go home and sleep. You have to entertain and you have to give something that people take home,' he said.[15]

And what about Shah Rukh? Atlee didn't hold back while discussing the secret sauce that went into making the biggest Indian film, with the biggest superstar of the country. 'You have to be a fan before a film-maker. I always used to say, "Sir, how much I love you, you will only know when the film releases." "I know, sir," he used to tell me.'

After the film became a hit, Shah Rukh hosted a press conference, where he spoke about what the film meant to him. He said, 'Jawan [the character] is emotion, Jawan is an Indian soldier, Jawan is an Indian mother, Jawan is an Indian girl, Jawan is an Indian vigilante. And you have to understand that Jawan, many times, is very weak because he is all of us. And many times, he is ready for a fight. Jawan is many times wrong, but very many times he is also right. Jawan, sometimes, will live in the darkness, sometimes Jawan will be the one who will be emitting the light. And finally, all of us, and every Indian, is Jawan, who is upright. Honesty, goodness, love—that's what the whole movie stands for.'[16]

Jawan is not the kind of film you review for its story, but for its experience and the emotion it invokes in you. In the darkness of a movie hall, it makes a gut-punching impact. *Jawan* is Shah Rukh versus the system, and in that, it's probably the greatest love story he has ever starred in.

It was not until earlier this year and three big blockbusters in 2023 later that Shah Rukh decided to tell his piece. It was at an award show for CNN-News18. The past few years had been professionally and personally trying for him. Like in the case of public figures, the lines are blurred between professional and personal success. The year 2023 was the win Shah Rukh and his family needed. In October 2021, his eldest son, Aryan, was apprehended by the Narcotics Control Bureau in relation to a drugs case, sparking significant controversy. Throughout this challenging period, the actor courageously defended his family, enduring sleepless nights and relentless media scrutiny. After nearly a month-long legal battle, Aryan was granted bail by the Mumbai High Court as the case fell apart.

At the event, when he received the award, he made it a point to remind everyone that he was the Indian of all seasons. He said a lot, but held back a lot more.

'It's been a bloody long time since I won an award now. I started believing I was doomed to win a Lifetime Achievement Award ...' he started with his trademark humour. With *Pathaan*, *Jawan* and *Dunki*, he had three blockbuster films that year and made his inevitable entry into the thousand-crore club. It's an oft-asked question—what goes behind the phenomenon Shah Rukh created at the box office? Quoting his character Vikram Rathore from *Jawan*, he said in the speech, 'I am hungry, and I have always been hungry...' That is what feeds his drive to stay hungry for success, to keep entertaining the 140 crore people of India year after year for over three decades. He described himself as an 'impetuous and impulsive modern actor, confident in his talent and hard work', cheekily mentioning that his wife sometimes calls him 'overconfident and cocky'.

Shah Rukh sees himself as a storyteller of hope and happiness, playing heroes who do good deeds and even ensuring that when he portrays a villain, that character meets a just end. He believes that goodness begets goodness, and that 'badness' deserves its due punishment.

He didn't hold himself back from talking about the challenges of the past few years, including the pandemic and personal struggles. But, most significantly, he answered what is perhaps the most-asked question: What did he learn? The importance of staying quiet, working hard and maintaining dignity, even when life throws unexpected curveballs, he said. In the speech and in life, he never misses a chance to encourage his fans to keep the faith during tough times, reminding them that just like in films, everything turns out fine in the end, and if it's not fine, then it's not the end—'*Picture abhi baaki hai, mere dost.*' The film is not yet over, my friend.

His final words that night were: 'I don't just feel like the Indian of the year, and I will be the Indian for all the years to come. I am actually the Indian for all ages. I thank you for making me the star that I am yet again ...'[17]

> "Main waada karta hoon, Papa, main iss parivar ka naam hamesha ucha rakhunga ... Main waada karta hoon, main aapko hamesha khush rakhunga"
>
> *Kabhi Khushi Kabhie Gham ...*, 2001

2

IT TAKES A VILLAGE, EVEN FOR A BADSHAH

Meer Taj Mohammad Khan's voice thundered, '*Aye badmash, idhar aao. Aye ullu ke patthey, tum itna hero bann ke ghumte rehte ho* [Hey, you naughty kid, come here. You walk around like you're a hero]. You should never take your freedom for granted. We have given it to you so we always maintain this freedom.'

A young Shah Rukh didn't know what his father meant by this. But the line stuck with him. He told Farida Jalal in an interview, 'At that point of time, I really used to think that by freedom, he meant from a foreign rule or something, but now I understand after having grown up that this freedom he was talking about was in terms of poverty maybe, freedom from misery.'[1]

Many years later, Shah Rukh would share this lesson with his audience. In 2016, at the annual day function of the Dhirubhai Ambani International School, Shah Rukh was invited as the chief guest. It was one of those evenings when everyone descended to hear the most well-spoken man in

Bollywood speak. He promised it would take twenty minutes to talk to the kids about life outside the gates of their school. And he spoke about how important it was to be free, echoing his father's words fondly. 'Feel free, because that's what essentially my talk is about—feeling free. The freedom to be yourself, to listen to your inner voice and never let anyone tell you who you are, who you ought to be, including me. These are the only years of your life in which you will be allowed to make regret-free mistakes,' he said.[2]

Going back to Meer Taj Mohammad Khan. Perhaps young Shah Rukh, who grew up in a small mohalla in Delhi, didn't know that his father was in and out of jail during the Quit India Movement. Or the fact that in 1947, his father had found himself listed in the Red Shirt freedom fighters' blacklist, leading to his prohibition from returning to Peshawar, which was relegated to Pakistan after the Radcliffe Line separated the two countries. Neither did he have any idea about the nights in Delhi University when his father's Hindu comrades would form a protective circle around Meer's bed, shielding him from potential anti-Muslim attacks.

But later in life, after 1947, Meer who aligned himself with Khan Abdul Ghaffar Khan's movement, became a nobody. He tried venturing into electoral politics, contesting against Maulana Abdul Kalam Azad, but did not emerge victorious. Departing from Peshawar, his home, at the tender age of sixteen, he never found another home and a settled life until he met Shah Rukh's mother, Fatima, thirteen years later.

Lateef Fatima Khan was born in Toli Chowki, Hyderabad. She distinguished herself as a first-class magistrate and a committed social worker. A vintage photograph featuring Fatima alongside former Prime Minister Indira Gandhi is often circulated on social media. Fatima's family came from Andhra Pradesh but resided in Karnataka. She was the eldest among four sisters and the daughter of Iftikhar Ahmed, a chief engineer of the Mangalore port who was educated at Oxford and was instrumental in its design and construction. Her proficiency in the four south Indian languages served as an additional advantage, especially with her work as a philanthropist, which took her to various places all over India.

While on David Letterman's Netflix show *My Next Guest*, Shah Rukh spoke about how he spent five years in the care of his grandmother in Mangalore before reuniting with his parents in Delhi. He was adopted by Fatima's mother because she didn't have any sons. Interestingly, the name 'Shah Rukh Khan' that the world knows him by wasn't his original name. Originally, his maternal grandmother (naani) had named him Abdul Rahman. However, this name wasn't formally registered, and his father later bestowed upon him the name 'Shah Rukh Khan'. Who knew then that this name would one day resonate throughout the world?

Meer was still unemployed when he crossed paths with Fatima in Delhi. At the age of twenty-nine, he met someone thirteen years his junior who contrasted with him in every aspect. Meer was tall and athletic, his fair skin almost translucent, revealing the blue veins underneath. He preferred simple attire, often flowing Pathan suits. He had a calm demeanour complemented by a mischievous sense of humour and the patience of a saint. He was largely unperturbed by life's curveballs. If he disapproved of something, it was mildly conveyed. A lover of literature and poetry, Meer could effortlessly recite lengthy Urdu verses. His speech, posture and perspective on life were all marked by a leisurely pace. Meer's constant companion was a small bag containing essentials for paan-making. Just like he would take his time making the perfect paan, for Meer life was a ritual, to be approached with elegance and kindness.

Fatima, on the other hand, was shorter and slightly plump, yet equally beautiful. Her fair complexion contrasted with her long black hair and she possessed a volatile temperament. Raised in Hyderabad, she had a demeanour akin to royalty. Her unique method of drying her hair was to lay her tresses on an upturned basket with incense and charcoal underneath. Fatima had three sisters, but of all of them she possessed a fierce and impulsive spirit.

Fatima's and Meer's paths crossed fortuitously, and for Meer, it was love at first sight. Fate intervened dramatically when Fatima was involved in a serious car accident near India Gate while Meer happened to be nearby. Pulling Fatima out of the wreckage, Meer rushed her to the hospital. In a twist worthy of a Bollywood epic, Fatima required a blood transfusion, and Meer's blood type matched hers. The unforeseen continued when Fatima's mother, pregnant with her fifth child, suffered a miscarriage upon learning of her daughter's accident. She, too, required a blood transfusion—and her blood type matched Fatima's. Without hesitation, Meer travelled to Bangalore (now Bengaluru), where the family resided, to donate blood.

Despite Meer's gallant efforts, Fatima's parents had reservations about the charming young man aspiring to marry their daughter. With a degree but lacking in family background and steady employment, Meer wasn't the best match. Unfortunately, his chivalry, too, came in the way of this match. The fact that Meer had previously donated blood made him a blood relative in the eyes of Fatima's parents, rendering him ineligible to marry into the family. Nevertheless, Meer persisted in his pursuit of Fatima's affections. He courted her with grand gestures, even borrowing his friend's car to take her on long drives. In February 1959, Meer and Fatima exchanged vows. Guests fondly recalled witnessing the typically strong and composed Meer blushing like a bride on the day of his wedding.

Once the wedding was over, the marriage began. Shah Rukh Khan entered the world on 2 November 1965 at the Talwar Nursing Home in Delhi as the second child of Meer and Fatima. His birth had complications as the umbilical cord had wrapped around his neck. However, he emerged unharmed. A nurse attributed his safety to blessings from Lord Hanuman, foreseeing luck in his future. She wasn't very off the mark in her prophecy.

The family resided in Rajinder Nagar at the time. But they soon had to vacate their home as they struggled with finances due to Meer's unsuccessful business ventures. Despite being an educated man, Meer's honesty often hindered his success in business. Fatima, on the other hand, had less tolerance for their financial struggles, occasionally clashing with Meer over his principled approach to business dealings.

That night at the Dhirubhai Ambani School's annual day, Shah Rukh told this bunch of teenagers about his parents. He said, 'My mother was top-class, she was really cool … She loved me and cared unconditionally, was beautiful like all mothers and believed that I will be the most famous man in the world, and I could do no wrong. In Delhi they say, "*Humaara bachha na*, is the apple of my eye." Some Punjabi ladies make it bigger, like "the pineapple of my eye". So I was the pineapple of my mother's eye.

My father was a gentleman ... He was very educated, [had a] master's in law, extremely intelligent, knew seven languages, had travelled the world, knew his politics, fought for the freedom of our country, India, and excelled at sports like hockey, swimming and polo. He could cook and recite poems, and knew the capital of every country in the world. My father was also very poor—he was unemployed and struggling to make ends meet for [the] fifteen years of my life that I had the privilege of knowing him ... Not being able to afford fancy gifts for me, he would wrap up something old that belonged to him in newspapers and declare it a birthday gift when my birthday came along.'[3]

Despite their financial difficulties, the household exuded warmth and hospitality, following the Pathan tradition of generous hosting. Shah Rukh and his sister Shahnaz (Lala Rukh) were shielded from the harsh realities of their life by their mother, who ensured they enjoyed some comforts. Shah Rukh had a calm demeanour from a young age. Despite being prone to illnesses and accidents, he was always a cheerful boy. His childhood was filled with imaginative play, including creating superhero scenarios and playing cricket with friends.

Meer fondly called his son 'yaar'. Both Shah Rukh's parents believed in a relaxed upbringing, with minimal rules and emphasis on academic success rather than strict discipline. While Fatima adhered more to religious practices, Meer embraced a secular outlook, fostering an environment of tolerance and respect for all religions.

Despite their financial struggles, life was tranquil. Summers were spent at their maternal grandparents' home in Bangalore, where Shah Rukh's early performances to Mumtaz's songs hinted at a future marked by his charm and charisma.

It is not often that he speaks candidly about his parents, but in a 2012 interview, he gave his fans glimpses of them. 'I think my father was the most successful failure in the world, and I'm very, very proud of him and I remember him as a gentle person who was six feet tall with brown hair and was very handsome. He taught me a lot of things. When he died when I was fifteen, and as years went by, I remembered things that he had told me. I remember he took me out for a movie. At that time, we were lower-middle-class. He took me and he didn't tell me money was out, so he made me sit at the roundabout near Kamani Auditorium and we bought peanuts. He told me in Punjabi, "*Yaara, yahan baithenge aur gadiyo ko guzarte dekhenge* [We'll sit here and watch the cars drive by]."'[4]

Shah Rukh admitted that night in 2012 that he could never be free, something he so poetically advocated to everyone. 'I've imbibed the fear of failure that I saw my father go through, and I didn't want to fail like him. I want to take my son out. If I promise him a movie, I want to show him a movie, not the cars around the roundabout. Though that was fun too. I think I have the enthusiasm and the energy that my mother had to earn money so that she could look after us.'

Shah Rukh, growing up in the era of the 'Angry Young Man', was a huge Amitabh Bachchan fan. He loved even the flop movies of the superstar. His companion during these movie outings was Amrita Singh, the actor who would go on to star in the hit movie *Betaab* (1983).

Amrita's mother, Rukshana Sultana, had connections with the Congress leader Sanjay Gandhi. Fatima worked as a special magistrate in the Juvenile Court, often collaborating with Rukshana in Old Delhi. Amrita attended the same school as Shah Rukh, and after school, the trio, which included his sister Shahnaz, would spend time at Amrita's home. Amrita unsuccessfully attempted to teach Shah Rukh swimming, but they bonded over their dreams of being in the movies and their mutual adoration for Amitabh Bachchan. Shah Rukh aspired to emulate Amitabh while Amrita dreamt of being romanced by him—dreams that eventually materialized for both.

Despite their limited finances, Shah Rukh and Amrita watched movies from the inexpensive first-row seats and engaged in detailed discussions and mimicry sessions, often at Amrita's house. They would purchase the soundtracks of Amitabh's films when they could afford them and memorize his dialogues, imitating his distinctive style. Shah Rukh's talent for mimicry gained him popularity at school, where teachers would invite him to perform impersonations of Hindi film actors during functions. At home, Shah Rukh and his friends would stage plays on the verandah, with Shah Rukh taking on the multiple roles of writer, director and lead actor.⁵

Around the age of seven, Shah Rukh began writing poetry, often inspired by everyday experiences, encouraged by his father. Meer introduced Shah Rukh to the works of great Urdu poets such as Mirza Ghalib and Mir Taqi Mir, nurturing his early poetic inclinations. Shah Rukh attributed his success as a romantic hero to these early lessons in unrequited love and longing.

He never wrote poems after his father's death. Maybe without his rhyming partner and muse, it all felt too painful.

> 'I have dreams like my father did. I am a believer ... gentle, thoughtful, often utopian like my dad.'

But Shah Rukh calls himself a pragmatic poet. 'I have dreams like my father did. I am a believer ... gentle, thoughtful, often utopian like my dad. But all the thinking and writing of all those poems ... I want to do that with a stomach full of food and a good car and a good house so I don't deprive myself. When I say I'm kind of capitalist, it is just that I am a survivor who wants to live well and think well.'⁶

In 1980, fourteen-year-old Shah Rukh travelled with his father to Pakistan. This was their second trip to the country—and would end up being their last trip together. Despite previous rejections, Pakistani authorities granted Meer a visa in the mid-1970s after his repeated requests. As a blacklisted freedom fighter, his applications were constantly denied until his sister, and later his bachelor brother, passed away, and he pleaded to meet with the rest of his family before it was too late.

The journey was lengthy and demanding. Father and son embarked on a train journey to Amritsar and then travelled to Attari, a small border town that served as the only official road crossing between India and Pakistan. From there, they walked across the designated no-man's land to Wagah in Pakistan and continued on to Peshawar, Meer's hometown.

During the journey, Meer shared stories of his childhood with Shah Rukh. The first visit, in 1977, when Shah Rukh was twelve, was a pleasant memory. The ancestral haveli was bustling with activity, housing several generations of the joint family. Shah Rukh enjoyed meeting distant relatives and playing with cousins his age. However, on the second visit, the warmth seemed to have faded. Quoting from his own memoir, which Shah Rukh claims he has been writing, he described this memory, 'This chapter is called "The Train to Pakistan". I finally learnt that life isn't a time to test where the goal is to make a list of "shouldas, couldas, wouldas" on 1 January and finish as fast as possible with every answer correct. My father got me back to Peshawar once again in 1980. The second time round was also turning out to be as exciting but without my knowledge there was something else taking place right under my nose. I was told by my father's friend that all this niceness that my cousins were showing me was to impress my father into leaving his share of property in their names. I still don't believe that was true but my father seemed to be dejected when we returned to India. My father was always very proud of his family and achievements, but in retrospect I think that going back to his family was not as great an experience as he'd anticipated. He was a very loving and gentle person, never having screamed at us or reprimanded us. He had left his house when he was sixteen … He had tried desperately to make things work in India. I think at times when he felt he hadn't succeeded with his duties to his family in India, he had taken courage from the fact that his family in Pakistan had brought him up well and he would be able to fight back.'

Whenever one sees Shah Rukh talk about his parents, this sense of poignancy and bittersweet sadness is unmistakable. He went on to talk about his recollection of that journey: 'Maybe his journey back home was to refresh this resolve and he had taken his little son along to give him a taste of his lineage. I think it was like trying to revisit his past and pass it on to his future. It's like when you are a little lost, you try to retrace your steps to figure out where you went wrong, but the past has changed with time. It was not the same for him. The memory of all the anecdotes and good times he had collected with pride over the years seemed tainted by the bickering and fighting for something as menial as the possession of his property rights. He had got his son along to introduce him to his proud past, but the past wasn't there and what was left of it was not something to be proud of either. Instead of finding out where he had gone wrong, he realized that the beginning itself was a mistake. He was too far gone to start all over, and neither side seemed to be his. He was in no-man's land. I remember him crying while walking along the no-man's land between Pakistan and India, and I felt sad for him. Little did I know by the time we got back, I would have to start feeling sad for myself. My father was beginning to die.'[7]

Many years later, Shah Rukh shot *Veer-Zaara* at the Wagah Border. He got emotional during the shoot. In a moment of vulnerability, he confessed, 'My father died while walking in this no-man's land.'

Neither was his past able to carry him through, nor was his future strong enough. When they returned to Delhi, Meer was diagnosed with throat and liver cancer. In the weeks before his death, he couldn't speak. So his kids would play dumb charades at Safdarjung Hospital, where he was admitted. Three months later, he passed away.

Like many sons, Shah Rukh held on to the belief that his father was a superhero. He didn't think his old man would die. In the days leading up to his death, Meer appeared to be improving. He was discharged from the hospital, he shaved and even enjoyed some ice cream at home. He looked healthier than he had in months.

When Meer was readmitted to Safdarjung Hospital, Shah Rukh remained calm, accustomed to the hospital environment by now. Around 2 a.m. on 19 September 1981, a nurse called the family to deliver the news of Meer's passing. Fatima didn't immediately disclose the news to fifteen-year-old Shah Rukh, simply saying that Meer wanted to see them. Upon seeing his father lying alone on a gurney in another hospital room, Shah Rukh tried to warm his cold body by vigorously rubbing his feet. The image of blood trickling down from his father's ear would haunt Shah Rukh for the rest of his life.

Fatima and Shah Rukh returned home early in the morning, with Shah Rukh unexpectedly taking the wheel of their Fiat. As they laid Meer's body to rest, a light rain started falling, as if nature itself was mourning the loss of a remarkable man.

Though devastated by the death of the man she had loved for twenty-two years, Fatima knew she couldn't afford the luxury of grieving for long. With limited financial resources and two children to raise, she took charge of the family's business interests, including running a small restaurant called Khatir and managing an agency that sold petrol cans, lubricants and other things for garages. Fatima's resilience and determination ensured that her family remained intact despite the tragedy.

The death of a parent affects everyone differently, and for Shahnaz, Meer's passing had a profound impact. Shahnaz, who had always been content with dreaming rather than taking action, was particularly close to Meer, who had chosen her middle name, Lala Rukh, meaning 'beautiful like a poppy'. Shah Rukh, in an interview with *Tehelka* magazine, reflected on how his sister's life changed after their father's death. He admitted that as a 'soul-selling commercial actor', he often uses his deeply personal experiences in films not to make money, but because life has taught him that it's okay to express his innermost feelings in that way. He recalled the moment his sister saw their father's lifeless body, how she fell, hit her head and then fell silent, staring into space for two years without speaking. This event turned their world upside down.

While his sister, who was highly educated with an MA and an LLB, struggled to cope with the reality of losing their parents, he developed a sense of detachment, false bravado and humour to cope with his grief. Much of what people perceive as his flamboyance and 'Bollywood' style is actually a mask for the sadness in his life.

During the filming of *Dilwale Dulhania Le Jayenge*, Shahnaz was hospitalized, and doctors feared she wouldn't survive. Shah Rukh took her to Switzerland for treatment while he was shooting the iconic song

'*Tujhe Dekha Toh Ye Jaana Sanam*'. She never fully recovered from the loss of their father, and the pain was compounded when their mother passed away a decade later. 'We are what among Muslims is called yateem and yasir—father-and mother-less,' Shah Rukh said. While his sister, who was highly educated, with an MA and an LLB, struggled to cope with the reality of losing their parents, he developed a sense of detachment, false bravado and humour to cope with his grief. Much of what people perceive as his flamboyance and 'Bollywood' style is actually a mask for the sadness in his life.

Shah Rukh adores his sister, describing her as a much better person than he could ever be—innocent and childlike. His children adore her even more than they do him and his wife. He admitted that he lacks the courage to be like her: 'I don't have the courage to be so simple, so hurt, so disturbed. So I keep working around the clock, making jokes about the things said about me. I act to avoid depression. It's much more than earning money, being a big star, dancing at weddings and doing endorsements.'[8]

The absence of his father left him grieving, exhausted and fiercely angry, but he swiftly rebounded, without hesitation and with renewed focus. His teacher, Seetha Venkateshwaran, said in Anupama Chopra's book *King of Bollywood*, 'He wasn't the type to miss school, and his mother wasn't the type to make him stay back. He just moved ahead.'[9]

St. Columba's School, located in central Delhi, was run by Irish brothers who were known for their strict disciplinary measures. Everyone remembers Shah Rukh as fearless. Undeterred by the daunting presence of cane-wielding priests and a stringent set of rules, Shah Rukh would have fun by pulling off elaborate pranks. By the time he was in eleventh grade, his pranks escalated. He once feigned an epileptic fit during a particularly dull class, prompting his friends to persuade the teacher to use a suede shoe to revive him, as was the Indian way to fix fits. His friends narrated this with much elation when they appeared on Farooq Sheikh's television show *Jeena Isi Ka Naam Hai*.

The most memorable aspect of Shah Rukh's school days was his clique known as the 'C-Gang'. On 9 September 1984, Shah Rukh and four of his closest companions officially founded the C-Gang, with the letter C representing 'cool'. They embodied the word 'cool' as a bunch, or so they erroneously believed. But the gang took their creed and reputation seriously. Vivek Khushalani, who was from a wealthy family, got his father to import T-shirts from the US—all personalized with the C-Gang logo and each member's name at the back. The logo, designed by his C-Gang friend Raman Sharma's cousin, was meticulously applied to their white uniforms to underscore their special status even within the school premises. Along with Shah Rukh, members included Bikash Mathur and his closest confidant, Ashok Vassan. Beyond the school gates, the designated C-Gang attire comprised grey Nike shoes, blue jeans and a white T-shirt. They also had laminated identity cards, crafted at a nominal fee at a shop in Connaught Place, bearing each member's photo and the date of the gang's inception: 9-9-84.

Despite the strict environment in their school, the C-Gang thrived, as their rebellious acts primarily involved posturing and defiance rather than engaging in illicit activities such as drugs and alcohol. Their defiance, while occasionally skirting the boundaries of legality, never veered into shameful behaviour. An instance of their rebellion involved sneaking out of their homes one night to watch planes land near the Delhi airport, only to be detained by the police while playing hockey on the road until dawn.

These were boys from diverse backgrounds, including the son of a pilot and of a businessman in the oil and gas industry, but the C-Gang's camaraderie transcended these differences. They frequented Nirula's café in Chanakyapuri, which was close to their school, played video games in the basement of the Chanakya movie theatre and occasionally splurged on bowling outings at the Qutab Hotel alley. It wasn't all good going, as the boys' parents were called in a couple of times. Shah Rukh's good scores and knack for excelling at sports saved him. His mother, too, was called in a few times—but as if he was ever a man who could be tamed!

On *Jeena Isi Ka Naam Hai*, his middle-school headmaster, Brother Eric D'Souza, said Shah Rukh was a 'boundary breaker' who adeptly skirted the rules without getting caught.[10]

Brother D'Souza was a charismatic figure in school. With his long hair and guitar-playing skills, the young priest defied the conventional image of a teacher and a priest. He is Shah Rukh's life guide in every sense of the term. He actively engaged with students outside of formal classes, providing an empathetic ear for their adolescent concerns. Known for his progressive ideas, Brother D'Souza introduced computers in the school curriculum and authored a textbook on the subject. However, he maintained high standards and didn't hesitate to discipline students by caning them when they didn't meet their potential. Nicknamed 'Crow' due to his hooked nose and dark skin, Brother D'Souza encouraged students to think innovatively and continually strive for excellence.

In 1983, Brother D'Souza cast Shah Rukh in his first significant role, as the wizard in the musical adaptation *The Wiz*, a play based on *The Wizard of Oz*. Despite tough competition, Shah Rukh secured the role.

The performing arts had always been Shah Rukh's domain. He was also in the *Chhabra Ram Leela*, an enactment of the epic Ramayana staged during the festival of Dussehra in Delhi. He played the role of one of the monkey warriors, experiencing the thrill of performing in a makeshift theatre set-up in an open field near his home. Despite the chaotic and unpolished nature of the performances, Shah Rukh cherished the experience, even earning a few rupees for reciting his poems to the audience during intermissions, marking this as his first paid performance. He told David Letterman on *My Next Guest* that the only word he had to say was 'Jai!' after Hanumanji's lines '*Siyapati Ram Chandra ki* …'[11]

For *The Wiz* musical, Shah Rukh attempted to sing the songs himself. Lamentably, his confidence didn't quite reflect in his voice. Brother D'Souza and another student, Palash Sen, who we now know as the face of the famous band Euphoria, provided the vocals for Shah Rukh's performances, marking Sen's own introduction to playback singing.

In a way, it was Shah Rukh's destiny to become an actor. It was his father's unrealized dream that he was meant to fulfil. Not many know that Meer, too, had tried his luck in the City of Dreams.

Partition saw an influx of talent into Bombay (now Mumbai) from Lahore. One of the most ambitious productions of the 1950s was *Mughal-e-Azam*, a cinematic epic based on the legend of Anarkali and Prince Salim (the Mughal emperor Jahangir, as he is known in the history pages). Directed by K. Asif, the film's production spanned fifteen years, marked by challenges ranging from financial constraints to cast fatalities. Despite setbacks, Asif spared no expense, employing elaborate costumes and renowned singers such as Ustad Bade Ghulam Ali Khan, elevating the film's grandeur.

Meer, intrigued by the allure of the film industry, visited the sets hoping for stardom. However, his aspirations were curtailed when he was relegated to the extras' line. He had hoped he had the looks to be a star, if not the acting chops for one.

Despite his dedication to acting, Meer found himself unable to endure the routine humiliations of the industry. He made one final attempt by seeking to meet Ashok Kumar, a prominent actor in those days, but was thwarted by watchmen. With his aspirations dashed, Meer chose to abandon his dreams of being part of the industry. Despite residing in Bombay for a year, he felt more and more disheartened with each passing day. He eventually gave up, after spending much of his time strolling along the picturesque Marine Drive. The truth was that he frequently began to fall sick and his friends convinced him to return to Delhi.

The joke, however, is that Meer was asked to go home and give birth to an actor. He did just that, serendipitously. 'My father was selected for a Pathan's role and he performed so badly that Asif sa'ab threw him out of the film. My father would say to me when I was small that Asif sa'ab told him to go back home and give birth to an actor,' Shah Rukh told the press in 2011 during the launch of his company Red Chillies Entertainment's first documentary, *Mughal-e-Azam: A Documentary*.[12] He was the narrator of the forty-minute film about the making and legacy of *Mughal-e-Azam*. He made it with Akbar Asif, K. Asif's son. The tagline of the movie read: 'A tribute from a son to his father'.

> # Bas Itna Sa Khwab Hai
>
> ## Yes Boss, 1997

3

THE BIG BOMBAY DREAM

It's hard to imagine Shah Rukh Khan as anyone other than the world-famous superstar he is today. But in the 1980s, Shah Rukh was certain he'd be a sportsman. 'But I injured myself. I was under observation for seven to eight days, and bedridden for a month and a half. I hurt my lower back and I felt very bad. For six to eight months, I was extremely depressed. I started going back to my school,' he admitted on Big CBS Prime's *India's Prime Icon*.

Acting was his mother's idea. She wanted him to feel better. 'My mom said, "Try and do something in the evening to fill your time." I started doing this play called *Annie Get Your Gun* at Lady Shri Ram College, one of the attractions being that it was a girls' college and I was one of the few guys who were chosen to act there—eight boys and eighty girls!'

The college enlisted the city's premier theatre company, Theatre Action Group (TAG), to stage the musical alongside the students. Barry John, the founder and director of TAG, led the production. Given the scale, male performers were recruited from outside the company through auditions. By the time Shah Rukh arrived, much of the casting had already been completed, and he ended up accepting the role of a singer-dancer in the chorus. However, by the time the show was staged, Shah Rukh decided to become part of TAG.

TAG was an English production company launched in 1973 by John, Siddhartha Basu, Roshan Seth, Lillete Dubey, Mira Nair and Pankaj Kapur. It had talents who were the crème de la crème of south Delhi. It was the first time in his life that Shah Rukh, who was a rank outsider, was faced with the task of making his mark and earning his spot among the members. Thereon, it became a habit for him.

His best friend in those days was Divya Seth, who later went on to become a well-known television star and acted in many films, including 2024's *Article 370*. Back in 2015, Shah Rukh tweeted a picture with her and said, 'My bestest friend Divya, who taught me acting. Don't hold the bad ones [performances] I do, only the good inspired by her teachings.'[1]

The two worked together in Lekh Tandon's TV series *Dil Dariya* (1988). In an interview, Seth said about Shah Rukh, 'We've always been friends and did so many plays together. He was always sure he would be successful. And he continues to work hard at it.'

Shah Rukh was studying for a degree in economics at Hansraj College in Delhi, but his true learning was at TAG, under John's tutelage. Despite being passionate about acting, Shah Rukh wasn't hoping to become the next Dilip Kumar or Amitabh Bachchan, though he was immensely in awe of them. Fair enough; it was not practical for a boy from a middle-class Gautam Nagar home in Delhi to consider Bollywood as an option. He didn't have the conventional looks to become a hero or the means to aspire so high.

But he and his Ammi had a ritual—they would watch a movie every night on their VCR. In those days, Shah Rukh hoped to make a killing in short films, TV and mostly advertising. His mother, like all Indian mothers, believed her son was made for bigger things in life. She let him follow his path, knowing well that great things awaited him down the road. Till today, Shah Rukh believes his mother is his first and most important fan.

Barry John has often been asked if acting can be taught. In 2016, in an interview to Huffington Post India, he explained that acting is a skill that can be learnt. In today's world, where modern actors need a wide range of abilities, training has become essential. But he believes that the film industry is crowded with untrained individuals, many of whom are relatives of industry insiders or simply possess good looks and sculpted bodies without any real experience. Like many aspects of life in India, the film industry is often a family affair, and while some talent may be inherited, the longevity of these actors' careers depends on the effort they invest, not their lineage.

Barry is clear that he isn't responsible for Shah Rukh's success. 'An actor must have talent, perseverance and a bit of luck. Shah Rukh had all of them. I can't take credit for what he is. His life is the stuff of dreams. It's like a fairy tale. There's tragedy, loss, comedy and success. He was destined to be somebody. He joined my Theatre Action Group in Delhi. I think I had a profound impact on his formative years as an actor. He was energetic, hard-working, intelligent and humorous. He had a great desire to learn, he was extremely committed and put in a lot of effort, just like he does today for any film.'[2]

Shah Rukh had always been a believer in the method and craft of acting. In fact, when he was shooting *Zero*, he asked his daughter Suhana to be on set and learn the groundwork. This insistence on getting the craft right comes from Barry. The latter's teaching style wasn't imposing and he gently guided his students towards becoming adept performers. He wanted to do a lot of workshops where his students could delve into characters and scenarios. Barry felt acting could not be dictated and pushed the younglings to work on their expressions and gestures to fine-tune the nuances of the characters they were playing. He promoted subtlety—fuss, frills and exaggeration wasn't his style. The most important learning from these classes, one assumes, would be Shah Rukh interpreting the character himself. The ground rule at TAG was: 'There is no right or wrong way to do a scene—"The Method" is what works for you. The barometer ultimately is how many people like it.'

Barry was the first man to suggest that Shah Rukh give movies a shot. This suggestion wasn't meant to be a compliment. In the five years Shah Rukh spent at TAG, it was apparent that he focused on the larger-than-life aspect more than on internalizing the story. From a craft perspective, there are actors who become the character and internalize a role. Shah Rukh has the ability of scaling up a character or making the story grander. Barry was probably the only man who realized that Shah Rukh might not have what it takes to be a flawless actor, but he had all the makings of a star.

In Delhi acting circles, a regular boy aspiring to be a star didn't often get multiple offers, or even the big ones. Shah Rukh's first movie was the small film *In Which Annie Gives It Those Ones*, directed by Pradip Krishen and his writer-partner Arundhati Roy. Set in a Delhi architecture school in 1974, the film was unusual, to say the least. It centres on the idealistic student Anand Grover, also known as Annie (played by Arjun Raina), who prefers dreaming up utopian solutions to India's problems rather than focusing on his studies. His girlfriend, the free-spirited Radha, is portrayed by Roy, while notable actors such as Roshan Seth, Divya Seth, Rituraj Singh and Manoj Bajpayee play supporting roles. It explores themes of youthful rebellion and college life. The film faded into obscurity until the release of Roy's book *The God of Small Things*. After she won the Booker Prize, the screenplay of *In Which Annie Gives It Those Ones* was published. In 2024, the Film Heritage Foundation announced that it was in the process of restoring the film and that it would release it in theatres soon.[3]

Shah Rukh's character had little screen time—four scenes—and no name. What the film showed him, though, was that he wasn't meant to be in films that didn't portray him in a larger-than-life persona—he was cut out to do hero parts.

Shah Rukh's breakthrough in television came with *Fauji*, helmed by the jovial Colonel Raj Kapoor, who appeared on *Jeena Isi Ka Naam Hai* to talk about the actor. Speaking about Colonel Kapoor, Shah Rukh said, 'I never thought I could act on screen. Let me share a story: After my father passed away, my mother and I were searching for a house to rent. When we found one, my mother insisted that I see it first before confirming. When asked where I was, she replied, "He's off acting." Kapoor's son-in-law Kamal

Dewan suggested I go to him, who was directing a serial. That's how *Fauji*, which was aired in 1989 and had thirteen episodes, came to be.'

Fauji served as Kapoor's homage to the Indian Army, presenting a realistic portrayal of cadet life as young men trained to become commandos.

Shah Rukh was already acting in another serial titled *Dil Dariya* at that time and shot for *Fauji* during lunch breaks—such shooting schedules were common for actors then who worked on multiple projects at the same time. The audition for *Fauji* involved a rigorous physical test, including a 1.5-mile run at dawn, followed by an impromptu boxing match. Shah Rukh impressed with his discipline, by not giving up on the race even when many co-auditioners dropped out. He was initially designated to land a smaller role while Kapoor's son Bobby was to play one of the leads, Abhimanyu. But Bobby, who was already the cameraman, had to bow out. It's the way of this industry, as Karan Johar points out in Zoya Akhtar's debut movie *Luck By Chance:* '*Industry mein outsiders aise hi toh aatey hai. Koi alag tarah ka role likhta hai, koi badaa star nahi karta hai and finally ek naye ladke ko break mil jata hai* [This is how outsiders get into the film industry. Someone writes a different sort of a role, big stars refuse to do it and then finally a newbie gets his break]. *Zanjeer* was turned down by seven actors before a struggling star, Amitabh Bachchan, picked it up.'

Shah Rukh has been destiny's child in that sense, or probably was always at the right place at the right time. His two big Bollywood hits, *Darr* and *Baazigar*, landed in his kitty just like that.

How Shah Rukh landed *Fauji*, over and above the rigour he showed, is funny, to say the least. At the launch of Samar Khan's and Sonali Kokra's book *SRK: 25 Years of a Life*, he recounted, 'I went there, I auditioned and he gave me a sweet role—in the whole *Fauji* serial, the Colonel orders me to go and count the crows on the tree. I would run and say, "There are four crows." This was my role in the whole serial. I thought this was so strange ... How could I tell my family that this was my role? ... I did that and it was one of the nicest roles, and they've all loved me like a family. I am not saying this with false humility, but maybe the goodness I have at this age is because of the wonderful men and women I've met in my life.'

Amina Shervani, who wrote and acted in *Fauji* (as Kiran Kochar), said that for its time, *Fauji* was an extremely expensive show to make.

It cost nearly Rs 2 lakh per episode to shoot. It was facing a four-year delay in its pilot launch. The *Fauji* team rallied in 1988 to ensure an early release the following year. They obtained permissions from the Ministry of Defence, Doordarshan and the Army headquarters. Despite challenges, the dedicated team pooled their talents and resources to bring the series to fruition. In an interview to ThePrint, Shervani said, 'I remember the Army was supposed to give us sten guns and other equipment to use, but they didn't let us touch anything. So I flirted with a commando to steal a broken, defunct sten gun, and made a mould of it. We made twelve aluminium moulds that looked quite real. And one day, I was carrying them back from the studio in an auto, and the cops stopped me, and there I was—with twelve real-looking guns. Fortunately, we had done films for Delhi Police before that, so the police commissioner knew what we were really doing.'

This was the late 1980s and the turmoil in Punjab meant that procuring materials such as fuel for the demolition and explosion scenes was difficult, as the authorities had put strict rules in place. And so, for the scenes in the show, these had to be sourced from Shah Rukh's mother, who owned a kerosene company. Dynamite was acquired through connections with friends who had contracts for stone and mica mining in the Aravallis, allowing the team to create their own explosives. One would think these would be the biggest challenges in the making, but the real hurdle was getting Shah Rukh to cut his hair. Shervani said, 'Shah Rukh just wouldn't cut his hair. He would keep smoking, and his mother would be worried that nothing would come of his passion for theatre.'

When *Fauji* was aired, it resonated with people in a big way. Shah Rukh's charm captivated viewers, propelling him to the forefront of the show. His character, Abhimanyu, became central to the story, showcasing Shah Rukh's knack for both romance and action. This was the first time he started becoming a household name. One of the many fans of Shah Rukh from that era is my own mother, Ellora Basu. When I first told her I am working on this book, she recounted to me how her love for Shah Rukh dates back to the late 1980s. 'Watching *Fauji* was like witnessing the birth of a superstar. Shah Rukh Khan's charm as Abhimanyu Rai was not to be missed, and we knew he was destined for greatness from the very first day the show aired.' As a child of that time, she told me how there was a general sense of fatigue with the trope of the 'Angry Young Man' that ruled movies and television then. 'I wasn't interested in television until *Fauji* came along. That was a young show. It had stories that my siblings and I could relate to. The show brought in young people to television viewing. A large part of our love was because of Shah Rukh. He was always a sincere actor, but more than anything else, he had the ability to charm you. It could be called screen presence, but in his unique goofy, boy-next-door way, he was someone you'd want to root for in a story. That's the sign of a hero!'

After passing out of Hansraj College, he enrolled in Jamia Millia Islamia for a film-making course. He was too busy to attend all his classes, but the marks rarely faltered. He was a bright student all along; some even said too bright to be lost to acting. He could have done his MBA and moved to the US, like many of his peers from school. But by that time, he was deep into the theatre circuit. TAG was taking up most of his time and the TV serials he starred in were flourishing.

In an interview to a channel in the US right before *Kuch Kuch Hota Hai* was to begin shooting, Shah Rukh recounted, 'I didn't want to do TV but I did it by chance. It was a different medium. Colonel Kapoor had seen a play of mine in Urdu and picked me up. I enrolled for film-making in Jamia Millia Islamia after college. It was a two-year course. I wanted to make films—make ad films, primarily. Someone saw me in a serial [*Fauji*] and gave me a call and that's how I went to Bombay.'

On Shah Rukh's fifty-fourth birthday, his professor Farhat Basir Khan from the Mass Communication Research Centre (MCRC) at Jamia Millia Islamia in Delhi, gave an interview about his most famous student. He told *The Indian Express* that when they (the professors at Jamia) first met Shah Rukh, he was already an accomplished actor and performer. He was immensely versatile and even portrayed a female character at an audition, leaving a strong impression on the professors. Shah Rukh's talent for conceptualizing was evident, as he had a remarkable ability to deconstruct ideas and present them simply.

During that time, Shah Rukh also began shooting for *Fauji*, dividing his time between his studies and the show. Due to his demanding acting schedule, he occasionally missed classes but made up for it by visiting Professor Khan's house to discuss course material. Despite his unconventional methods—which the professor didn't always agree with—his charm and understanding of the subjects shone through. One assignment stands out in Professor Khan's memory—when the entire class went out on a field shoot to engage with people and grasp on-ground realities. Everyone was supposed to return to the van at a designated time, but Shah Rukh was late. Concerned, the professor sent people to look for him. Eventually, they found him at a beautiful location, waiting for the perfect moment when the sun was at a particular angle so he could take a photo. The professor was impressed by his attention to detail.

As fate would have it, Mayanagri, as Mumbai is often called, was bound to entice a rising star like him. It was 1990 when Shah Rukh first landed in the city he would eventually call home.

I wish the story were just as dreamy as one would have hoped. When Shah Rukh landed in Bombay to do a role for a company named Iskara, there was no one to pick him up at the airport. The thought that this was all a hoax and that he had come to the city for nothing played on his mind. On the brink of stardom is a precarious place to be. One has the sort of hope that rides on anxiety: What if it doesn't happen for me? Shah Rukh was no different. He panicked as he looked around. Was this a fraud? He knew going back wasn't an option. He couldn't fail. Desperate, he locked himself inside a phone booth, looking for coins with which to place a call to his mother. He wanted to break down and tell his Ammi about the cruel joke that had been played on him. Overcome with shame and rage, he broke down. People crossing the booth saw a man in a shambles. That's when a few women on their way to perform Hajj recognized the 'Fauji boy' and stopped. 'Don't worry, beta,' they comforted him, hands raised in prayer. 'We'll remember you during our Hajj pilgrimage. You'll become a big actor one day.'

Eventually the individual entrusted with picking Shah Rukh up at the airport showed up. And the actor made his way to meet Kundan Shah and Aziz Mirza, who would go on to become two of his early collaborators in Bollywood. Aziz thought Shah Rukh looked like his son Haroon and immediately developed a soft spot for him. Shah Rukh even started living out of his Prabhadevi home and became thick with Haroon. Looking back, he once joked in an interview, 'When I write a book, I will romanticize my struggle. There was none. Everyone struggles within themselves. More than writing stories about that, I spent days on the roads of Mumbai before anyone cast me; I ate cockroaches before I got proper food. Then I got a break and everyone was rude to me. And now I am going to make it stick.'

He continued, musing, 'I don't have a story like that. I had a significant number of naysayers who said I wouldn't make it. But I didn't come to be a star.

In those days, Shah Rukh was sure that television was where his audience was. 'Television is about instant popularity. I had a set idea and wanted to work on my own terms. I didn't want to care about the size of the banner. If my role was good, I was game. I didn't want to get launched. I always chose variety.'

I had a lot of faith in the goodness of acting. I had done a lot of reading on acting. There was a belief in me that I knew the grammar of acting. Not the essential thing to become a star, but important to be a good actor. I am not a grammatical actor. I know how it's done, but I always try it differently.'[4]

Shah Rukh's days were divided between Delhi and Bombay as he started work on three major TV productions—*Circus*, *Wagle Ki Duniya* and *Umeed*. For Sumita Dhar (name changed), a seventy-five-year-old homemaker in Mohali, the Shah Rukh of *Circus* was better than the Shah Rukh of *Fauji*. 'I am the queen of watching television. I watch everything, from the Pakistani drama *Dhoop Kinarey* to *Fauji* to Turkish dramas and now even K-dramas. But I still remember seeing Shah Rukh as Shekharan for the first time. We already knew him, but in *Circus*, he was finer and better. There was a spark in his eyes that told you he was destined for greatness. Every time he appeared on screen, you couldn't look away.

I knew I was watching the beginning of something extraordinary! I wasn't surprised at all when he got into Hindi films and became such a big star. I would tell my late husband, "This boy is made for more!" I was right. My husband, who was in the army, and I would have passionate debates on *Fauji* versus *Circus*. In all of it, Shah Rukh always won in the end!'

In those days, Shah Rukh was sure that television was where his audience was. 'Television is about instant popularity. I had a set idea and wanted to work on my own terms. I didn't want to care about the size of the banner. If my role was good, I was game. I didn't want to get launched. I always chose variety.'5

Shah Rukh didn't aspire to be in films. Bombay, and Bollywood, was his stop gap, even though by then film offers were coming fast, with *Circus* making good noise for him. Parallel cinema director Mani Kaul offered him *Ahmak*, based on Fyodor Dostoevsky's novel *The Idiot*. There was Ketan Mehta, who was taken by the bratty young actor and thought he would be a good fit for *Maya Memsaab*. The prospect of dancing with the heroine against the backdrop of snow-capped mountains was what lured Shah Rukh to Ketan's movie. But he did Mani's film for emotional reasons: *The Idiot* was a book his father had gifted him. This was his hat tip to his maker!

Mani's film got him the eyeballs and made him friends with producer Viveck Vaswani, a well-known Cuffe Parade boy who had the means to make movies and the passion for it too. In an interview to Film Companion in January 2024, Vaswani said, 'We would sit and smoke. I could match him, cigarette for cigarette, coffee for coffee, lack of sleep for lack of sleep. I guess we were matched.'

In an old *Lehren* interview from 1992, Shah Rukh said, 'I wasn't interested in films. *Maine karna hi nahi chaha* [I never wanted to do it]. I was doing my Mass Communication (MA). After *Umeed* and *Circus*, Hemaji [Hema Malini] called me for *Dil Aashna Hai*. Films were an experiment.'

Shah Rukh and Hema Malini could have ended up having a spat over a newspaper piece. In a 2016 interview, Shah Rukh recounted, 'The headline was "Hema Malini Does Not Know How to Direct" [attributed to him]. I did not say that, but it's possible that I was that bad-mannered—I say a lot of things that I regret later. But I didn't mean it and I didn't feel it.' He sheepishly and nervously went on set the next morning. Nevertheless she called him and told him to sit next to her. 'I sat down and thought, "Oh, she's going to kill me." She asked, "What did you say in that interview?" I was just hoping that the ground would swallow me up and this moment would end. Instead, Hemaji matter-of-factly said, "Either you are famous, or I am very famous. I have stopped working. So, it has to be your fame. So when you're famous, people write nonsense. So get ready."'

It was in those days that Shah Rukh told a friend, 'I'm going to be a successful star. You see, Amitabh Bachchan has retired, Dilip sa'ab is very old, and after that I can see only one person, and that is Shah Rukh Khan.'

While success was courting him, back home things were taking a turn for the worse. His mother was dying.

Shah Rukh was shooting in Goa when he found out that his mother wasn't keeping well. She had a lingering ankle ache. He called his mother, and she told him it was nothing. He believed her. Perhaps the twenty-five-year-old believed fate wouldn't be that cruel to him. But just like heroes in epics, sometimes the gods throw in a curse, testing the mettle of the hero.

An ulcer on her foot landed Fatima in hospital, and in two months she was gone. The cause of death was multi-organ failure due to septicaemia. It made no sense to Shah Rukh.

When she died, he was filled with rage against life itself. The one person who had believed in him and felt that he had what it takes to be a star was gone before she could see it. He had tried to arrange an in-hospital viewing for his mother of a few episodes of *Circus*, but unfortunately, Fatima was too sick to make sense of them.

He told Simi Garewal in a *Rendezvous* interview that he was desperate to pull his mother back from death.[6] When Fatima slipped into a coma, the doctors urged her family to come immediately. He knew it was a matter of hours. He was in anguish—he didn't want to let her go. He prayed in the hospital parking lot: *'Nasrun minal lahi wah fatahun kareeb'*, meaning 'God, give me the strength to win.' He uttered it 869 times that day.

When he managed to reach his mother's side, she was nearly gone, perhaps holding on only to see him one last time.

He held firm to the belief that death only claimed those who were completely content. Desperate to keep Fatima with him, he recited a litany of all the terrible things he would do if she left him—neglect his sister, fail as an actor, deliberately cause chaos in their lives. A solitary tear escaped her eye, and she was gone. He tenderly combed her hair, kissed her and then let her go.

At the burial ground, Shah Rukh wasn't quite himself. He almost came to blows with the maulvi over a non-issue. The truth was that he couldn't begin to fathom how this could be the last time he was seeing the face of someone he loved the most in the world. As they laid Fatima to rest, he finally allowed himself to weep.

> 'When my father died, I didn't cry. I thought it was heroic. I was one of the pall bearers. I thought I had become a little big man. But I felt cheated despite the fact he had prepared me for his death ... And my mother's death made me realize that nothing is permanent. I stopped hoping for anything. I cried a lot. Nothing shocks me any more.'

He later said in an interview to *Filmfare* magazine, 'When my father died, I didn't cry. I thought it was heroic. I was one of the pall bearers. I thought I had become a little big man. But I felt cheated despite the fact he had prepared me for his death ... And my mother's death made me realize that nothing is permanent. I stopped hoping for anything. I cried a lot. Nothing shocks me any more.'[7]

The weeks that followed weren't easy for him. The grief was making him nauseous; his own city, his own house was making him claustrophobic. He was barely eating and felt shattered. His sister, who still wasn't over their father's death, also grieved this irreversible blow. But what worried everyone was that Shah Rukh didn't even go to visit his mother's grave.

They say that in times of extreme emotion, things and decisions can go either way. Shah Rukh's grief had turned to anger and, in his darkest moment, he decided he wanted to run away from anything that reminded him of the pain in his heart. He packed up and left Delhi. In a way, this was the last time he called Delhi home. At 5 a.m. on 26 June 1991, he landed at Viveck Vaswani's house in Mumbai and said, 'Let's make movies!'

Vaswani said in an interview to *Film Companion*, 'One day the bell rings at 4 a.m. Shah Rukh was standing there with two big bags. He used to go up and down, and usually, as a matter of routine, I would go and pick him up from the airport. It was a tradition. He was standing there and I asked him, "Why didn't you call me? I would have come picked you up!" He straight asked, "Will you do a film with me?" I said, "I have been saying [this] for two months, and you have been rejecting it." I asked him to come in. He said, "No, will you do a film with me?" I told him I swear I will do the film. At 4 a.m., we kept our bags inside, went to The President, got kona coffee and cigarettes, and he asked what kind of film. It was to be his launch film, and it had to be him. That's where *Raju Ban Gaya Gentleman* was born!'[8]

Vaswani told him he would make Shah Rukh a star.

Shah Rukh entered Bollywood exactly a year after Amitabh Bachchan announced a break from films. Bachchan took a five-year sabbatical after *Khuda Gawah* (1992) to recover from his failure as a political figure and understand where his heart lay. Yes, Shah Rukh was at the right place at the right time. There was room for a new kind of leading man. The old guard was passing the baton to the new order.

Growing up, Shah Rukh had been smitten by two figures—Dilip Kumar and Amitabh Bachchan. Dilip Kumar knew his father. In an interview to *Filmfare* in 2013, Shah Rukh said, 'Actually, I knew Dilip sa'ab as a kid. Dad knew him. They used to live in the same galli in Delhi. I've met Dilip sa'ab many times in my childhood. We have been to his place often. Actually, Sairaji doesn't remember this, but her medicines used to be sent by my aunt from London. Years later, when I was working with Ketan Mehta, I saw a picture of Dilip Kumar in his office and I was like "Oh! That's me." He looked so much like me in that picture. Or, rather, I looked so much like him. But my relationship with Dilip sa'ab goes beyond films. Dilip sa'ab and Sairaji have always thought of me as their son.'[9]

In some ways, Dilip Kumar was the reason Shah Rukh made it to Hindi movies. As a convent-educated boy, Hindi wasn't Shah Rukh's strong suit. His mother knew that movies were his weakness. She challenged him to score well in his exams, and if he did, he'd be taken to the movies. The first movie he ever saw in a theatre was *Joshila*. After he got full marks, they went to Vivek cinema hall to watch it. He later discovered that it was directed by Yash Chopra and produced by Gulshan Rai. 'So, my connection with Yash Chopra goes back to that time,' he said in an interview.

Shah Rukh's mother was a movie lover, and those were the days of VCRs. They would watch movies on a black-and-white TV, since they didn't have a colour television. A man named Vinit, who later acted in two movies, sold VCRs in Chandni Chowk, and Shah Rukh became friends with him due to their common love for films.

His mother suffered from leg pain, so every night he and his sister would massage her legs while they watched movies—a ritual they cherished. 'We used to watch all kinds of films. She loved Dilip Kumar and thought I looked like him. Every time a new movie was released, mom, sister and I would watch it at Uphaar theatre. After my father's death, watching films was "our" thing.'[10]

Dilip Kumar and Shah Rukh never worked together, but Kamal Haasan brought them very close to it. Haasan wanted to re-make one of his most loved Tamil films, *Thevar Magan*, in Hindi, with Dilip Kumar and Shah Rukh as father and son. But Dilip Kumar declined. 'He found the theme too violent. And he had sworn never to do violent films,' Haasan told journalist Subhash K. Jha in an interview.

As a child Dilip Kumar had witnessed the savagery and brutality of Partition in his home town, Peshawar. His family had been butchered. He had managed to escape the bloodshed by hiding under a bed without food and water for many days. And you know what kept him alive? A little sparrow that had perched itself near his hiding place and reminded him there was life outside. Dilip Kumar could never face violence after that, even on screen. Alas, Shah Rukh and his dream of sharing a screen remained unfulfilled.

But they stayed friends. Would that be the correct way to label their relationship? Maybe not. Saira Banu, Dilip Kumar's wife, thinks of Shah Rukh as their *mooh bola beta* (adopted child). He chides her when she doesn't run her fingers through his hair in blessing. He is there to support her through good and bad times. When Dilip Kumar passed away, Shah Rukh was the first to reach their home.

Maybe it's his way of holding on to his parents—both of whom were attached to Dilip Kumar. Or perhaps it was his way of showing his appreciation for the thespian's art. Shah Rukh believes that Dilip Kumar's biggest gift to Indian cinema was his silence. Sometimes it speaks louder than words—a virtue he believes he doesn't possess. 'He booms even when he whispers,' Shah Rukh said while giving a tribute to him in 2001 at the Zee Cine Awards.

Of the many things that Dilip Kumar taught him over the years, he never forgot two things. 'The first time we met, he lightly tapped me on my cheeks and said, "Work hard." That, and the fundamental rule that Indian films tend to forget: "No actor can be bigger than the substance he portrays—character, story and screenplay. For any enduring performance, Shah Rukh—a good story, good character equations, conflict and an opportunity to then wade through it. Then you have substance to deal with, not just shadows!"'[11]

Taking that as a learning, Shah Rukh has always empowered his writers to develop material that has substance. His last writer, Sumit Arora, who wrote *Jawan*, says, 'The dialogues had to justify the persona of the star that Shah Rukh Khan is, and yet they have to hold within the world of the story. It couldn't have looked fake or manufactured at all.'

In another interview, Arora, who is a Meerut boy, said that his life went from walking down Bandstand staring at Mannat to doing meetings with Shah Rukh inside the bungalow. Inputs from the star were always available. 'Shah Rukh sir and I worked together to find Azad and Vikram Rathore's language. We'd sit with the dialogue draft, and Shah Rukh sir would explain the line to Atlee in English. Sometimes, Atlee would convey the emotion he wanted for the scene, and we'd capture it in our own rhythm.

That's the amount of work he puts in personally to perfect the substance, so to speak. And over these three years, Shah Rukh sir has taught me the most important thing about art—to be open to others and respectful of everyone. You create better when you are welcoming of others.'

Shah Rukh's life is what can be described as that of a hero—a man plagued by personal loss only to emerge stronger; a man destined for greater things; a man who was born to rule the world. From the modest beginnings of television to the grandeur of the silver screen, his ascent epitomizes the essence of determination, talent and the audacity to dream big.

In an industry that is often perceived as a closed fortress, Shah Rukh appeared as a swarthy youngster, challenging conventions and rewriting the rulebook of the Hindi-film hero. In many ways, Shah Rukh's rise to stardom coincided with a transformative era in India—the country was changing its ways. The old hero was fading into oblivion, the older values weren't sitting with the new crowd. As the nation embraced economic reforms, opportunities burgeoned and dreams dared to soar higher. The angry hero of the 1970s was not what the common man wanted—they wanted someone who was softer and had stars in his eyes. And Shah Rukh was that quintessential Indian guy.

Every year on Eid, as you walk down the crowded Bandstand area, you hear an announcement: '*Shah Rukh sa'ab aa gaye bahar* [Shah Rukh sir is outside his house now].' The crowds run towards Mannat to catch a glimpse of the star. It makes one think: Why do these hordes of people, who come from across the globe, stand outside his home all day just to catch a glimpse of him? A part of the reason is the nature of the Indian fandom. It is all about putting someone on a pedestal and revering them.

Most of those who rise fall just as hard—we have seen that happen time and again. This ties back to the nature of fandoms at large. But not with Shah Rukh Khan. The common man wants to see Shah Rukh win. Mannat is a shrine not because a superstar lives in it—Mannat is the story of hope. That a man from nowhere, an absolute nobody, has become someone whom the world knows—a king among men.

Mannat stands as this terrific success story that is a homage to the dreamers, the believers and the relentless pursuers. No dream is too audacious, no obstacle too formidable. Shah Rukh is not just a superstar—he is the very essence of our aspirations, our hopes and our collective faith that greatness can be achieved.

The story of Mannat itself is pretty fantastic. On 8 October 1995, Shah Rukh presented his wife, Gauri, with a historic bungalow overlooking the sea. It was constructed in 1896, situated on a sprawling 26,300-square-foot property. In a metropolis where a snug 500-square-foot apartment is deemed comfortable, owning a standalone bungalow is a huge feat. Mannat, or Villa Vienna, as it was called then, was in a dilapidated state and mostly used for film shoots. Over the next five years, the property underwent a remarkable transformation.

It wasn't an easy purchase for Shah Rukh either. He had to do films he didn't particularly like to buy the bungalow. In an interview in 2016, Shah Rukh even admitted that pre-Mannat, he did films for money. '*Main naam nahi lunga, par sirf ek film maine paison ke liye ki thi. Maine abhi tak saat films ki hai. Aur mujhe maalum bhi tha, maine producer ko bhi bol diya tha, maine ghar liya tha uss film ki fees se, mujhe bahut zaroorat thi. Jab meri halaat theek-thaak ho gayi, toh jab maine recently apni saare films vapas khareedna shuru kiya, woh pehli film thi jo maine vapas li... mujhe aisa lagta hai ki maine uss film ki payment vapas ki hai* [I will not take its name, but I have done only one film for money. I have done sixty films till now. I bought my first house from the fees of that film. I needed the money. But when I got financial stability and I started buying my films, that was the first film I bought. I feel I have returned the payment for that film].'[12]

Mumbai regulations prohibit alterations to heritage properties, hence the exteriors and facade of Villa Vienna remained unchanged. However, the interiors became a stylish residence fit for a star. Renowned Indian artist M.F. Husain crafted a painting to complement the elegant white-and-cobalt-blue living room.

The villa belonged to gallerist Kekoo Gandhy. Initially christened 'Jannat', meaning 'heaven', Shah Rukh later altered its name to Mannat, meaning 'prayer', as the residence proved auspicious for his career. Not many know that Mannat was first offered to Salman Khan. In an interview with Bollywood Hungama, Salman said, 'It had come to me when I had just started off. My dad [Salim Khan] said, "*Itne bade ghar mein tum karoge kya* [What will you do in such a big house]?"' And then he added, laughing, 'Now I want to ask Shah Rukh, *itne bade ghar mein karta kya hai tu* [what do you do in such a big house]?'

In her book *My Life in Design*, Gauri Khan answered it for Salman. 'Shah Rukh spends a lot of time in his library and study. He brainstorms there by himself and sometimes in a group—reading and writing, having meetings and work discussions. We have created a comfortable yet serious ambience. Needless to say, a majority of Shah Rukh's day, when he's not shooting, is spent in the library.'[13]

The current valuation of Mannat is more than Rs 200 crore. But Shah Rukh always says, 'Even if I was broke one day, I would sell everything but not Mannat.'

One would guess it reminds him of how far he has come in life. The physical space probably makes him work harder every day. But the answer is slightly more spiritual. We discovered it on a quick Twitter AMA. When a fan cheekily asked him of his plans to sell the house, he wrote back, '*Bhai Mannat bikti nahi. Sar jhuka kar maangi jaati hai ... yaad rakhoge toh life mein kuch paa sakogay* [Brother, Mannat is not sold. One has to lower one's head in prayer and ask for it. Remember this, and you might achieve something in life].'

> *Mujhe yakeen hai ki main sirf isliye janma hoon ... ki tumse pyaar kar sakun ... Tum sirf isliye, ki ek din meri ban sako*
>
> *Chalte Chalte, 2003*

4

A LOVE STORY FOR THE AGES

What are the broad beats of a classic desi romantic saga? Hear this one: A young boy and girl meet and fall in love. They date for a few years. It is all clandestine until the families find out. Parents are unhappy. The girl is locked up and told she can't see the boy. She decides to sacrifice her love and go away to Mumbai. He follows her to the big city to win her love again. He finds her right when the sun is about to set at a beach in suburban Mumbai. He whisks her off her feet and declares how much he loves her and how he can't live without her.

Sounds like a fairy-tale romance.

Well, I just narrated the love story of Shah Rukh and his wife Gauri Khan née Chibba. And the best romance writers will attest to the fact that this is a story made for the big screen.

Shah Rukh first laid eyes on her at a common friend's party in Delhi. Gauri was dancing with her friend when he saw her. When a popular song played, it was customary for the boys to invite the girls to dance. The highlight of the evening often revolved around the intimate act of slow dancing.

She was fourteen. He was eighteen. She was wearing striking maroon corduroy pants that caught his eye. She was fashionable, sassy and attractive. When he approached her, she lied that she was waiting for her boyfriend. He was a little disappointed, but soon discovered it was her ploy to keep boys out of her way.

In an interview, Shah Rukh remembered how Gauri was very talkative at that time. 'She talked a lot, which is strange, because you know Gauri—she doesn't talk much. Then she explained that she wasn't waiting for her boyfriend but for her brother. She just used that line so she wouldn't have to dance with any cheapskate,' he said to Preity Zinta on her chat show, *Up Close & Personal with PZ*.

Shah Rukh got her phone number the third time they met, on 25 October 1984.

Their first date lasted only five minutes. Gauri came from an affluent south Delhi home in Panchsheel Park. The colony was all about elegant bungalows and row houses. The two met at the Panchsheel Park Club, and sat next to the pool and sipped colas. On their way back, the scooter Shah Rukh and his friend were riding broke down and they had to drag it down the street.

But Shah Rukh and Gauri connected. Love blossomed and the years began to pass. Gauri lived in a joint family. She was constantly surrounded by uncles, aunts and cousins, and was accountable to far too many people about her whereabouts.

The couple came up with a complex system to communicate discreetly. Direct phone calls from Shah Rukh were out of the question, as frequent calls from a boy would arouse suspicion. Instead, Shah Rukh enlisted other girls to call and ask for her, using the code name 'Shaheen', which Gauri would understand as a signal. Despite not being permitted to date, Gauri would rendezvous with Shah Rukh at parties, often accompanied by her friends. He assisted her with her history studies and even taught her how to drive. They would go for cute cola dates and stroll through the expansive Jawaharlal Nehru University campus, hug a bit, laugh a lot and eventually come back to their respective homes.

Our wonderfully progressive Shah Rukh wasn't always the green flag he is today. He was overbearing and possessive in the early years of their relationship. He had a problem with Gauri wearing white shirts and preferred her hair to be tied up to avoid drawing too much attention to herself. He vehemently opposed the idea of her wearing swimsuits and got enraged if she interacted with other boys. Despite being a Delhi boy, he was suffering from what he calls the 'small-town, middle-class mentality'. Tired of his behaviour, his Gauri reached a breaking point and decided to distance herself from him. They didn't meet each other for six or seven months after a fight. She refused to answer his calls. Then, without informing Shah Rukh, she went on a holiday to Mumbai.

Upon learning that she was in Mumbai, undeterred by reason, he pursued her by landing up in the city of dreams for the very first time.

Shah Rukh later said in an interview[1] that the day before she left, she came to see him. It was her birthday and he had decorated his room with balloons and bought her many gifts. When she arrived, she cried, and he thought it was due to the overwhelming tension she was feeling. He confided in his friends, Ashish and Benny, and later told his mother about it. 'She told me to go and bring back the girl I loved,' he said. She also gave him Rs 10,000.

> 'She came over, and we hugged and cried. It was then that I realized I was being unreasonably possessive. I also realized that no one could ever love Gauri the way I loved her, and that gave me tremendous confidence.'

Together with his friends, he went to Mumbai. For the first two days, they stayed at a friend's house, but after that, they slept on the footpath near the Oberoi. He vividly remembers how they used to wash up in the Taj Hotel, sneaking into the bathroom early in the morning as it was being renovated at the time. They spent most of their days walking around searching for Gauri, especially along the beaches. 'Gauri loves beaches,' Shah Rukh says.

At the time, he didn't know much about Mumbai. On their last day, they met a Sardarji taxi driver who mentioned Aksa Beach. Desperate and out of money—Shah Rukh had even sold his camera—they decided to take a chance and go there. The cab dropped them off at Aksa, leaving them with just about twenty rupees. Someone then suggested they check out Gorai Beach, so they took a ferry across and searched extensively but couldn't find her. He went around describing Gauri to people there, focusing on her hair—he always loved her hairstyle, though she had cut it short just to spite him—and explaining that she was a friend he had lost. As they were heading back by rickshaw to catch the ferry around midnight, they heard people shouting. The rickshaw driver said there was a private beach nearby. Feeling a surge of hope, Shah Rukh asked the driver to take him there. When they arrived, there she was, standing in the water, wearing a T-shirt. 'She came over, and we hugged and cried. It was then that I realized I was being unreasonably possessive. I also realized that no one could ever love Gauri the way I loved her, and that gave me tremendous confidence.'[2]

Who knew that doing a show such as *Fauji* would come in handy in a courtship? Even though Senior Chibba didn't think much of Shah Rukh and his career, Abhimanyu Rai of *Fauji* left a mark on Shah Rukh's future father-in-law. 'Her parents had seen me on television and were quite fond of me. But they thought my name was Abhimanyu and then they got to know that I was Shah Rukh Khan. Her brother would threaten me in his best Amrish Puri voice: "Keep away from my sister, or else ..." Finally when I saw him I was in for a shock. He was this fair kid with blue eyes, who was not even remotely intimidating. In fact, when my friend Ashok saw him, he said, "There must be more to him, *yaar*, he sounds real deadly on the phone."'

For Gauri's father, Ramesh Chibba, watching *Fauji* was pure nostalgia, transporting him thirty years back to his own days at the Indian Military Academy. In an episode where Shah Rukh delivers drill orders to his subordinates, Ramesh was impressed with both his acting prowess and adeptness at mastering a challenging routine that even seasoned army men often struggle with. At that time he was not aware of the actor's relationship with his daughter. Ramesh found himself admiring Shah Rukh's skills without any idea of their personal connection. On one occasion, while dining out, Gauri's family spotted Shah Rukh at a restaurant, wearing a shirt that their garment export company had recently made for a French client, something not yet available in the market. Gauri's mother, Savita, remarked, 'There's the *Fauji* boy wearing our shirt,' leaving Gauri's uncle Tejinder to ponder if it had been pilfered from the factory. Meanwhile, Gauri, present at the table, pretended ignorance of both the man and the shirt she had gifted him.

Eventually, the unsettling rumour of a Hindu–Muslim romance reached Gauri's household, leaving her parents bewildered and distressed as they grappled with the spreading gossip. Not particularly devout, Ramesh and Savita were not inclined towards elaborate religious rituals or pujas. Their own marriage was a product of love, a departure from the prevalent trend of arranged marriages in their generation. They prided themselves on being progressive and affectionate parents, but the prospect of Gauri falling in love with a Muslim boy was beyond their comprehension. Gauri had always been an undemanding child. The notion that the same child could now be involved in such a controversial relationship seemed inconceivable to them.³

There was ample bagaawat. Shah Rukh and Gauri even called it off for a bit. Shah Rukh told *Filmfare*, 'Things weren't working out … Gauri was locked up at home like Simran in *Dilwale* [*Dulhania Le Jayenge*]. She would keep telling me, "Shah Rukh, you don't know my parents … you take things so lightly." And I would tell her that ten years down the line, we'd be laughing about all the trying times. And that's just what we do today. Sometimes in the nights, we sit and think about all that has happened and have a good laugh.'

The couple made the decision to confront their family members. Shah Rukh initiated the process by approaching Gauri's aunt, Neeru. He met Gauri's aunt and uncle at a restaurant and tried his best to impress them. At one point, he even joked about converting and calling himself Jeetendra Tully. Something about that meeting worked. Both Gauri's aunt and uncle suggested Shah Rukh attend a party at Gauri's home.

At the party, many guests recognized Shah Rukh as the actor from the television series *Fauji*. Intrigued, Gauri's father, Ramesh, engaged him in conversation, inquisitive to know more about him. He was unaware that this was the boy his daughter had been dating all along. Caught off guard, and intimidated, Shah Rukh initially fumbled for words. Sensing something amiss, Ramesh pressed for Shah Rukh's real name, to which he eventually confessed that he was Shah Rukh Khan. Recognizing the gravity of the situation, Ramesh advised Shah Rukh to leave to avoid causing a scene. Before leaving, he met Gauri's mother and thanked her. She was left puzzled and wondering why this well-mannered boy would leave out of the blue.

For Ramesh, the dealbreaker wasn't that Shah Rukh was a Muslim man, but the fact that he was an actor. Having served as an aide to President of India Zakir Husain, Ramesh had met film actors earlier and formed an unfavourable opinion of them. Even in the 1980s, it was uncommon for middle-class Indian children to aspire for careers in Hindi films. Bollywood was viewed with suspicion.

Savita admired Shah Rukh as a television star, but he wasn't an option as a prospective son-in-law. Desperate to thwart the relationship, Savita went to several astrologers, only to be informed that intervention was futile. Meanwhile, Gauri's older brother, Vikrant, was determined to protect his sister's honour, particularly from a Muslim boy with an absent father and limited job prospects. Vikrant resorted to threatening Shah Rukh with a gun, but his intimidation tactics failed. In contrast, Tejinder, believing in Shah Rukh's worthiness, advised Ramesh and Savita to reconcile their differences and not be swayed by religious or societal judgements. '*Banda dekho kaisa hai* [Assess the boy's character],' he urged them as tensions within the Chibba household reached a breaking point.

Why didn't they elope, you'd ask? Shah Rukh lived the plot of *Dilwale Dulhania Le Jayenge* long before he did the film. 'Like Raj and Simran, we never wanted to go against the wishes of our parents. The thought of running away from home never crossed our minds. But we knew we'd get married for sure. When I met Gauri's parents, I couldn't bring myself to say that I loved their daughter. That I thought was a stupid thing to say … because I could never love their daughter as much as they loved her. They had given birth to and brought up Gauri … My love could never be a substitute for their love.'

Pandemonium broke out at Gauri's home; her mother stopped eating, and the entire atmosphere felt like a period of mourning. Shah Rukh visited her father and felt a profound sense of guilt. During their conversation, it became evident that the family had no choice but to take a chance. 'I can understand Gauri's parents' apprehension. After all they were a Punjabi joint family. About fifteen people and Gauri was the youngest, the most sheltered one. Imagine she announces that she wants to get married to this ruffled-looking guy belonging to the wrong religion, having the wrong attitude and working in the wrong profession. There wasn't a right thing going for me. I don't blame them. They may have thought that any day they would have got a better deal for Gauri. Let's put it this way ... if my daughter brought in somebody like me, I would hit the ceiling.'

In another interview, Shah Rukh recounted his experience from the day of his wedding. He had both a Hindu-style wedding and a court marriage, the latter being essential for inter-religious unions. Although court marriages are usually kept discreet and only announced after some time, news of his marriage to Gauri emerged within three days. This led to protests from some Muslim organizations opposed to his marrying a Hindu.

'Things weren't working out ... Gauri was locked up at home like Simran in *Dilwale [Dulhania Le Jayenge]*. She would keep telling me, "Shah Rukh, you don't know my parents ... you take things so lightly." And I would tell her that ten years down the line, we'd be laughing about all the trying times. And that's just what we do today. Sometimes in the nights, we sit and think about all that has happened and have a good laugh.'

The situation was ironic given that his mother, a social worker and special executive magistrate, had facilitated around twenty-five intercaste marriages at their home. Initially, they had hoped for a simple, intimate wedding, but Gauri's parents preferred a traditional Hindu ceremony. Ultimately, he agreed, reasoning that marriage was a once-in-a-lifetime event. Typically, the groom arrives on a horse and does not see the bride until the ceremony is complete. However, the car meant to transport Gauri after her make-up broke down. With the wedding time fixed, Shah Rukh picked her up himself, took her to the venue, returned and arrived on a horse. Halfway through, he switched to an elephant, which was challenging, with friends helping him climb on to it.

By the time Shah Rukh got married, he had lost both his parents. 'When my mother was alive, she would call me anti-social. I used to never attend any functions or weddings. My mother used to always warn me that nobody would come for my wedding,' he said. He was determined to enjoy his own wedding to the fullest; he decided to dance for the entire one-kilometre stretch to the venue. At the wedding, he stood on his toes and wouldn't allow Gauri to place the garland around his neck. His friends, aware of his sense of humour, repeatedly cautioned him, saying, 'Shah Rukh, don't make any jokes there because people might misunderstand your intentions.' As this was his only opportunity to experience a wedding up close, he asked the pandit to explain each ritual, which went on for several hours. Despite his friends' warnings not to take things too seriously, there was a particular ritual where Gauri was supposed to wash his feet, which he was not comfortable with.

He donned his *Raju Ban Gaya Gentleman* suits for the ceremonies of the Hindu wedding. At the sangeet, he became the life of the party, trying to lift the otherwise gloomy atmosphere. Gauri's mother, known for her dancing and lively presence, did not dance at her own daughter's sangeet. By the end of the wedding, he had endeared himself to everyone. Gauri's father had arranged for an army band to play songs from Shah Rukh's upcoming films, including *Deewana* and *Raju Ban Gaya Gentleman*. 'It was the first time I wore suits, and the first sign of Gauri's mother thawing was when she told me that we never thought you were so nice looking. I wore a tuxedo for my reception and I gelled my hair. My logic was that the person who should enjoy the most at my wedding should be me,' he said.

When it was time for the bidaai, Gauri cried as she sat in the car that would take her away. Soon her mother started crying too, and her father and brother followed. 'So then, in all seriousness, I said if you are all feeling so bad then you can keep her—I'll come and see her regularly. Since we are from different religions, and me being the way I am—when they look at me nobody can ever think I can be responsible about life—I could imagine how insecure her parents were feeling.'

That was the first time in seven years that they went home together. It had been an uphill task for them to get to this point. 'For the first time after having known each other for seven years we spent the night together. Before this we had always been worried whenever we went out, even for a stroll, as to what if somebody saw us. It was quite an exciting feeling that we were sleeping together and that when I wake up the next morning, she will be there. Can you believe the next evening I took a flight back to Bombay, and the day after that I shot for *Dil Aashna Hai*? Actually I had gone to the set because the unit wanted to congratulate me, but they asked me to do one shot and, before I knew it, one shot became five and I was late coming back home and we had a big fight.'

> 'It was the first time I wore suits, and the first sign of Gauri's mother thawing was when she told me that we never thought you were so nice looking. I wore a tuxedo for my reception and I gelled my hair. My logic was that the person who should enjoy the most at my wedding should be me.'

Very few guests from the film industry attended their wedding—only Rajiv Mehra, Viveck Vaswani, Aziz Mirza and G.P. Sippy. Juhi Chawla and her mother hosted a party for the couple when they came to Mumbai.

Gauri wasn't very happy about living the Bombay life. With a husband in films and no friends in the city, she was lonely. While she has been seen as the rock behind her husband's career, in an interview in 2012 to designer duo Abu Jani and Sandeep Khosla, she admitted she had wanted his films to flop so they could go back home. She was not happy about him moving to Bombay and didn't even realize when he became a star. It was very shocking for her to be involved in the film industry and everything related to it. The experience was incredibly difficult. Getting married at twenty-one, everything about films was completely new to her. She thought it would be better if nothing succeeded. At times when his films did well, she was unaware of the impact. When *Deewana* succeeded and *Dilwale Dulhania Le Jayenge* followed, it was astonishing. 'I didn't even know when he became a big star,' she said.

Gauri thanks her stars that she chose the right life partner, though. 'He has been the only man in my life, and he has kept me immensely happy.'

As incredible as the journey to Bombay was, life proved to be very challenging. She recounted that although she enjoyed the experience, it was a new place with new people. Initially, they frequently returned to Delhi. For the first six months, they stayed at Aziz Mirza's place. After that, they rented an apartment near Mount Mary, which was completely unfurnished—no sofa, chair or bed. Her mother came from Delhi and was shocked at the condition. Shah Rukh and Gauri had to provide her with a mattress to sleep on. What was supposed to be a temporary arrangement lasted a year, during which the couple had to drink water from pots. Eventually, the couple bought a small apartment in Bandra. They finally had a flat with furniture, and gradually they transformed it into a home before eventually moving to Mannat.

Gauri has the best analogy for their oft-romanticized love story. 'It's like growing up together. We married young, and dated for a while before that. I have grown with him. Till date, I feel I am getting to know him. A few months ago, I told Karan [Johar] there's something [new] I discovered about him. Any relationship is always growing.'

But Shah Rukh has a different take on that. He feels he and Gauri have stayed the same. 'It's like having a child and everyone telling you the child is getting taller. The relationship must've changed. We came to the city twenty years ago, and just by the way had two kids. Initially we had the attitude that we were too young. We were not sure what we were doing.'

The quiet dates and anonymity of Delhi is missing now. Unlike Gauri, he doesn't miss chaat at Gole Market. 'I don't want to have pav bhaji at Chowpatty either. I am very happy being a star. I love what comes with it and also appreciate working hard for it,' Shah Rukh said.

What set this young couple apart from their peers then was how they conducted their relationship publicly. Aamir Khan, who debuted in films four years before Shah Rukh did, initially kept his marital status private. Although his then-wife, Reena, briefly appeared in his debut film *Qayamat Se Qayamat Tak*, Aamir chose not to publicly disclose that he was married. It was only after the film's success and his rise to stardom that he revealed his marital status. In contrast, Shah Rukh openly showcased his relationship with Gauri.

There were rumours that producer F.C. Mehra had urged Shah Rukh to delay his wedding until after the release of his film *Chamatkar*.

While the director, Rajiv Mehra, denied these rumours, there's a story suggesting that Shah Rukh threatened to quit the film instead of postponing his wedding.⁴ Shah Rukh was vocal about his affection for Gauri. Later in a chat he even said, 'My producers said not to marry. "*Bachelor hero ki fan following zyada hoti hai* [A bachelor hero has a larger fan following]." But I said, "*Mushkil se pataya, shaadi karni padegi* [It took a lot of effort to woo her, I must marry her]."'⁵

In a 1992 interview with *Stardust* magazine, Shah Rukh said, 'My wife comes first. And I can tell you this much that if ever I am asked to make a choice between my career and Gauri, I'll leave films. I mean I would go insane but for her. She's the only thing I have. I am hooked on her.'

> **'It's like growing up together. We married young, and dated for a while before that. I have grown with him. Till date, I feel I am getting to know him. A few months ago, I told Karan there's something [new] I discovered about him. Any relationship is always growing.'**
> **—Gauri Khan**

He didn't understand why it had to be an either-or situation. Why couldn't he have both? 'I really don't understand this big sh*t about sacrificing this for my career and that for my career. I mean, why can't you have both? Why are you looking for excuses for your neglect towards your family or wife or girlfriend? And even if you have neglected your personal life for your professional one, what makes you so proud of it? You have no right to hurt the people who love you.'

He made it amply clear to colleagues, peers, the press and the world that he would never do that to Gauri. Nothing mattered more than her!

Early on in his career, Shah Rukh appeared with Gauri on magazine covers, and Gauri participated in interviews. In June 1994, she said to *Aura of the Stars* magazine, 'Being with Shah Rukh brings me complete fulfilment and boundless happiness. I have no regrets about marrying him. I cannot envision a life without him.'⁶

And for Shah Rukh, the family he has now is the only family he has left, and together with Gauri he has built a world that anchors him. It's a marriage where he is not afraid to admit that she is the boss. She calls the shots and he follows them. He often talks about how he loves Gauri because she is so honest and complements him perfectly. She has taught him how to be diplomatic, often advising him to speak less because his words are sometimes misunderstood by others who don't know him well. She has also taught him practical habits such as turning off the lights before going to bed, having dinner at the proper place and keeping his clothes organized, and helped him improve his dressing sense. He credits her with transforming him from an 'animal' to a man and appreciates how she spoils him. He calls Gauri 'the stabilizing force in his life', balancing his tendency to be extreme. It's not his achievements that she respects or likes; rather, she values him because he makes her laugh. 'And, boy, do I make her laugh!' he says.

After the first few years, Gauri retreated from interviews and, instead, was seen more at celebrity gatherings. They went through a few initial miscarriages before conceiving their first child. Shah Rukh was in the middle of shooting *Pardes* when Gauri had a miscarriage and he had to rush back home from a shooting of the song *'Yeh Dil Deewana'*.[7]

It was on that trip that Shah Rukh first showed how far he would go for his fans. Narrating an incident on a chat show, Shah Rukh mentioned how a lady stalked him across the airport to get an autograph from him. He was panicked and anxious, unable to be his gracious self. The fan was relentless and chased him down. He gave in but was in for a surprise when the fan said, 'I love you, Akshay Kumar.' Bemused, he didn't say a word and signed the autograph on Akshay's behalf. He even shook a leg to Akshay's famous song *'Tu Cheez Badi Hai Mast Mast'* for the fan.

Shah Rukh and Gauri's son Aryan was born on 12 November 1997, followed by their daughter, Suhana, three years later, on 22 May. Shah Rukh, naturally not a fan of hospitals, had the worst thoughts running through his mind when Gauri was delivering Aryan. 'I've lost my parents in hospitals—so I don't like being in hospitals. When I saw her [Gauri] in the hospital, they had put in tubes and stuff. And she was becoming delirious and she was really cold. I went with her to the operation theatre for her Caesarean ... And (*takes a deep breath*) I thought she'd die. Didn't even think about the kid at that point in time. It wasn't important to me. She was shivering so much ... I just got a little scared.'[8]

You'd assume that kids would have changed their romance. Shah Rukh explained, 'Kids don't change the equation of a marriage. They are the manifestation of romance, love, lust, whatever you call it. I see her in the babies. She sees me, I am sure. It personifies this intangible relationship,' Shah Rukh said. On 27 May 2013, the couple welcomed their third child, AbRam.

Unlike many Bollywood celebrities, Shah Rukh has managed to evade scandals. While gossip magazines sporadically linked him to co-stars, there were no persistent rumours of extramarital affairs. 'There are some promises in my heart about our relationship,' Shah Rukh said, 'and those I think I have maintained.'

> 'Kids don't change the equation of a marriage. They are the manifestation of romance, love, lust, whatever you call it. I see her in the babies. She sees me, I am sure. It personifies this intangible relationship.'

On *Rendezvous with Simi Garewal*, Shah Rukh explained why dalliances don't cross his mind. 'The greatest gift God can give you is to make you happy with yourself. The only reason I stick to her, I don't want to be responsible for taking Gauri's calm and peace away. I don't want to make her unhappy.'

At a time when affairs and flings were common, Shah Rukh made it amply clear that he was not interested in the leading ladies of his films. They were his colleagues, whom he admired and respected immensely, but was not interested in romantically.

To *GQ* magazine, he said he does not cheat and has never had the desire to deceive anyone—whether financially, emotionally or romantically. While he doesn't consider himself the most morally upright person, he views cheating as a lowly act. His issue is that he finds it difficult to say no and is overly courteous, which makes it challenging for him to avoid people he doesn't want to be with. Forming a sexual relationship and then trying to disengage from it would disturb him greatly. He believes that the time for affairs or cheating has passed. 'Because I never cheated, half the people said I'm gay. But I'm too old now. In fact, if I do cheat now, people will say, "*Jhoot bol raha hai, saala* [He is lying]."'

He said that when he arrived in Mumbai, there were many misconceptions about the film industry, and he felt it was important to dispel those myths.

Shah Rukh said that long ago, he had made a promise to his wife that she could walk into any party with him without worrying about whether he had slept with any woman in the room. He said, 'There's no girl who will come up to you and say hello, knowing me better than you know me.' This was a promise he made to himself. Although he has affection for many of the women he works with, he believes that physicality is not an aspect of these relationships.

Once Farida Jalal asked him what he would do if Gauri left him. '*Waise toh aisa hona nahin chahiye* [This is unlikely to happen]. I am a henpecked husband. But if it were to happen, I would tear my shirt and sing a song for her, "*Oh gori gori, oh baake chhori, kabhi meri gully aaya karo.*"'

Their marriage has been one of friendship. The couple, above all, are a unit. They are two people who grew up together. 'She doesn't even like my acting too much. When I get depressed after a film doesn't do well, she says not every movie will do well. She supports me but it is not overt, it is ambiguous. It must be difficult being married to a film star, who, apart from her, has millions of other girls behind him for his success. But she trusts the fact that I love her. She is real. In this world where we work, everything is unreal. From the moon, stars, rain, everything. She doesn't beat around the bush. She is clear-cut!'[9]

And he has been a family man through and through. And of all the hats he dons, he has always maintained that he is the best father in the world. It's something his wife complains about: 'He spoils the kids too much.' Archival interviews from before Aryan and Suhana were born has Shah Rukh saying, 'If it's a boy, I want him to be a badmaash. He should do all the bad things by the time he is sixteen, so that he can sober down after that. If I have a daughter, I'll give her all the love that's stored within me. Though my wife thinks I'm mad, I know I'll drop my daughter to the parties she's invited to. I'll want her friends to say, "Wow, what a handsome father you have!" When she's with her boyfriend in the back seat of our car, I'll be at the wheel, driving her around. My parents were my yaars. Similarly, I'll be my baby's best buddy.'

As romantic as the story sounds, Shah Rukh's idea of love in real life is a lot less grand than in the movies. 'I am pathetic with relationships. I am so pathetic that I am comic. If somebody said what do you say to him or her when he or she said this, my answer would shock you. They are like "but how could you?", and I say, "I don't know how else to relate to this." I am very bad with relationships, I am awful. I am extremely one-sided, perhaps even selfish. Actually, I am very detached. I am "demotional", emotional and detached. I don't know how it works. I won't be able to say anything that I've done in my films to a girl, or even in relationships. I am extremely closeted, introverted, shy, reclusive and completely shut off about my emotions.'[10]

During the promotions of the film *Jab Harry Met Sejal*, he revealed that his personal life, filled with love from the start, has made romance somewhat easier for him. He's unsure whether romance comes to him naturally or with effort. He said that because his life has been so beautiful in terms of romance and other aspects, he feels emotions more deeply. He believes he might be particularly sensitive and emotionally inclined, akin to how women understand love better. He finds that women have a different perspective on romance compared to men. Having always been shy around women, he feels unsure about how to romance in real life, although he does have a good sense of humour. While he can converse well with women, he finds that his long-standing role as a romantic hero in films has led many to assume he must be inherently romantic. 'But I don't know if I am romantic or not. I am very dignified, for sure. First, I know that I will never cross the boundaries of decency with a woman in any way, no matter if she is an older or a younger woman or even a little girl. I think being shy is romantic. I remember a lot of people saying that girls love bad boys, but I am not a bad boy.'

For all those out there wondering whether good guys finish last, please look at Shah Rukh Khan.

> "Mujhe andhera pasand hai ... tumhare aane waale kal ki yaad dilata hai"
>
> Don 2, 2011

5

THE ANTI-HERO

In the September 1992 edition of *Stardust* magazine, the cover lead read: 'Can the industry digest Shah Rukh Khan's arrogance?'

Shah Rukh was always clear on his stand: '*Agar self-respect ko arrogance boltey hai, toh haan main arrogant hoon* [If they call self-respect arrogance, then, yes, I am arrogant] ... When I sign a film, *main logo ko pareshan karta hoon* [I drive them up the wall]. I insist that *woh puri kahani likh ke laye* with dialogues. *Main stage ka actor hoon, aap mujhe character dijiye, main play karunga. Aapko Shah Rukh ke liye kahani likhni nahi hai. Pehle jab main detailing ki baat karta tha, log boltey they yeh samajhta kya hai? Ab hit ho gaya hoon toh boltey hai lambi race ka ghoda hai* [I insist they come to me with the entire story written, with dialogues. I am a stage actor, give me a character, and I will perform it. You don't have to write a story for Shah Rukh. Earlier, when I used to talk about detailing, people used to say, "What does he know?" Now that I have become a hit, they say, "He's in it for the long haul"]. It depends on the actor's position.'[1]

At a time when debutants carried the demeanour of someone looking for a favour or a break, Shah Rukh could look them in the eye and tell them what he was worth. But then Shah Rukh wasn't your ordinary debutant. Folded hands were never his style and he was never found hunching in front of producers at parties. The fact that he had tasted success (with *Fauji*) and won people's love wasn't new for him. He was confident of his affable screen presence, which even in his early days had the ability to cut across demographics.

Shah Rukh made his big Bollywood debut in June 1992 with *Deewana* opposite Divya Bharti and with the veteran Rishi Kapoor as co-star. Though he had signed a few films back to back, *Deewana* was the first to be released. The film was melodramatic and had neither the subtlety of theatre nor the tone of *Fauji*. It was a Bollywood masala flick about a widow finding love again in Shah Rukh, only to be posed with a dilemma when her husband (Rishi Kapoor)

> **'I am my worst critic and when I saw myself on the screen, I was appalled.'**

returns from the dead. There was little scope for this to be underplayed or dealt with with subtlety. Shah Rukh wasn't a raw newcomer. Of the many things he knew, he knew acting the best. He was intense and the screen loved him. His exaggerated performances led critics to hail him as the new star on the block.

Years later, in an interview with *Filmfare*, he reflected on *Deewana*, admitting he did not think highly of it. While he was pleased with the film's success, he didn't believe he had contributed to it. He criticized his own performance, describing it as 'loud, vulgar, and uncontrolled'. He said that he overacted and took full responsibility for it. He believed that this was the result of working without a clear direction or script, as he had been scheduled to start shooting later but had to rearrange his dates due to other commitments. 'I am my worst critic, and when I saw myself on the screen, I was appalled. Isn't it amazing that people have liked me in the film? Perhaps that's because I am a fresh face. It's not a performance I'd care to repeat or remember.'[2]

He also reflected on the role of music in the film's success, calling it a major factor. He wished people could say, 'The film's music is good, but Shah Rukh is even better.' In *Deewana*, however, the music overshadowed everything else. He credited director Raj Kanwar for his effective song picturization and praised the performances of Rishi Kapoor, Divya Bharti, Deven Verma and Amrish Puri, but emphasized that the film would be remembered primarily because of Nadeem–Shravan's music. He said, 'A lot of films have been running because of their music. I'd love to be in their shoes now—be as successful as an actor as they are music directors.'

For a young star like him, owning this early success was crucial. He laid claim to it and gave quite a few interviews. In one, he spoke about being the best. He wasn't running anyone down. He didn't need to. But he made it a point to announce that he didn't feel the need to compete with his peers. 'I am the best and I have to compete with myself. I don't believe in the rat race because I am not a rat. ... At night, before I go to sleep, I tell myself I won't let the sun go down on me.'

He was already a known face when he was working in serials, but Shah Rukh's career boomed after he came to Mumbai. Viveck Vaswani took him to a party thrown for Shashi Kapoor's *Ajooba*. Everyone from Dimple Kapadia to Rishi Kapoor to Rajiv Rai were present. Vaswani made sure he introduced this new shining star to everyone. It was at this party that Shah Rukh met Rakesh Roshan, who at the time was making *King Uncle*. The film was already sold. Vaswani's idea was to get Shah Rukh to appear in any one of their films to build him up as a saleable star. The socializing landed the boys a meeting with Rakesh Roshan.

Vaswani recounted in an interview, 'Rakesh asked him, "Why should we cast you?" Shah Rukh might have been a newcomer from TV, but he spoke like a veteran. He explained that Jackie Shroff was already on for the film. Casting Salman and paying him more money would have raised the price of the film. Casting Shah Rukh at lesser money would reduce it. The perception that he was a new boy from television broke.' Roshan ended up signing Shah Rukh for a three-film deal, out of which *Koyla* and *Karan Arjun* were eventually made. In a matter of a few months, Shah Rukh had signed *Dil Aashna Hai*, *Deewana*, *Chamatkar* and *King Uncle*. But the first shot Shah Rukh ever gave for a film was for *Dil Aashna Hai* at Rajkamal Studio. He was on a roll.

Shah Rukh was unlike anything the industry had seen before. He wasn't seeking the blessings of industry veterans, wasn't hopping from office to office to score brownie points. His pitch was simple: Hire me, I am good. Subhash Ghai, who directed him in *Trimurti* and later *Pardes*, recounted an incident in the book *King of Bollywood*, 'I told him "I hear you act well." Shah Rukh replied, "Yes, sir, I do."'

Ghai observed that Shah Rukh's body language stood out as compared to other aspiring actors. He pointed out that newcomers typically arrived with a humble posture, hands folded in a gesture of submission. And as they rose to stardom, their hands often moved behind their backs, displaying a sense of arrogance. In contrast, Shah Rukh's hands remained by his side, and his eyes exuded unwavering confidence.

Shah Rukh knew his worth from the word go. He believed he could act. He believed he had what it takes to be a star. He wasn't desperate for a film. He demanded that a film match his worth. Until that time, this was uncommon in Bollywood. Most newcomers who entered the industry were either star kids or outsiders with no experience. Shah Rukh was neither. He didn't come from money, nor did he have the backing that most of his peers did. And yet, he was already well known among the masses without having done a single film. That social currency of familiarity with the audience backed the confidence he brought to the table. For any producer to hire him was an easy decision because he guaranteed a certain assurance of bringing people to the theatres. '*Arrey woh* Fauji *wala ladka? Yeh uski film hai* [Oh, that boy from *Fauji*? This is his film] ...' This helped gain footfall for his first few films. And because Shah Rukh didn't see acting as a long-term plan but more like a pitstop until the next move, he was never fearful to gamble it all.

The 1990s saw a strange equation between the press and the stars. Entertainment journalism, for the most part, was more about discussing the secret lives of stars and less about their films and body of work.

Shah Rukh didn't have much to feed the gossip circles. He was very public about his love for his wife. Used to tales of dalliances of a whole generation of male actors, who spent most of their energy hiding details of their lives on set from their wives, Shah Rukh was hard to make sense of. Naysayers found this love story too good to be true.

A theory cropped up that he was gay. A man comfortable with his sexuality, a hit with his female co-stars but not having an affair with any of them—he must be swinging the other way. Shah Rukh addressed it publicly. He had nothing to hide. He said, 'I work with Juhi, Madhuri, Manisha, Shilpa, Sonali, Nagma, Suchitra Krishnamoorthi, Urmila … I didn't go to bed with them. I didn't go to bed with Kajol. I respect my co-stars. Somehow girls don't turn me on. I'm not gay, but I'm not carried away by a beautiful face. It should have more to do with a woman's character, intelligence and not purely physical attraction. Gauri has all of these, so why should I chase other girls?'[3]

The press in the early 1990s was writing contrary things. The common thread running through all of it was character assassination. It was the easiest tool to bring down a star in those days. Perceptions mattered and chastity was a virtue that appealed to the Indian masses. Since stars were larger-than-life figures, usually put on a pedestal, there was a direct link between actors' popularity and their personal lives.

In 1992, Shah Rukh nearly went to jail when he misbehaved with a journalist. He was working on Ketan Mehta's *Maya Memsaab,* in which he portrays the youthful paramour of an older married woman disillusioned with the mundane aspects of life, living in her own fantasy world. It's a relationship that brims with passion and yet is laden with conflict, jealousy and aggression. One notably explicit scene depicts the couple engaged in lovemaking, a departure from the typical Hindi films then. Actor Deepa Sahi, also the wife of director Mehta, appears topless in the scene.

Cine Blitz magazine ran a story titled 'Shah Rukh and Deepa's Steamy Scenes Revealed!', alleging that Mehta had created a situation where Shah Rukh and Sahi had to spend a night together in a suburban hotel before filming the scene to 'get totally comfortable with each other'. Shah Rukh, allegedly, had kept this entire episode hidden from his wife Gauri. All hell broke loose when Shah Rukh read the piece.

Sometime later, Shah Rukh bumped into Keith D'Costa from *Cine Blitz* at a film event and lashed out at him. There was a verbal confrontation, and Shah Rukh wasn't polite. But he didn't stop at that. Later that evening, Shah Rukh called Keith's residence and threatened him with physical violence. The next day he followed through on his threat, confronting Keith at his home in front of his parents. Shah Rukh was aggressive and crude. Keith filed a police report against the actor and sought police protection, while Shah Rukh continued to harass him with abusive phone calls.[4]

Shah Rukh recounted on David Letterman's *My Next Guest* that early in his career, he was highly reactive to news coverage about him. He got very angry about a particular news item and called up the editor, expressing his frustration by saying, 'You wrote this.' When the editor told him it was a joke, Shah Rukh threatened the editor, made outrageous comments and ended up shouting and screaming. The incident led to his brief arrest; the police, who were very calm, took him to the lock-up and he was granted bail that evening.

When Letterman pressed for more details, Shah Rukh revealed that he was allowed one phone call while in jail and chose to call the same journalist again, even after being reprimanded by a senior officer at the station. He recounted, 'I told him that since I was already in jail and no longer scared, it was now his turn to be very scared.' After his release on bail, he went to the journalist's house, where he found many police officers stationed outside. Shah Rukh greeted them and, with a matchbox they provided, lit a cigarette right outside the journalist's window, reflecting on his own immature behaviour at the time.

The matter was forgotten, even forgiven, by both the parties when Shah Rukh realized a few years later that Keith hadn't written the article. The actor called him and apologized profusely.

After *Maya Memsaab*, Shah Rukh never did an intimate scene in a film again. It wasn't until *Jab Tak Hai Jaan* (2012) that he kissed on camera. As disdainful as he was of tropes such as two flowers coming together on screen instead of the scene showing an actual kiss, Shah Rukh always ensured his scenes reflected romance without seeming raunchy.

However, his behaviour with Keith made sure the arrogant tag stuck. Shah Rukh's tempestuous temper only added fuel to the fire. He wasn't a breeze in his early projects. In *Kabhi Haan Kabhi Naa*, he and director Kundan Shah almost came to blows. Though hailed as one of his finest performances, and his own favourite, Shah Rukh didn't have a ball at the shoot. Set in Goa, the film sees Shah Rukh playing a man smitten with his friend, but, unlike the usual Hindi-film narrative, he doesn't win the girl in the end. Shah Rukh and the director got into quite a few altercations, and their creative disagreements sometimes escalated alarmingly to the brink of physical fights. But Shah Rukh had committed to doing the film during the launch of *Deewana*, and stuck with it.

The film also ran into financial trouble, which delayed its release. Most of the film was ready in 1992 except for five scenes, but it was released only in 1994.

Shah Rukh and Kundan Shah first met in Delhi in 1989. In a 2015 interview, Kundan Shah recounted their early interactions. At the time, Shah Rukh was working on the serial *Umeed*. He appeared in two episodes of a comedy show directed by Vikas Desai, which Kundan had produced. He also did an episode in *Wagle Ki Duniya* and later worked on *Circus*, which was directed by both Aziz Mirza and Kundan.

Kundan was impressed by Shah Rukh's performance in *Fauji*, but it was his role in Lekh Tandon's *Doosra Keval*, based on the 1984 Sikh riots, that reflected his emotional depth as an actor. He recognized Shah Rukh's versatility and invited him for a meeting. Shah Rukh was excited, as he and his friends were big fans of Kundan's film *Jaane Bhi Do Yaaro*. Shah Rukh read the script overnight and returned it the next morning.

By the time shooting for *Kabhi Haan Kabhi Naa* began, Shah Rukh had committed to multiple other projects, which was a cause for concern with the producers due to the lack of a formal agreement. They approached Shah Rukh at the mahurat of his film *Deewana* at the Juhu Centaur (now Tulip Star) hotel with a consent letter. The room was crowded, so they spoke in the corridor. Shah Rukh signed the letter on the floor without a table, and they gave him Rs 5,000 as the signing amount, with his total fee for the film being Rs 25,000. Later, Shah Rukh bought the film's rights in 1992. Despite the film being ready even before the releases of *Baazigar* and *Darr*, and despite those films turning out to be hits, distributors were hesitant to pick up *Kabhi Haan Kabhi Naa*. Eventually, Shah Rukh managed to convince producer Vijay Gilani to purchase the film. Gilani, Venus (Worldwide Entertainment) and Shah Rukh became joint producers, ensuring the film's release in Mumbai. Shah Rukh's efforts were crucial in getting the film to this point.[5]

It was rather unheard of in those days for an actor to take on the responsibility of an entire film. Actors were then hired hands who left most of the heavy lifting to the producers. Even when a film couldn't be completed, they were happy to leave it halfway and move on to their next. It was a common idea that actors had shelf lives—so they made the most of the few good years they had and then led a cushy life. They never bothered themselves with the ground-level logistics of a film. As someone who came from a theatre background, Shah Rukh's approach and value system were different. He had worked on independent projects more than commercial ones. Film-making on such sets was both collaborative and intimate. Everyone was expected to do everything. If you have an input on the story, you say it. If a light stops working, you fix it. Actors had multifaceted roles on such sets. And independent films were first and foremost passion projects. Profits were a secondary conversation in them. Shah Rukh continued to be that actor. So if a film couldn't be completed, he'd pitch in his own money to get it started. It didn't mean that he had money in surplus. He just cared that much. Word got out soon enough that there was a new audacious actor in town who would pull out all the stops to take a film to the finishing line.

Kabhi Haan Kabhi Naa is one of Shah Rukh's most loved films till date. My friend Prerona Sanyal, an educationist based in Delhi, says the film was her hope on bad days. 'Growing up, *Kabhi Haan Kabhi Naa* was the film that made me believe that marks don't define a person's worth. Imagine being young and struggling in school, feeling like life is at its lowest point—and then you see Shah Rukh Khan on screen. He wasn't just a character—he was a reflection of us. School was tough, and in that moment he became the symbol of each one of us who ever felt like they didn't measure up. On every rewatch, I realized that this film made me believe that life would get better. The connection I formed with Shah Rukh in that role has stayed with me to this day. I remember first seeing him in *Fauji, Doosra Keval* and *Circus,* and thinking he was such an attractive, next-door kind of guy. I even had a bit of a crush on him back then. But with *Kabhi Haan Kabhi Naa*, it wasn't just about admiration—I related to him deeply. And then, when he became Raj in *Dilwale Dulhania Le Jayenge*, we watched him succeed, both as an actor and through his characters. At some point, his roles and his real self seemed to merge, and for me, that intertwining process began with *Kabhi Haan Kabhi Naa*.'

Earlier in 2024, Shah Rukh tweeted about the film. 'I really believe this film is the sweetest, warmest, happiest film I have done. I see it and miss everyone involved in the film, especially my friend and teacher Kundan Shah.' Shah Rukh posted a picture from the film and wrote, 'At that stage ... in that age ... raw ... uncontrolled ... craft still undefined ... surrounded by the best cast & crew in India and a director who I miss every day! Taught me that sometimes you lose the moment ... but win everything else ... I am sure somewhere, some world Sunil did too!'[6]

> Shah Rukh knew his worth from the word go. He believed he could act. He believed he had what it takes to be a star. He wasn't desperate for a film. He demanded that a film match his worth. Until that time, this was uncommon in Bollywood.

However, Kundan and Shah Rukh never worked together again. Shah Rukh moved on to greener pastures and found other collaborators, from successful film-makers such as Yash Chopra to Abbas–Mustan and later Karan Johar. His ecosystem changed, but he never forgot his roots or the people who helped him stand tall.

When Kundan passed away in 2017, in his tribute, Shah Rukh called it 'one of the greatest losses of his life'. At the age of twenty-five, when he moved to Mumbai, he stayed at Kundan's house, was cared for by his family and received emotional support from them. He recalled that his theatre friends in Delhi had advised him to touch Kundan's feet and give him a hug when they first met. He credited Kundan, whom he regarded as one of the greatest directors in the Hindi television and film industry, for much of his success. Despite the director's frequent reprimands, numerous retakes and occasional confrontations, Shah Rukh wrote about how much he valued those experiences. He mentioned that he had posters of several films at home, including one of *Jaane Bhi Do Yaaro*, which Kundan had long declined to sign.

Just days before Kundan's passing, Shah Rukh had planned to ask him for the signature but was unable to do so. Shah Rukh reflected that he would always cherish Kundan's memories, love and the way the director had treated him. 'Every time he came to hit me, every time he shouted at me, fed me at his house, told me how bad I am, every time he told me how I'll never do good work in my life, reminded me of my mother. I'll miss Kundan like a mother that I didn't have for the longest time,' he said.[7]

The romantic-hero image or the moniker of the 'King of Romance' was a later acquisition for Shah Rukh. In 1992, he was eagerly looking for a story that was dark and violent. Shah Rukh wanted to do action and he was eager to push the boundaries of bad boys in Bollywood. In a 1992 interview, Shah Rukh spoke to *India Today* about Mani Kaul's *Ahmak*, based on Dostoyevsky's *The Idiot*. He played the role of Raghurajan in *Ahmak*, modelled on the character of Rogozhin, the villain. Rogozhin is a wealthy merchant's son who squanders his father's fortune and becomes obsessively enamoured with the infamous beauty Nastasya Filippovna. Their tumultuous relationship is marred by jealousy, culminating in Rogozhin's fatal stabbing of Nastasya. Critics have likened Rogozhin's dark appearance and malevolence to the embodiment of evil, in stark contrast to the novel's protagonist, Myshkin, portrayed as a Christ-like figure. Shah Rukh's youthful charm contrasted with Raghurajan's heinous deeds, bringing out a deliciously sinister side to the character. In the climactic scene, Raghurajan chillingly remarks on how there is so little blood despite the deep stab wound. To *India Today*, Shah Rukh said, 'Yaar, shooting for Mani was something else. I didn't understand the movie but I loved the art-film environment. You bite into a samosa and ask yourself: Who is God? What is life? Who am I?'[8]

But after that movie, he admitted that his aspiration was to do something more. The interview piece read, 'Shah Rukh is aware of the power of pulchritude, but would like to be known as more than just a pretty boy. He is convinced that audiences don't come to see his films because he is playing a hero: They come to see him. His one big desire now is to play a villain and "give the Hindi movie creep a whole new dimension".'[9]

It can be said that Shah Rukh almost manifested *Baazigar*. Director-duo Abbas–Mustan were lured into watching *A Kiss before Dying*, adapted from Ira Levin's novel, by their nephew. The film portrays the chilling narrative of a calculating college student who orchestrates the murder of his girlfriend and subsequently endeavours to charm her sister. Halfway into the film, they wanted to do a remake. This was an era prior to adaptation rights.

> 'My whole logic is if you tell *Sholay* from Gabbar Singh's point of view, the murders will seem correct.'

Adapting ideas from Hollywood has been a long-standing tradition in Bollywood. And in those days to Bollywood-ize Hollywood films, sex was replaced with melodrama. For instance, in *Baazigar*, the hero, or the anti-hero, was given a tragic background that could justify his malicious actions. At the outset it is shown how the boy's family is destroyed when his father is cheated by his business partner. The anti-hero seeks revenge by stalking the partner's family and engaging in relationships with both his daughters, killing the older one and committing multiple murders before dying in his mother's arms.

In the 1990s, stars had to be pristine, chaste and without faults. The audience was a lot less forgiving. So playing a guy who murders the heroine's sister and multiple other people, and eventually dies a dog's death didn't appeal as a heroic story to anyone.

Aamir Khan declined the role, as did Anil Kapoor. Salman Khan's father, scriptwriter Salim, felt it was premature for his son to explore negative roles.

That's when Abbas–Mustan thought of Shah Rukh—that boy with too much attitude. He was far from the conventional hero, but he was striking and his television work had made him popular. However, producer Ratan Jain wasn't convinced. It definitely felt like a step down, given that both Aamir and Salman had debuted with blockbusters and were ruling heroes at the time. Jain told *The Times of India* in 2023, 'At the time of *Baazigar*, he [Shah Rukh] was a new actor. He had done a few films. And I found only Shah Rukh Khan was ready to do something new. He was experimenting with everything. He was not interested in doing regular romantic or action films. I approached a lot of actors but nobody was ready to do that role in *Baazigar*. Everybody was scared that the role would go against their image. Shah Rukh knew what I was making. In my first meeting with him, he said, "Okay, I will do this role and I will do it better than everybody." And he did.'[10]

In September 1992, Abbas–Mustan provided Shah Rukh with a detailed narration of the story. Shah Rukh didn't have a day's doubt. He enthusiastically discussed his approach to certain scenes. He relished the prospect of portraying a villain. The makers were a little surprised by his excitement, since everyone thought of this film as professional hara-kiri.

Shah Rukh had his reasons. He believed in the diversity of storytelling. In an interview with Anupama Chopra, he explained where he was coming from at that time. 'My whole logic is if you tell *Sholay* from Gabbar Singh's point of view, the murders will seem correct.'[11]

Abbas–Mustan, amused at his line of thinking, were, however, still cautious. Since Shah Rukh had put his faith in them, they didn't want to be responsible for his doom this early on in his career. They made it amply clear that the audience might not sympathize with Shah Rukh's character if he were seen killing a well-known actress. Initially, both Ayesha Jhulka and Madhuri Dixit turned down the girlfriend's (Kajol's) role. Sridevi agreed, but suggested that the sisters be written as twins so she could do both roles. Abbas, in 2017, told Film Companion, 'Sridevi was popular. Bumping her off wouldn't go down well with the audience. The film would have not landed with the audience if a mass favourite actress like Sridevi was killed before the interval of a film.'

Consequently, new actresses were cast. Shilpa Shetty played the girlfriend Shah Rukh kills. Shetty was seventeen then. Tanuja's daughter Kajol, who had already signed three films, was roped in for the role of Shetty's sister, the female lead.

Shah Rukh was a lot less wary than everyone else around him. He had no inhibitions about playing a man who murders his young girlfriend and two of her friends to protect his secret. He went full-throttle at it, giving the Hindi movie creep a new dimension, as promised. His bloodshot eyes, bloody face and body language brimming with rage all played up to give the character a scary effect on screen. Right before he throws his girlfriend off the roof of the marriage registration office, he gives her a chilling look and innocently says, 'I'm sorry.'

He was having way too much fun being bad. Dalip Tahil, who plays the girlfriends' father in the film and the prime antagonist, wasn't sure of the level of gore shown. But Abbas–Mustan were certain that sympathy for Shah Rukh's mother in the film would win the audience over.

After the film was released, the team went to London for its promotions. This was Shah Rukh's first trip abroad. The overseas distributor, Eros International, planned six premieres in three days. Shah Rukh and Gauri stayed at the lavish St. James Court hotel. In the wee hours of the second night, Shah Rukh received a phone call from India that roused him from sleep. It was producer Yash Johar, delivering the exhilarating news that *Baazigar* had become a superhit!

One particular dialogue had stuck: '*Haar ke jeetne wale ko Baazigar kehte hai* [A daredevil is he who wins even when he loses].'

Shah Rukh would dance to the song '*Yeh Kaali Kaali Ankhein*' everywhere! He knew that in the long run, swimming against the tide would pay off. In an interview to *Forbes* magazine in 2013, he spoke of the fear that people were trying to put in him. Thank god he didn't fall for it. 'I don't think about the short term. I have this belief. It could be because I've had repeated failures in the past. And then I have taken high-end risks and succeeded in them. Like everyone told me my career was over when *Baazigar* released. My best well-wishers told me—you can't be a hero again after you've killed a woman. But it paid off. In the long run, everything is sustainable if you stick to it.'

The popular industry theory is that if one wants to stand out, the best way to do so is to shock everyone. Shah Rukh's initial roles were just that—shocking, with lots of shades of grey, sometimes too much of it.

These roles were hitherto unseen, unheard of and intrinsically challenged the fabric of what a Hindi-film hero should be like.

Who would have known that a few years later, this very 'bad boy' would be the new archetype of the Bollywood romantic hero. It is fair to say that Shah Rukh knew how to move with the times and, more than anything else, how to leave a mark.

In *Baazigar*, Bollywood found a star. And in *Darr*, Shah Rukh found an opportunity—to prove that he was capable of going beyond. Film historian Dilip Thakur told *The Times of India* in 2023, 'Yash Chopra started *Darr* after *Lamhe*, [which] turned out to be a flop. Rishi Kapoor was the first choice because he had acted in Chopra's *Chandni*. Kapoor, Mithun Chakraborty and Jackie Shroff rejected the offer, and eventually Sunny Deol agreed to play the role. Divya Bharti was rumoured to be cast in *Darr* but it did not materialize. Juhi Chawla was signed. Sudesh Berry said no to playing the role, which eventually went to Shah Rukh Khan. Aamir Khan's controversy created a lot of buzz because he said no to playing a negative role. Shah Rukh was shooting in Lonavala where Yash Chopra went to meet him and sign him. It was a huge opportunity for Shah Rukh Khan.'[12]

The 1989 thriller *Dead Calm*, which depicts a married couple's sailing excursion being turned upside down by a deranged criminal, served as a loose inspiration for *Darr*. A little-known fact about the film is that it was first discovered by Hrithik Roshan and Uday Chopra, who introduced Aditya Chopra to it. In fact, the title 'Darr' was initially chosen for an amateur film Hrithik had shot. When Aditya decided to make *Darr*, he decided to use it here instead.

Rahul, Shah Rukh's character in *Darr*, marked a departure from typical Bollywood roles, portraying a lonely and mentally unstable man who speaks to his deceased mother from eighteen years ago. His relentless pursuit of the heroine takes a sinister turn when his unreciprocated love transforms into murderous intent. In the climax of *Darr*, Rahul tracks

Sunil (Sunny Deol) and Kiran (Juhi Chawla) on their honeymoon, brutally attacking Sunil and attempting to force Kiran into marriage. The film reaches a crescendo as Sunil retaliates by mercilessly beating Rahul and ultimately shooting him dead.

In the Netflix series *The Romantics*, Shah Rukh recounts his experience working on *Darr*. He was watching *Lamhe* when his manager informed him that Yash Chopra wanted to meet him. Shah Rukh had envisioned the director as a tall, long-haired, semi-hippie figure, but was surprised to find him to be a simple and straightforward man, quite different from his expectations. Yash Chopra told Shah Rukh, 'I think you are a great actor. This is a bad guy role.' Chopra was candid about having initially wanted someone else for the role, but since they were unavailable, he believed Shah Rukh was perfect for it. Shah Rukh agreed to take on the role, expressing his desire to break away from the good-guy roles he was typically offered. He had recently seen *Cape Fear* with Robert De Niro and was drawn to its aggressive and intense portrayal. 'In today's time and age, I think I'd be put behind bars if I did a role like that,' he said later.

In 2009, Yash Chopra, in an interview series with his son Uday, decoded *Darr*. He said, 'I generally made romantic films. I have just one word—an obsessed lover. The film went through a lot of changes. I had approached Aamir Khan. Then there were Sanjay Dutt, Ajay Devgn … Then I approached Shah Rukh Khan. I told him, "It is a negative role." He said, "Before you narrate this film, I want to tell you I am already doing two films where I am the negative hero. So you hear the stories and if they match yours, then don't narrate yours to me." There was *Anjaam* and another film with Raveena Tandon that never happened. Apart from being a very good actor, he is a wonderful human being. He considers the other person's problems and if he understands someone loves him, he will go all out for that person.'[13]

Shah Rukh always called *Darr* a psychological film. For him, at no point was it a love story. That set the tone for how it played out on screen and what went into layering the performance, with Shah Rukh adding his own nuances to it. 'My character is different and unusual. It's a character

I have never done before and it's likely I will never do a character like this again in my life,' he said in *The Romantics*.

Shah Rukh, Yash Chopra and Aditya Chopra formed a lasting collaborative partnership. During the making of *Darr*, Shah Rukh became close with Aditya Chopra, initially mistaking him for the chief assistant director rather than Yash Chopra's son. Shah Rukh shared his thoughts on character development, inspired by a study on stammering he had encountered. He suggested incorporating this aspect into his role, while Aditya proposed that he stammer specifically on 'Kiran', the name of the woman he loves.

> 'Everyone told me my career was over when *Baazigar* released. My best well-wishers told me—you can't be a hero again after you've killed a woman.'

In *The Romantics*, Shah Rukh describes Aditya Chopra as his sounding board. He saw that Aditya, as a young collaborator, was open to discussing all sorts of ideas and interpretations. Shah Rukh recalled presenting some unconventional ideas, such as making a phone call while hanging upside down, to which Aditya responded that his father might not approve. They served as filters to each other. 'We helped each other with Yash-ji. *Darr* did very well, people loved it. It became quite a phenomenon …' Shah Rukh said on *The Romantics*.

Darr and *Baazigar* were shot simultaneously. This could have been a bad idea. If the performances didn't land, Shah Rukh could have vanished from the film industry overnight. The films finally released within a month of each other, and by the time they became box-office hits, Shah Rukh had redefined the Hindi-film hero. Much like Amitabh Bachchan's Angry Young Man, this was the new version of the Anti-Hero. This hero wasn't a saccharine goody two shoes—he was passionate, dark, selfish and violent. In *King of Bollywood*, Shah Rukh says, 'The Hindi film hero has changed. He can die in the film and lose the girl. He can kill people. We don't have to like him, just the story he is telling.'

In Rajat Sharma's *Aap Ki Adalat* in 1994, Shah Rukh was asked if he had thought about the effect these films would have on people. On the show, Shah Rukh was informed of a nationwide survey conducted by a magazine regarding his portrayal of negative characters in films. If these characters were called villains, it was fine, but if they were called heroes, it was a problem, Rajat told Shah Rukh.

Shah Rukh explained how some roles fell between extremes, and called them 'human characters' rather than strictly negative or positive ones. These roles weren't black-and-white but involved both lies and truths, good and bad. He admitted to having virtues and flaws, and described how he uses a love angle in his films, portraying characters who love so intensely that they might even kill for that love. He also pointed out how these films did not end with any sympathy for these characters.

When asked whether *Baazigar* glorified murder and *Anjaam* torture, he clarified that it would be glorification if the characters got away with their actions. However, by the end of the films, his characters were shown to significantly suffer. He acknowledged the criticism that films can negatively impact children, but pointed out that while men might dismiss his films, women often responded emotionally and found them impactful. 'After *Baazigar*, I saw men come out and say this film won't work. The women came out crying. They felt for the film and they liked it.'

Regarding the portrayal of stalking, he stated that, as an actor, he could not take full responsibility for the character's actions. He described the character as mentally unbalanced and psychotic, recognizing that such behaviour was abnormal. He noted that in Hindi films, the hero often represents a superhuman ideal, which does not reflect his own personality. 'It was a mentally disbalanced, psychotic character. No normal person would do what these men are doing. I do understand the detrimental effect movies can have. But I also understand that the biggest villain of a Hindi film is the hero—because he is a super human being. I am not that guy.'

To the mainstream heroes before him, actors were slaves of the masses. But not to Shah Rukh. 'I am not a slave of the masses. I am a performer, it's my job to entertain you. I am not going to tell a joke which you have asked me to tell you. I am going to tell a joke that I think will make you laugh. If it doesn't, oops I am sorry! I will try again. I am not going to do what someone is telling me to do. You are paying to see me; you are not paying to see yourself. I can't be told, "Oh, dance like my uncle." I can't be told not to play a negative role. I am not your slave. Neither are you my slave. You are paying to see me for two and half hours and for those hours, maybe I won't give you what you came to see. It is possible you came to see a hero who is nice to a girl. Maybe you see a guy who has thrown a girl off the third floor and is happy about it. But when you go back, you should know you had a good evening.'[14]

The truth about *Darr* is that women loved it. It was the first film to address stalking and obsession. The film sparked a national conversation on these issues and prompted many people to speak up about their own experiences, which until then had never been legitimized by a mainstream film.

It also paved the way for Bollywood films to explore darker themes and more complex characters, which were relegated to indie cinema until then.

The film won the National Award for Best Film that year (popular film providing wholesome entertainment). *Darr* dominated the international box office in 1993, raking in Rs 5.58 crore. On a global scale, it earned Rs 21.31 crore, which translates to a whopping Rs 366 crore after accounting for inflation in 2017. Even in India, *Darr* performed very well. It earned a domestic gross of Rs 15.73 crore, with a net income of Rs 10.74 crore. Considering inflation and adjusting for the year 2017, this translates to an estimated domestic gross of Rs 184.4 crore.[15]

One may still wonder how a seemingly 'problematic' film such as *Darr* hit home with women. In a post on Medium, classical dancer Meera Nair explained, 'Two days ago I watched *Darr* in our college class room with a projector. This is the first time I watched a villain role of Shah Rukh Khan, and that too after 30 years of its release. In the beginning, it was hard for me to picturize him in that role. Because before screening, our professor and we discussed how focused [a] stalker he is, which was kind of traumatising. While watching I realised why he said "his character in this movie was one of the most celebrated characters by the women back then". … Bollywood heroes are usually depicted as virtuous and honourable characters who fight for justice and love. Shah Rukh Khan's portrayal of Rahul brings down this archetype. He played a character who was deeply flawed and morally ambiguous. He was not a hero but a villain. And yet, he was able to make the audience empathise with him.'[16]

Shah Rukh's character died a violent death, so there was no endorsement of his actions on screen. Yash Chopra was always sure that the character had to die in the end. But what he and his leading man Shah Rukh did was humanize the villain enough for him to be deemed an anti-hero.

A column in Daily O rightly explained this. '*Darr* established a method to Rahul's madness. A bad guy with a heart of gold is an old trope in Bollywood. But Rahul's heart was no gold. Yet, and the makers had convinced us of this, it's not his fault—because of a traumatic childhood and an uncaring father. Could this be a prelude to depression? I think so.'[17]

On the surface, it might sound like everyone wanted to make excuses for Rahul, but this film marked the advent of wholesome storytelling in mainstream movies. Characters were just characters, doing things and meeting their fate eventually. Perhaps for the first time in the history of Hindi cinema, the audience went into the psyche of the bad guy. The story rose above the mundane ideas of good and bad, and evolved into a conversation about what makes people do what they do. In 2003, novelist Gregory David Roberts told us all about good and bad men in his bestselling novel *Shantaram*. 'The truth is that there are no good men or bad men,' he said. 'It is the deeds that have goodness or badness in them. There are good deeds and bad deeds. Men are just men—it is what they do, or refuse to do, that links them to good and evil. The truth is that an instant of real love, in the heart of anyone—the noblest man alive or the most wicked—has the whole purpose and process and meaning of life within the lotus-folds of its passion.'

In 2016, plans were under way for a spin-off web series titled 'Darr 2.0'. A teaser trailer hinting at a five-episode miniseries was launched on YouTube in August 2016. This modern take on the classic film would explore the dark side of technology, focusing on cyberstalking and digital crimes. Y-Films, the youth division of Yash Raj Films, was attached to produce the series, with Vikash Chandra in the director's chair. Nikhil Taneja and Shubham Yogi were on board to write the screenplay and dialogue. Unfortunately, the project was shelved. It was deemed that anti-heroes wouldn't have a ball in the woke world. In 2020, Rahul wouldn't stand a chance with love. He would have been shredded to bits.

An ardent fan of Shah Rukh, Divya Tripathi, who hails from Hyderabad and calls *Darr* her favourite film, thinks otherwise. She told me, 'I think it's the perfect film. Rahul would have had a chance even in 2020, as long as the writing and the actor is on a par with the original. Rahul is not shown as glorious. Rahul is a creep who dies. The writing was such that I could understand Rahul and the void in his heart. At no point did Shah Rukh or Mr Yash Chopra make him a hero. He is the villain of the piece. And yes, I stand by the fact that it's one of my favourite films. It shows an actor's ability to do something that is risky. We say we are bored of cinema and people aren't going to the theatres. Why should they? Are you taking bold risks and making outrageous movies? No, you aren't. People who risk big, win big, and *Darr*, *Baazigar*, *Anjaam*, all stand for that! Cinema is meant to evoke something. If it was flat, it would be called life.'

There's a deeper reason to Shah Rukh's lack of adherence to society's idea of a hero, or any stereotype at large. On NDTV's *Spotlight*, talking about his struggle in the initial days, he said that the reason he took up the roles other heroes turned down, such as *Darr* and *Baazigar*, was because he thought he wasn't good-looking enough to be a hero, so he should just be a villain and get a job.

His early producers told him all sorts of things: 'Oh, your hair is all wrong', 'You don't look like a star', 'You speak too fast.' Shah Rukh also revealed that a director referred to him as ordinary and ugly. 'There's a wonderful director friend of mine, and he met me and he said, "You are so ordinary and ugly." He told me to my face "that I can use you for anything that's very interesting about you", and I believe that. Not because he told me, but I believe that. I took on the roles because I just wanted to act. Please go ahead and do whatever you really believe in ... Just do it. And I think it will turn out right.'

In a way, the idea of his arrogance stems from his own self-assuredness and confidence. He did address the tag in an old interview. '*Mujhe aaj tak samajh nahin aaya ki mujhe log arrogant kyun kehte hain. Mere ko woh womanizer nahin keh sakte, mujhko alcoholic nahin keh sakte, drug addict nahin keh sakte, money hoarder nahin keh sakte, badtameez nahin keh sakte, kuch nahin keh sakte. Toh unhonein socha arrogant keh dete hain isko* [I still don't know why they call me arrogant. Since they can't call me a womanizer, an alcoholic, a drug addict, ill-mannered or a money hoarder, they thought let's call him arrogant]. But there is no negative quality in me except for the fact that I smoke. Which is a bad quality, which nobody should do. So arrogant *mujhe bhi nahin maloom kyun kehte hain. Mujhe nahin lagta main arrogant hoon* [So I don't know why they call me arrogant. I don't think I am].'

But the truth wasn't all that simple. People weren't merely making up stories—they were just unable to make sense of the man Shah Rukh was. As an industry, Bollywood is always eager to label people. The film industry is nothing but a microcosm of society. Anything that can't fit into its neat boxes is then labelled as something that does make sense to it. And Shah Rukh's epithet was 'arrogant'. The industry was finding it hard to tame him. He was making his own rules, breaking the old ones and having fun along the way. His heroes were nothing like heroes. His early films weren't interested in pleasing people by acting holier than thou. And to top it all, his swagger was charming the audience.

Naysayers had little to shut him down with. Their theories about what classically worked had been proven wrong by him. Even when he didn't know success the way he does today, he knew what he wanted and went for it with single-minded focus, not once sparing a thought for the noise around him. Even as a struggler, he wasn't at anyone's mercy. 'I wanted to come to Bombay for a year, make one lac rupees and buy a house and go back to Delhi. I haven't gone back yet,' he said at the Locarno Film Festival in 2024, adding that he had wanted to go back and become a journalist.[18]

This was a man who knew his worth. Money didn't lure him. He made it amply clear after the success of *Darr* and *Baazigar* that while some actors came to the industry to earn money, fame and glory, and were known to throw their weight around, he wanted to act and have a good work-life balance. He acted for the thrill of it. He would say, 'I do not care much for the frills that come along with this profession. I do not want to go astray and lose myself to this world like the others. I want to keep in touch with reality. I want to keep in touch with myself.'

Little did he know that exactly a year from *Baazigar*, his reality would become bigger than he could ever have imagined. In 1995, *Dilwale Dulhania Le Jayenge* was released to the world, arguably the biggest hit India has ever seen!

> "BADE BADE DESHON MEIN AISI CHHOTI CHHOTI BAATEIN HOTI REHTI HAIN, SENORITA"
>
> *Dilwale Dulhania Le Jayenge*, 1995

6

EVERYONE WANTS A RAJ

'I was shocked. I didn't know what to say. They narrated this namby-pamby film to me. He is in love and he doesn't even run away with the girl. It's not about like or dislike. This wasn't the film I wanted to hear,' Shah Rukh says in Netflix's *The Romantics* about the movie that made him the global superstar he is today—*Dilwale Dulhania Le Jayenge (DDLJ)*.

During *Darr*, Aditya Chopra and he brainstormed eccentric ideas and discussed how to pitch them to Yash Chopra. Following the completion and imminent success of *Darr*, Aditya moved on to his own directorial debut. He discussed a film titled *Auzaar* with Shah Rukh. In those days, Shah Rukh was in his bad-boy-is-cool mode and assumed it would be a typical 'macho cool dude' movie. The name, which meant 'weapon', certainly suggested so. However, in 1994, Aditya surprised him by offering him the lead role of Raj in *DDLJ* instead.

Shah Rukh was in no mood for Aditya's goody-two-shoes hero. At the time, Aamir and Salman, two of his most successful peers, were doing similar films. Sooraj Barjatya's *Hum Aapke Hai Koun...!* had become a recent success, and Aamir had debuted with *Qayamat Se Qayamat Tak* and had stayed on that path. Shah Rukh had convinced himself that he shouldn't make the choices they were making. If he had to stand out, he would have to be bold with his own. His own successes had assured him that to stand out, he would need to do films that his peers wouldn't imagine picking up.

For the first six months, he kept Aditya on hold. Aditya, on his part, would drop by every week on a different film set, and Shah Rukh would politely entertain him but not say yes—he didn't know how to say no to a friend. 'I am very shy and I don't think I am good with romance. Mostly, I don't even believe in that kind of romance,' Shah Rukh said on *The Romantics*, remembering his early reservations about *DDLJ*.

At the edge of his patience, Aditya knew he had to push Shah Rukh for a definitive answer. He went to the sets of *Trimurti* to meet him. Fans had collected to meet Shah Rukh after the shot. Aditya narrates the incident on *The Romantics*. 'There was an old fragile lady. About eighty. She told Shah Rukh, "*Beta tu bohot accha hai. Tu accha kaam karta hai aur mujhe bohot pasand hai. Par tu har film mein marta hai aur har film mein tera khoon hota hai. Mujhe accha nahi lagta* [Son, you are very good, and your work is very good. I like you very much. But you die in every film or get killed. I don't like that]."' Fifteen minutes later, Shah Rukh and Aditya found themselves in a corner. Aditya told Shah Rukh that he knew the latter was hesitating and struggling to refuse the role, but advised him not to close himself off to doing a love story, explaining that in the country, a superstar embodied some intrinsic qualities, that he should be every mother's son, every sister's brother and every college girl's fantasy.

There was something from that day, mostly the old lady's earnest, innocent plea, that stuck with Shah Rukh. The next time he met Aditya, he told him that he would do the film.

DDLJ was the classic anti-casting. In the fourteen films that Shah Rukh had already appeared in before *DDLJ*, he was neither the classic hero nor a romantic persona. In fact, in three of the films—*Darr*, *Baazigar* and *Anjaam*—he had played a man who was far from pleasant. He had even signed a two-hero film, *Karan Arjun*, in 1995, which was action, drama and all things masala. But Aditya told him to simply trust him. And trust he did.

Shah Rukh admitted in a 2016 interview that he used to be rather indecisive in the early years of his career. 'I am indecisive at times. And I have been wrong about my own choices.' One of the most significant, he noted, was *Karan Arjun*. The film, with its intense fight scenes and dramatic tone, was far from the kind of projects Shah Rukh typically gravitated towards. He struggled to connect with the movie and couldn't fully understand it, but director Rakesh Roshan assured him that it would resonate with the audiences. When Shah Rukh watched the film with distributors, he was taken aback by the audience's reaction—there wasn't a moment during the entire screening when people weren't either clapping or crying. The film turned out to be one of his biggest successes. This experience taught him that he couldn't always predict how a movie would turn out. Later, Shah Rukh also had his doubts about *Swades* (2004), a film he didn't initially believe would do well. He had wanted to work on *Jodhaa Akbar* (2008) with Ashutosh Gowariker instead. He even told Gowariker that while *Swades* was a good film, he thought it would fail commercially. However, Gowariker was confident about the project, explaining that he wanted to make the film because it was his father's wish. It was this personal motivation that convinced Shah Rukh to take on the role, despite his initial scepticism, as it gave Gowariker the chance to honour his father's legacy.[1]

Why Shah Rukh agrees to do a film is largely instinctive. He doesn't ask too many questions. If he likes it, he will do it regardless of the logistics and market pressures. But in 1995, Shah Rukh was utterly unsure of *DDLJ*. He had his heart set on an action film Aditya Chopra wanted to make. Moreover, *DDLJ* as an idea was completely out of the blue for India, and Raj, as a hero, though modelled on Shah Rukh, wasn't the Bollywood archetype. It was a sharp deviation from the virtuous Prem of *Hum Aapke Hai Koun..!* played by Salman, which until then was largely the romantic-hero norm. Would women want something different?

Right from the start, Shah Rukh was sceptical of the story. Raj Malhotra had none of the usual virtues that a hero would have. And he wasn't 'grey' either—the guy was strangely both idiotic and loveable. In one of the film's earlier drafts, Raj was a casanova too, who goes to Simran's father's store to buy condoms before kicking off a night of debauchery. In hindsight, that would have justified the hate the senior had for him. But Aditya decided that would be a little too ahead of the times. He settled for beers in the final cut.

But the one part of the film Shah Rukh was sure of was the climax—Simran's father gives his daughter's hand to Raj. Turns out Aditya didn't write the action sequence of the climax. That was Shah Rukh coaxing Yash Chopra into having his way. Shah Rukh said on Netflix's *The Romantics*, 'Anupam Kher was supposed to come for shooting, but he got stuck somewhere, so I went to Yashji and Adi, and said, "Can I have one action sequence in the film?" They said I can't because there's no need for it. I said, "Please let me shoot it, [then] throw it out." Yashji loved me too much, so he couldn't say no. He said, "Okay. You have one hour." One hour later Yashji said, "*Ho gaya ab* [Enough]. Now we will make the film we are making."'

When word got out that Shah Rukh was doing a romantic film, he was warned: No one will accept you as a romantic hero.

It could have happened. He had thrown Shilpa Shetty's character down from the terrace of a very high building in *Baazigar*, and had stalked and tormented the beautiful Juhi Chawla for three hours in *Darr*.

Shah Rukh said in an interview in 2020, 'I was told by many people that I looked unconventional, very different from what the perception of a leading man was. I did feel, maybe, not being handsome enough—or, as they called it back then, "chocolatey"—would make me unsuitable for romantic roles. I had no idea how to go about it, and also if I would be able to do it well. It was one of those roles that I realized I can do … using a version of my real self. So you might see some quirks, habits and mannerisms that were true to my off-screen persona—especially the sense-of-humour part. I always felt that I can play more unconventional roles because of my looks, but *DDLJ* belied that, and I still struggle to make that one macho unconventional kicka** character that suits me, or so I thought.

But it's been a struggle to not be considered romantic and sweet for the last twenty-five years—a struggle, I guess, I am happy to lose ...'[2]

For Karan Johar, who served as Aditya Chopra's right-hand man on the project, this film marked his entry into the industry and the beginning of his career in film-making—something he hadn't even considered until that year. Interestingly, at the time, Karan wasn't a fan of Shah Rukh—he was more inclined towards Aamir Khan. Karan admitted recalling how he didn't like Shah Rukh in *Deewana*. He and his friend Apoorva Mehta, now CEO of Dharma Productions, would often have heated debates, with Apoorva questioning Karan's admiration for Aamir, saying, 'Aamir is so boring, what do you like about him?' Their arguments about Aamir and Shah Rukh were intense, as if they were defending their own family members.

Karan also remembered a Parsi friend who had once told him that Shah Rukh had 'the cutest ass and an Adam's apple to die for'. Later, when Karan met Shah Rukh on the set of *DDLJ*, he shared these remarks with him and even gave Shah Rukh a pair of Levi's jeans to wear, suggesting he open the top few buttons of his shirt to highlight his Adam's apple. Karan mentioned that his friend thought Shah Rukh had a great physique, but never showcased it properly, advising him to wear tight jeans. Shah Rukh was taken aback and embarrassed by these comments, and Aditya Chopra nearly fell off the sofa laughing. Reflecting on the incident in his memoir *An Unsuitable Boy*, Karan wrote, 'Shah Rukh went all red with embarrassment. But it's so strange how everything pans out in your life.'[3] Karan incidentally has more memories of this film than of his own debut movie *Kuch Kuch Hota Hai*—from the time the song 'Mere Khwabon Mein Jo Aaye' was shot in Filmistaan to the premiere of the film, when he couldn't stop bawling seeing the magic of what they had created on the big screen.

The ensemble cast, featuring stalwarts such as Satish Shah, Amrish Puri, Farida Jalal and newcomers Mandira Bedi and Parmeet Sethi, among others, forged a strong bond during the making of the film. The 1990s were a time when egos took a back seat, allowing actors to collaborate and giving them the space to become emotionally close. At the heart of filming was the off-screen warmth among the cast and crew that made it an experience that was not just professionally rewarding, but also life-changing for each of them.

The leads were both big movie stars by the time *DDLJ* started filming; there was just one newbie on the set—Mandira Bedi. She was also the first to notice Shah Rukh's ability to put people around him at ease. '*DDLJ* was my debut movie, and Shah Rukh made me feel so special. There is a scene in the film where we are playing antakshari and I have to feel shy because Shah Rukh holds my hand by mistake, as he thinks Kajol is sitting next to him. It was so difficult, and I told Adi that. Shah Rukh had to practise the scene so many times so that I could get my expressions right *(laughs)*.'

She says it was even harder to pull off the iconic '*Mehendi Laga Ke Rakhna*'. Mandira was leading the dance with Shah Rukh and the weight of getting the steps right and giving the song the right look was on her shoulders. It was Karan who taught her the thumkas to save her from choreographer Saroj Khan's wrath. 'Shooting for *Mehendi Laga Ke Rakhna* was a nightmare, because that was the first thing I shot for the movie. I am a typical south Mumbai girl and I didn't know how to do latkas and thumkas. Whenever I would dance, I would shake my shoulders, not my hips *(laughs)*. I am sure our choreographer Saroj Khan must have looked at me as a gone-case! I shot for twenty days and that was the most nervous time in my life. Karan helped me rehearse those moves. One afternoon, he called me home for lunch and taught me how to shake my hips,' she recounted in an interview.[4]

While the film reflected a mix of tradition and modernity, the set saw a clash of old and new. Cinematographer Manmohan Singh remembers being entirely unconvinced about the final sequence. 'There was a clash of ideas while we were planning the climax of *DDLJ*. Yashji and I weren't convinced, as we thought it was very clichéd. Adi thought so too, but he still wanted to end the film on that note, where Amrish Puri lets Kajol go with Shah Rukh Khan. He was adamant about it. He asked us to give him a better climax, but Yashji and I could not come up with any other ideas. Today, when I look back, it is one of the best climaxes in Indian cinema.'

Farida Jalal believes it is the climax that has all the magic. 'DDLJ is relevant even today because of its freshness. I don't think there is any film that has such an epic climax. Normally, you would like a boy eloping with the girl. You would never see a mother promise her daughter that she will not let her suffer as she did. Also, the pairing of Shah Rukh Khan and Kajol was bang on. They looked so beautiful together on screen. No other actor could have pulled off this film. Amrishji's classic dialogue, "*Jaa Simran … jee le apni zindagi*", may have been used by so many fathers in real life. This line made a difference in so many people's lives.'[5]

The film's success was unprecedented. Given the nature of the film, which refused to conform to traditional tropes, not many expected it to be as big a hit as it ultimately turned out to be. Satish Shah was perhaps the only actor in the cast who had no doubt that the film would be a great hit.

'I had predicted that *DDLJ* would become a superhit. Yashji would come to the set almost every day. Once, we were shooting for the song "*Mehendi Laga Ke Rakhna*" and I went up to Yashji and told him, "Yashji, a year ago, I was shooting for *Hum Aapke Hai Koun...!* in the same studio and that film went on to become a big hit.

When word got out that Shah Rukh was doing a romantic film, he was warned: No one will accept you as a romantic hero. It could have happened. He had thrown Shilpa Shetty's character down from the terrace of a very high building in *Baazigar*, and had stalked and tormented the beautiful Juhi Chawla for three hours in *Darr*.

I'm getting the same vibe with *DDLJ*. I am sure this film will be a huge success." Yashji did not agree with me. … After the film, Yashji told me, "*Yaar tu toh bhagwaan hai. Shooting ke time bata diya tha ki yeh film superhit hone wali hai* [You are god. You had predicted that the film would become a superhit even while it was being shot]." And he gave me a tight hug.'

On its twenty-fifth anniversary, in 2023, *Dilwale Dulhania Le Jayenge* was re-released to massive fanfare. On the very first day, fans gathered in the thousands to rewatch the classic and mouth their favourite dialogues along with the actors. *DDLJ* really is the most discussed film in Bollywood and definitely the most talked about in Shah Rukh's own filmography. It is his—and Bollywood's—longest-running film in theatres till date.

What's most interesting about the re-release is that when it hit multiplexes across India on the Valentine's Day weekend, Shah Rukh's latest release, *Pathaan*, was also running in full force at the box office. Shah Rukh even cheekily tweeted, '*Arre yaar itni mushkil se action hero bana ....* and you guys are bringing back Raj ... *uff*!! This competition is killing me!!!! I am going to see *Pathaan* ... *Raj toh ghar ka hai* [I have become an action hero after so many difficulties and now you guys are bringing Raj back!].'

Manoj Desai, owner of the Maratha Mandir theatre in Mumbai, has sworn that he will run the film until the day the theatre exists. 'Some of the theatregoers have watched the film so many times that they know every dialogue,' Desai says.

The film's ticket is priced at Rs 40, and it continues to be played at the coveted 11.30 a.m. slot. The crowd is usually young college-goers and teen couples who have just started dating. Weekends are still sometimes houseful, Desai tells us. 'You would assume that no one wants to watch this film any more. It might feel dated but people still flock in, sometimes in large numbers.'

In 2015, there was talk that the film would be pulled down. The outcry was so huge that Desai had to roll back the plan. And since then, despite the lull of the Covid-19 months when screens were shut for almost a year, the film has only thrived. Maratha Mandir has now become synonymous with *DDLJ*. 'Some people come with their children to show them the movie that their parents watched when they were in college. Some come with their parents to revisit the movie that was their first, at the exact place where they saw it first. And then there is the new crowd—those who come to understand what's so special about this film that it's been running for nearly twenty-five years. The young ones surprise me the most. They can't figure out what's so charming about this film. It is not a love story that Gen Z gets. But then next week, they come again with more people and they all try to understand why. This cycle continues and now Raj is charming to them too and Simran is cute,' Desai says.

Desai's theatre also benefits from its location. Situated bang opposite the Bombay Central Station, dreary travellers make a pit stop to watch the film in the middle of the day. Doctors from the area drop by to catch the movie because it's soothing and familiar. 'It's their comfort watch in the middle of an exhausting day,' he says. Sometimes, it is just a spot for afternoon nappers who want to doze off to the iconic Jatin–Lalit tune on the ukulele.

Desai isn't exaggerating the popularity of *DDLJ*. The film's footfall was memorable even last year. On 10 February, *DDLJ* raked in Rs 2.5 lakh across PVR, Inox and Cinepolis. The following day, there was a remarkable 300 per cent surge in collections, soaring to Rs 10 lakh. According to reports, similar figures were anticipated for 11 February. It earned a total of Rs 22.5 lakh over the three-day weekend.

Upon its original release, the movie had amassed a staggering worldwide box office collection of Rs 2 billion ($60 million). Accounting for inflation, the film ranks among the top-grossing Hindi films to date. Its domestic net earnings of Rs 533 million in that era translate to roughly Rs 4.613 billion ($62 million) when adjusted for inflation.

In the middle of the political furore of the early 1990s—from the Babri Masjid demolition, which led to nationwide riots, to the Bombay blasts—and its social complexities, *DDLJ* offered some much-needed respite to audiences. It beautifully balanced India's journey of embracing modernity while honouring its cherished traditions. Shah Rukh's character, Raj, epitomized the best of both Eastern and Western cultures. He effortlessly embodied diverse identities, appealing to a wide audience. Raj cherished and promoted traditional Indian values without being preachy. He navigated the balance between tradition and modernity, a struggle familiar to many urban Indians in the 1990s. In Aditya Chopra's cinematic vision, contradictions between the past and the present, wealth and poverty, urban and rural, and global and local identities peacefully coexisted and enriched each other.

DDLJ underwent several conceptual changes, from depicting an immigrant's loneliness to highlighting the diaspora's desire to return to India, while also showcasing a steadfast commitment to Indian values abroad. Centred on a love story, the film is inherently conservative, revolving around the restoration of cultural and ethical norms. The opening sequence shows Amrish Puri as an elderly member of the diaspora in London longing to return to his homeland as he feeds doves and reminisces about India.

The 1990s witnessed a surge in the number of films that catered to the diaspora for various reasons. India's economic liberalization in 1991 empowered the middle class, shaping the era's cultural landscape. The struggles of NRIs grappling with commercialization and a culture shock resonated with many, symbolizing broader societal challenges.

Aditya Chopra believes Indian films serve as a medium for fostering connectivity among Indians worldwide. These films not only cater to the diaspora's pride and cultural nostalgia, but also appeal to cultural anthropologists.

The diaspora in the 1990s presented a lucrative demographic, prompting film-makers to explore narratives catering to their experiences. These films, depicting distant locales through an Indian lens, became a platform for India to assert its globalized identity and celebrate commercialization while offering a sense of familiarity.

Set in London, *DDLJ* revolves around two starkly contrasting NRIs—Raj, a wealthy and Westernized party enthusiast, and Simran, a traditional, grounded girl. At one point in the film, Simran's rather strict father admonishes Raj, saying, 'You call yourself an Indian? You give India a bad name.' However, when Simran returns to India for her arranged marriage, Raj and Simran strive to convince her father to accept their love. Beyond the central romance, the film resonates with viewers for its exploration of patriotism and family bonds. Themes of nationalism and longing for one's homeland are evident in the poignant portrayal of Indian expatriates' emotional attachment to India. Choudhry Baldev Singh (Amrish Puri) constantly refers to India and Punjab as '*apna desh*' and '*apna Punjab*'.

In an article in *The New York Times*, Rajinder Dudrah, a professor at the Birmingham Institute of Media and English, and an NRI himself, said, '*DDLJ* deeply resonated with NRIs who were navigating multiple cultural identities. The movie mirrored the struggle individuals faced reconciling Indian traditions with Western influences.' Dudrah highlighted the film's theme of '*dil hai Hindustani*', emphasizing that regardless of geographical location, individuals of Indian descent maintained a deep-rooted connection to India.[6]

The film juxtaposes Punjab's rustic landscapes with London's cosmopolitan backdrop, reflecting the characters' dual cultural identities. Baldev's fusion of Western and Indian attire mirrors his life in London, influencing his family's upbringing with a blend of traditions from both worlds.

Baldev Singh's struggle with his national identity is highlighted in his efforts to reconcile with India, exemplified by his desire that his daughter Simran marry in Punjab. In contrast, Shah Rukh's character, Raj, represents a more cosmopolitan, affluent upbringing, but is someone who also maintains a deep connection to his Indian roots. The story track of Simran asking her father for permission to go on a trip is an intrinsically Indian issue, which NRI kids deeply related with in 1995, when *DDLJ* was first released.

Despite being second-generation NRIs, throughout the film both Raj and Simran embody Indian ethics and show an inherent respect for their cultural values. Raj's adherence to Indian customs, particularly in matters of honour and marriage, and his willingness to confront Baldev Singh's disapproval and respectfully seek his daughter's hand in marriage reinforce his Indian roots. Simran, on the other hand, is the ideal Indian daughter who displays a strong adherence to her heritage and family expectations. Her deep cultural connection with Indian values makes her initially agree to marry a man she has never met.

Aditya's film was inspired by Shah Rukh's real-life love story and how he won over Gauri's family. But Raj's nature was defined during the screenplay stage. The charm and goofiness of the character was all Shah Rukh. In Shah Rukh's portrayal, the NRI audience saw Raj as a modern, flawed and alluring character who, despite his contemporary demeanour, deeply values family and tradition.

The film portrays the Indian diaspora as a community that embraces and preserves the Indian value system, even in the face of Western influences, affirming the enduring strength of Indian cultural identity across borders. And this played a major role in *DDLJ*'s raging popularity among NRIs.

Cultural influence aside, *DDLJ* also became synonymous with the romantic locales of Switzerland. In the country today there's a tour known as the DDLJ Trail. Travel influencers Shivangi Johri and Saket Saxena first went on it in 2019. 'That year, we were travelling by train and many of these *DDLJ* locations were not accessible if you didn't have a vehicle of your own,' Shivangi told me over a call from Norway. It is a natural assumption that she is a fan of Shah Rukh and the film. 'Actually my husband Saket is crazy about Shah Rukh Khan. He has watched *DDLJ* 1,000 times. It was his dream to do the DDLJ Trail. When we couldn't finish it in 2019, he was bummed. Last year, we decided to go back to Switzerland and go to each and every spot on the list. He had this child-like glee on his face. I have never seen him so happy.'

The duo went from Zweisimmen (where Kajol misses the train while buying a traditional Swiss bell) to Gstaad (Early Beck bakery and *'Zara Sa Jhoom Loon Main'* shooting venue) to Launen Enge and Launen Rohrbrücke (*'Ho Gaya Hai Tujhko Toh Pyaar Sajna'*) to Lauenensee (Yash Chopra Lake) to Saanen (the spot for the famous 'palat' scene) to Montbovon (the famous church scene) to Interlaken (the red-rose prank scene).

Shivangi says that on the trip they met scores of other Indians who had come to Switzerland only to visit the places their favourite film was shot in. 'The movie has left a deep imprint on the people who have watched it. It was an awakening of sorts in how romance was being seen by young people. The syntax of love changed with the film. Even on our trip we met people who were there only to experience the magic of Raj and Simran. People from all over the world, primarily Indians, were singing *DDLJ* songs in an unknown country and bonding with each other over their favourite scenes and songs. It is one of my most special memories from a trip till date.'

Cinematographer Manmohan Singh believes that *DDLJ* made Switzerland mainstream. Foreign locations were no longer an escape into dream sequences, but a legitimate location to shoot chunks of a film in. Singh said, 'The unique part of shooting *DDLJ* in Switzerland was that most of it is captured through the train and road journey that Kajol and Shah Rukh take. Normally in Yash Chopra films, you would see songs being shot in Switzerland. For a change, I enjoyed capturing *"Tujhe Dekha Toh Yeh Jaana Sanam"* in the mustard fields of Gurgaon more than Switzerland *(laughs)*. Even today, film-makers try to emulate it.'

It would be an understatement to say that *DDLJ* redefined the portrayal of romance on the silver screen and the vein of desi storytelling. Since its release in 1995, it has become the touchstone for modern romances in India and served as a blueprint for countless films that followed.

Gone was the angry young man of the 1970s and the 1980s embodied by Amitabh Bachchan's Vijay, and here was a chill hero, comfortable in his own skin, modern, well travelled and yet traditional in his values. Call it the optimism of the 1990s or the new sense of buoyancy India was experiencing then, but *DDLJ* loudly proclaimed that there was a new hero in town, and he was here to stay.

Raj was the boy next door instead of the aloof, troubled man that the audience was used to seeing on the silver screen. Raj was witty, charming and comfortable to be around. In a departure from traditional gender roles, he did the unusual, even unthinkable, for those times. He befriended the women of the house—he was complimented by the aunts, peeled vegetables with the mother, became a buddy to his girlfriend's sister and kept a Karva Chauth fast with his girlfriend. This found its way into the larger popular culture. An Indiatimes article in 2013, 'How SRK Ruined Karva Chauth for Husbands', read: 'There's little to do for poor husbands out there but to grin and bear it. Because you might not believe that God is watching, but we can guarantee that some (if not all) of your wives and girlfriends have watched Shah Rukh Khan. And now that the bar's been raised, you have no option but to try and be half the filmi husband he is.'

This portrayal of Raj as a sensitive, vulnerable, yet strong man challenged the chauvinistic attitudes embodied by characters such as Simran's father and fiancé, showcasing the evolving identity of the modern Indian man.

As one of the posts on film critic Bardwaj Rangan's blog says, 'More than anything else, it was what Shah Rukh and Kajol did to change the definition and myth of a hero and heroine simply by their presence which is unconventional yet uniquely charismatic, which added to the greater halo anointed on them.' Aman Basha, the writer, notes that the film marks a significant departure from the convention of eloping to live life on one's own terms, without regard for societal expectations. Despite Simran's pleas to Raj to take her away, he refuses, which could be seen as both adhering to tradition and subtly confronting patriarchy. Basha points out that had Simran eloped, it would have validated her father Baldev's worst fears, potentially turning him into a more tyrannical figure, which would have had dire consequences for the other women in the family, Lajjo and Chhutki. The irony, as Basha notes, lies in how Baldev, with his disdain for Western values, is challenged by the same method Gandhi used against the British—passive resistance. Raj and Simran never directly confront Baldev. Instead, they endure his tyranny, symbolically turning the other cheek. This passive resistance questions not only Baldev's actions, but also the moral correctness of his decisions. Raj's justification to Simran's mother emphasizes the importance of choosing the right path. Basha concludes that, much like Gandhi's charm, Shah Rukh's portrayal of Raj in the film left a lasting impact on audiences.[7]

The film was subtle in its rebellion against patriarchy. Basha explains, 'For such a revolt against patriarchy, it seems natural that Raj would find greater companionship among the women of the household. It is pertinent to note that no other male character in the film or in earlier films, was found so constantly in domains of work and space traditionally associated with women. It was perhaps from here that the boundaries of on-screen masculinity would change, a theme constant in all the characters SRK would go on to play.'

The film's second half unfolds in Punjab, with rigidly defined gender roles. The world of women revolves around cooking and housework, while the domain of men encompasses hunting, camping and chess. This strict social division is reflected in the film's scenes. Raj's arrival disrupts this established order. Determined to spend time with Simran and her family, he spends most of the second half surrounded by the family's women. He readily assists with wedding preparations, carrying food, offering opinions on outfits and even participating in an all-female song-and-dance routine. Notably, he doesn't just perform these tasks, he seems to genuinely enjoy them.

As an opinion piece in the *Reverie* magazine, titled 'A Gendered Retrospective on DDLJ', explains, 'Raj is good at and enjoys doing activities that define womanhood in Indian culture and the film doesn't view him as any less of a man for it. He heavily contrasts [with] Simran's betrothed who is the model of traditional masculinity—a tall, chiselled hunter who values tradition—and the film asserts that Raj is the more desirable of the two. He places value in the happiness of the women and takes an interest in their goings on, making him not only a better romantic interest, but a better person overall.'[8]

Raj was a welcome change from on-screen men who were either seeped in misogyny or conditioned by patriarchy, duelling for *khandaan ki izzat* and, by and large, avenging the rape of the women close to them. Instead of being a traditionally stoic figure defined by physical prowess and unwavering machismo, Bollywood's leading man now had charm, vulnerability and emotional expressiveness. Raj wasn't afraid to shed a tear, break into a spontaneous dance or prioritize a woman's desires. This resonated deeply with an audience seeking a more nuanced portrayal of manhood. He wasn't just a hero who conquered villains—he was a man who respected a woman's agency, championed her choices and valued emotional connection. This softer masculinity, devoid of the usual hyper-masculine posturing, struck a chord with a changing India. Raj's character became a prototype for a new generation of heroes, one that continues to influence actors and audience expectations today. And that is a big part of the enduring legacy of *DDLJ* and Raj in our lives.

The film's influence is evident in the proliferation of its tropes and motifs throughout Indian cinema. From the portrayal of charming, flawed protagonists to filming in scenic European locales, *DDLJ*'s imprint can be seen in numerous Bollywood romances that followed its release. Its iconic moments, such as the unforgettable train-station climax, and timeless musical numbers, have been ingrained in the memories of audiences across generations.

A host of Hindi films have based their scenes, and sometimes their whole plot, on *DDLJ*. *Jab We Met* is often called the spiritual successor of this Aditya Chopra classic. The train motif that is central to *DDLJ* has been adapted to Geet's (Kareena Kapoor's) story. She even says, '*Ek ajeeb sa darr lag raha tha … bechaini si, jaise kuch galat ho raha hain, jaise koi train chhoot rahi hain* [A strange fear had seeped in … like something wrong was happening, like I was about to miss a train].' To cement the reference, director Imtiaz Ali added a sequence where Shahid Kapoor's Aditya helps Geet on to a moving train.

In 2013, Rohit Shetty recreated the *DDLJ* train scene in his action-comedy *Chennai Express* starring Shah Rukh and Deepika Padukone, but put his typical comic spin on it. The scene, which introduces Deepika's character Meena, shows Rahul (Shah Rukh) extend his arm to Meena from a moving train to help her get on and then moves on to show Shah Rukh helping four gangsters into the train in exactly the same way, all to the background of the *DDLJ* soundtrack.

Deepika was thrilled about filming the scene. 'I got to live the *DDLJ* moment with Shah Rukh. The fact that while growing up it is every girl's dream to romance Rahul and Raj on-screen, and I got an opportunity to do that as well in the film.'

In an interview with Huffington Post India in 2018, Kajol, the original Simran, spoke about what actually went into creating that iconic scene in the first place. 'Honestly, we were worried about the heat and getting cranky, my hair was frizzling out, the train wasn't moving at the right speed that it should have. We couldn't do retakes because the train had to go ahead and come back, which would take some twenty minutes. It was a mess. Actually, Raj should have just pulled the chain instead of making me run like a crazy person,' she said.[9]

Other than *Chennai Express, DDLJ* also paved the way for another successful franchise. In 2014, Karan Johar's stable released the Alia Bhatt–Varun Dhawan-starrer *Humpty Sharma Ki Dulhania*, helmed by director Shashank Khaitan. Nearly every aspect of this film mirrored *DDLJ*, with a notable parallel in the climax, where Alia Bhatt's character proposes to Varun Dhawan's in a manner reminiscent of Raj's proposal, albeit with gender roles reversed. At the trailer launch of the film, Karan said, 'It is an ode to *DDLJ*, not a copy. One will see glimpses of *DDLJ*, but the love story is different. We have made this film with honesty, integrity and with an intention to entertain people. We are not claiming any originality or an out-of-the-world twist in the film. From frame one to the last scene, the endearing quality is its sincerity in simply trying to entertain you. The reason why we have put that frame of *DDLJ* is because it is a film-maker's heartfelt desire to use an ounce of *DDLJ* in the first film he makes.'[10]

Karan, who was an assistant director for *DDLJ*, bonded with director Shashank Khaitan because of the film. He said, 'I have a lot of memories of *DDLJ*. I started my career from there. It is and will be the largest part of my career. The film, with its epic love story and innocence, had set the barometer which no other till date could match. When I met Shashank he told me he had grown up on that film. Most of these young kids have grown up on that fodder. Love for many people in this generation is *Dilwale Dulhania Le Jayenge*. SRK's charisma and Kajol's innocence and fragility from the movie are memorable.'[11]

In 2015, *DDLJ* marked the twentieth year of its release with a grand celebration. On the eve of its 1,000-week celebrations, Yash Raj Films held a grand screening of the film at Maratha Mandir. Shah Rukh and Kajol hosted a press conference, in which they explained their own equations with the film. 'In a strange sense, we all detach from the film. Everyone realizes that this film no longer belongs to us. It belongs to the people ... [They] have taken it and made it their own. This is dream-like,' Shah Rukh said.[12]

The film rightfully belongs to the fans. 'I don't want to meet Shah Rukh ever. For me he is Raj. There is a bubble in my mind that I have constructed from whatever I have seen of him in that film. I want to maintain that image,' says Arundhuti Ghosh, a graphic designer from Kolkata.

Raj has shaped the romantic expectations of most women of our generation. For some, he is an illusion, for others he is unattainable and for many he is the benchmark. Eighteen-year-old Dolly Dube tells me that her mother, Pinky Dube, has hoped all her life that her husband would become Raj from *DDLJ*. 'She is in her forties and my father is in his fifties. She works as a house help in Patna and he is a carpenter. I have seen my mother watch this movie every week now for years. She now jokes, "You have your cartoons to blow your mind—I have this." My mother got married when she was just fifteen. My father is an average Indian man. I don't think most of them are capable of being Raj. My mother cannot understand why he can't be a little like Raj or just do a little better. There was this one time when my aunt (mother's younger sister) was visiting us and my father didn't help with chopping vegetables for a pooja we were hosting at home. My mother turned to her sister and said, "*Aise aadmi kabhi Raj Malhotra ban hi nahi saktey. Shiksha hi galat mili hai unhe* [Such men can never be Raj. They have not received the right kind of education for it]." *DDLJ* still plays at home every week and my mother never forgets to tell me, "*Aadmi aisa khojna jo tumhari izzat karey* [Find a man who respects you]." She isn't wrong—love does fizzle out, but respect should remain. Just last week she told me my father made a cup of tea for her for the first time in all the time they have been married. It didn't taste the best, but the effort was definitely appreciated.'

At the film's 1,000-week celebrations, Shah Rukh talked about how the cast and crew of the film did not set out to change the world—they were simply telling a story that they felt was true for them. He said, 'It was the love, passion and simplicity of what Adi believed India is like—what a boy should be like, a girl should be like. Adi never made a villain in his films. Everyone is good in his movies, just circumstances are bad. And while making the film, it all gets better.'

And his fans believe him.

Strangely enough, Shah Rukh himself hasn't watched the film too many times. In *The Romantics*, he tells the story of the first time he watched it after its release. It was at Raj Mandir in Jaipur, and he was shooting for *Chaahat* and had gone with Pooja Bhatt, Mahesh Bhatt and Anupam Kher. 'It had been eight days since the release and Adi felt the last part of the film was too long. When I was watching the movie, I realized people were chatting in the hall. I almost felt like going back and telling Adi that we should cut that part and make the movie crisper. But then Bhatt sa'ab said, "They aren't chatting. They are repeating the dialogues of the film."'

After almost three decades of the release of the film, the dialogues now just roll off the tongue. I remember meeting a cab driver in Paris named Patrick Hines. He was picking me and three other journalists up from the airport to take us to our hotel. We were in the city for a junket for another Aditya Chopra film, *Befikre*. Within minutes of us getting into the car, he could tell we were Indians. The first question he asked us was if we were from the 'Land of Shah Rukh Khan'. I asked him how he knew Shah Rukh Khan. 'I have watched *DDLJ*. "*Raj, agar woh tumse pyaar karti hai toh woh ek baar palat ke zaroor dekhegi … Palat … Palat,*"' he repeated the iconic dialogue from *DDLJ* in broken Hindi. Over the next one week, we met him a few times and exchanged stories about *DDLJ*. One of the things he said, which has stayed with me till date, is, 'Men think being brash is cool, but it is not. I love *DDLJ* because it had a hero who showed people he cared, he loved. Women don't get attracted to hot-and-cold behaviour. You are making them feel insecure. Even if you do marry a woman you have won like that, you won't be happy. You'll complain she is nagging. Why is she nagging? Because you aren't putting her at ease. You are making her feel unsure of your affection. You want a solid man like Raj. I am a man like that, and I tell the men I am friends with to watch the film so they know how to love a woman. It's not very difficult to be decent.'

Kajol and Shah Rukh are right when they say that people remember the film a lot better than they do. '*Humein dialogue yaad nahi hai. Par log humein aake humare dialogues boltey hai* [We don't remember the dialogues, but people come and repeat the dialogues to us],' she said. They remember the words and what the words made them feel.

At the Maratha Mandir 1,000-week event, Shah Rukh said one of the truest things about the film: 'Between Kajol and I, we have five children, and none of them is older than this film. *Humara sabse accha bachcha* DDLJ *hi hai* [Our favourite child is *DDLJ*].'

The iconic poster of *DDLJ* has its own story. In an interview Kajol told the content platform Curly Tales, 'He [Shah Rukh] had to carry me on his shoulder. I was feeling so bad and asking him continuously if he would manage it. I think it took a hit on his masculinity. He was like, "How can you say this? I am a guy."' Kajol recalled the incident with a loud laugh. 'Later he had a frozen shoulder.'[13]

It was a stroke of fate that the celebrated on-screen pair went on to shoot Rohit Shetty's *Dilwale* (2015) the same year as the film's twentieth anniversary. Shetty recreated the iconic poster of the film that had Shah Rukh carrying Kajol on his shoulders. Shah Rukh posted it on Twitter with the caption, 'All looked happy that I picked Kajol again.'

The film and Raj both belong to the people who made it as big as it is today. Everyone has the memory of where they first saw the film and what Raj did for them. The fact that Austin Colby was chosen to play the character of Raj in the Broadway adaptation didn't go down well with fans. In fact, they were furious. A fan on Twitter wrote, 'I hope you realise that no white man will ever be SRK.'

Over the years, Shah Rukh and Raj have become one for his fans. And they do have a lot in common. They are not afraid of being vulnerable, are respectful towards women and make people feel seen. They are both men we admire and not necessarily lust for. They are men we can take home to our families and rest assured that they will charm our parents.

As such, it is next to impossible for fans to be rational about seeing a new Raj. They are emotional in their response. *DDLJ* on Broadway opened to average reviews, but the magic was just not there. To separate the artiste from the character is nearly impossible and, even if it's achievable, requires immense reconditioning for the audience.

Shah Rukh, in a 2005 interview with NDTV, had a simple take on why a film such as *DDLJ* cannot be recreated. He said, '[It was a time in our lives when] all of us were friends or becoming friends. Some of us knew each other from before that, and now, after ten years, we are still friends. I think that level of comfort for everyone, not just the hero-heroine, was very fresh. *Haste khelte kuch bann gaya* [In the midst of fun and laughter, something was made], and I think that is what makes *Dilwale Dulhania Le Jayenge* special. I don't think we will ever be able to make *DDLJ*, including us, again, unless you [have] that level of friendship and happiness.'[14]

Resham Baduri, a communications executive from Mumbai now settled in the US, and a die-hard fan of the film, also feels *DDLJ* can never be recreated, not because of the actors but because the fans won't stand for it. She talks about how, after her divorce, going back into the dating pool has been a challenge for her. And as she oscillates between her hopes of finding a man like Raj and having them dashed, she realizes *DDLJ* has become a time capsule to her. 'We no longer live in a world of Rajs. We live in a world of animals. In such a world, where green flags are obsolete, Raj is reduced to a fantasy. Everyone says *DDLJ* is a comfort watch. It is comfortable because it helps us travel back to a time that no longer exists and will perhaps never come back as long as we are alive. People have become so different from who they used to be. Romance has been invaded by social media. I am a hopeless romantic and I do believe I will find my Raj someday. But until then, I am going to protect the experience of the film in a rather militant fashion. I don't want it to be remade. I don't want to see someone else as Raj—definitely not a gora [Caucasian]. Why change it? The makers and the actors should just be proud that they made a movie that cannot be topped. Someday when I have a daughter, I am going to take her to Maratha Mandir to make her meet Raj—the man who got me through every bad day with the belief that love exists.'

> Shah Rukh and Raj have become one for his fans. And they do have a lot in common. They are not afraid of being vulnerable, are respectful towards women and make people feel seen. They are both men we admire and not necessarily lust for. They are men we can take home to our families and rest assured that they will charm our parents.

> *Kehte hain agar kisi cheez ko dil se chaho, toh puri kainaat usse tumse milane ki koshish mein lag jaati hai*
>
> Om Shanti Om, 2007

7

THE WORLD IS HIS OYSTER

It would be an understatement to say that *Dilwale Dulhania Le Jayenge* marked Shah Rukh's ascent to global stardom. By his own admission, the film changed his life. Shah Rukh's charm was channelled into a highly marketable package somewhat unconsciously by the star. 'He is at once the biggest and most versatile of Bollywood heroes, a star said to command a larger fan following than any other working actor in the world today, a man who does psychological thriller, screwball comedy, earnest romance, ditzy rom-com, serious biopic, and, lately, testosterone-fueled action. He's said to be five-feet-seven [*sic*], shorter than some of his female co-stars, seemingly still in full possession of his springy hair, and is physically muscular yet lithe, with a dancer's grace, as if Gene Kelly had dabbled in steroids. At 57, he still conveys a whiff of the unconflicted naïveté of 1990s Bollywood superstardom, when gold was an absolute good and fame an incontrovertible blessing,' described a piece in the *Vulture* magazine titled 'The Thoroughly Goofy, Undeniably Seductive, All-in-One Charm of Shah Rukh Khan'.[1]

His rise in the early 1990s coincided with a phase when Bollywood had started gaining visibility outside India, particularly among the Indian diaspora. The migration of young Indians in the 1990s was a major contributing factor in establishing his global appeal. As these young professionals and students settled abroad, they carried with them a love for Bollywood films. *DDLJ* was pivotal to this. The cult classic resonated deeply with Indians abroad by making them feel seen.

The growing Indian communities abroad created a demand for Bollywood films in the international market, and the man leading the brigade of Bollywood's foray into the world was Shah Rukh Khan. The demand inevitably led to a wider distribution of films, with screenings in countries with a significant Indian population, such as the US, the UK, Canada and the Middle East.

DDLJ had already set the stage for the West being a lucrative market and setting for film plots. The UK and the US became rich sources for full-fledged narratives, with millions of viewers willing to pay in dollars and pounds to watch these films. By the early 2000s, Hindi films were as likely to be set in New York as in New Delhi.

As the international market grew, savvy directors began creating films specifically designed for overseas audiences. These 'overseas-friendly films' featured big star casts, extravagant music numbers, lavish productions, romantic storylines and minimal action. Directors sidestepped violence and gore in favour of family values. NRIs sought comfort. Writer Suketu Mehta describes it well. 'The diaspora wants to see an urban, affluent, glossy India, the India they imagine they grew up in and wish they could live in now. They want love stories with minimal conflict, even between rivals.'[2]

The post-*DDLJ* effect was beginning to show in Hindi films as well. Yash Chopra's *Dil To Pagal Hai* (*DTPH*), released in 1997, starred Shah Rukh this time as Rahul, a flamboyant playwright and theatre director who lives in a studio apartment in Mumbai. Though Mumbai has a few of them, none of them are styled like the Manhattan makeover they got in this film. It was similar to Shah Rukh's studio from Subhash Ghai's *Pardes*, where he played an NRI based in the US. Rahul in *DTPH* is a cynic who serendipitously falls in love with Pooja (Madhuri Dixit), whose faith in romance beautifully contrasts with Rahul's pragmatic and cynical nature. The film proposes the idea of a soulmate—that there is someone, somewhere who is made for you. *DTPH* was a massive hit, making Shah Rukh the poster boy of feel-good cinema.

DTPH opened to record-breaking business, with 100 per cent collections in its first week across India. The film maintained this in the second week, and merely dropped to 97 per cent in the third. It grossed Rs 59.82 crore ($16.47 million) in India and Rs 12.04 crore ($3.3 million) internationally, bringing the worldwide total to Rs 71.86 crore ($19.77 million) against a budget of Rs 9 crore ($2.48 million), including print and advertising costs. The film had a worldwide opening weekend of Rs 4.71 crore ($1.3 million) and grossed Rs 8.97 crore ($2.47 million) in its first week. It was the third-highest opener of the year, after *Border* and *Koyla*. It was also the highest-grossing film of 1997 overseas.[3]

The film had a massive pop culture impact. Like mental health advocate and youth-focused platform Yuvaa co-founder Nikhil Taneja writes, 'I remember Karisma Kapoor's hotness ushering me into adolescence through *Dil To Pagal Hai*. I remember learning what love truly was as my heart skipped many beats when the lips of Madhuri Dixit and Shah Rukh Khan came dangerously close to each other. I remember feeling heartbroken myself, as I hoped Akshay Kumar would have a happy ending with Karisma Kapoor in an alternate universe. And I remember, thereafter, using the movie's "*Rahul ... Naam toh suna hoga*" line to disastrous effect in real life.'

DTPH, from a film-making perspective, tried something new. It is one of those rare Hindi films in which the lead actor and actress meet for the first time around the interval. Yash Chopra ensures that the friendships between Rahul and Nisha, as well as Pooja and Ajay, are not just side notes. Instead, he gives these relationships ample space and depth in the first half, establishing a solid foundation for the conflict that unfolds later in the film.

The film's songs are a highlight. American wrestler John Cena singing a song from the film went viral this year. Wrestler Gurv Sihra shared a video on X of John Cena singing *'Bholi Si Surat'* during their gym session. Cena is a huge Shah Rukh fan and, over the years, has shared several posts dedicated to the actor. Shah Rukh responded to this, saying, 'Thank u both.... Love it and love u John, I'm gonna send u my latest songs and I want a duet from the two of you again!!! Ha ha.'[4]

At Anant Ambani and Radhika Merchant's wedding earlier this year, Cena had the opportunity to meet Shah Rukh in person. The WWE superstar said in an interview, 'It was just such an emotional moment to be able to shake a person's hand that affects your life so drastically and tell them specifically what they did. He [Shah Rukh] did a TED Talk that found me at the right time in my life and his words were beyond inspirational to me. They helped orchestrate a change in my life. And since that change, I have been able to recognize all the jackpots that I have been given and been grateful and work hard to make sure I don't waste them.'[5]

Subhash Ghai's *Pardes* released the same year as *DTPH*, but had more in common with *DDLJ*. It dealt with a lot of the same themes. The movie, much like *DDLJ*, reflected the identity crisis faced by the children of immigrants. Marriage choices became a battleground where these children, raised between two cultures, grappled with reconciling their parents' desire for tradition with their own modern aspirations for love.

While the anxieties of immigrant parents regarding their children's romantic choices might seem specific to their situation, *DDLJ* portrays them as a reflection of a larger question for all of India. The film asks: How does one define oneself as an Indian in a globalized world? This struggle transcends geographical boundaries and resonates with everyone in India, whether they have migrated or not. *DDLJ* cleverly positions the problems of NRIs as problems of identity for all. The film emphasizes the Indian family system as the core institution that defines what it means to be Indian. This remains true regardless of where you live. The family acts as the anchor, holding together tradition and individual desires even amid the complexities of a globalized world. Unlike *DDLJ*'s optimistic view of maintaining Indian identity abroad, *Pardes* takes a darker approach.

While *DDLJ* suggests Indian identity can adapt and even strengthen with visits home, *Pardes* wrestles with the allure and corruption of the Western world.

The film reflects the immigrant's dilemma—emotionally tied to India, yet drawn to the material comforts of America. In a paper published on the likeness of the two movies, titled 'The Diaspora Comes Home: Disciplining Desire in *DDLJ*', Patricia Uberoi says that the *Woman's Era* magazine captures this struggle perfectly: 'Immigrants yearn for both worlds—the emotional depth of India and the financial security of America.'⁶

Here, in the land of dreams, Shah Rukh's journey began in earnest, marked by a relentless drive and a magnetic charm that would make him a global icon. His life, much like his persona, defies convention, reflecting the very essence of India's diverse cultural tapestry.

While *Pardes*'s ending suggests a possibility of preserving Indian values abroad, the film inherently believes that cultural identity is tied to a specific place, and dislocation inevitably leads to loss.

And while these films became an archetype for India, and Indians, Shah Rukh, too, became one with India and its people.

The global potential of Indian films was first noticed in 1998, when *Dil Se..*, helmed by Mani Ratnam, was released. Set against the backdrop of insurgency in Assam, the film follows a radio personality, Amar (Shah Rukh), in India who is captivated by a free-spirited woman, Meghna (Manisha Koirala), he meets on his travels. It was a big deal for Shah Rukh to be doing a Mani Ratnam film. He wasn't an obvious casting choice. When asked why Shah Rukh, the film-maker said, 'It was just a feeling. I hadn't seen too many of his films before. You feel that you want somebody who would be a common man, who would represent All India Radio, which is the voice of the ordinary citizen, and still be able to carry the film on his shoulders. I needed somebody who would take us across the line. It was a difficult subject, it was the 50th year of Indian Independence but there are corners which still have darker areas. We tried to cover it and this film was trying to explore the gray thing. And we wanted this happy mood to control that side of it. So he somewhere represented that kind of mood.'[7]

Shah Rukh and Mani Ratnam were working on another script—the Tamil film *Alai Payuthey*. It was later adapted in Hindi by Shaad Ali as *Saathiya*. It was originally planned with Shah Rukh. It was a simple city-based love story, but the script didn't fall into place, so the duo moved on to something else, which ended up being this film.

Dil Se.. is Shah Rukh's only collaboration with director Mani Ratnam. The producers at the time were concerned that its tragic ending might not sit well with audiences. One of the film's major highlights was the dance number 'Chaiyya Chaiyya', and producers feared that viewers might leave the theatre after the song. To counter this, they decided to play the song again at the end of the movie. Ram Gopal Varma, who was one of the film's producers, narrated the story of how they were planning to end the film. 'Bharat Shah told me that "*Bahut gadbad ho gaya hai* (We have made a huge mistake). There's one way of saving the situation." According to him, the moment Shah Rukh and Manisha Koirala hug each other, we'll cut the part where the bomb goes off. And we'll add the "Chaiyya Chaiyya" song. He reasoned that it's the most liked song of the film and the audience would get happy on seeing it twice.'[8]

When RGV, as Ram Gopal Verma is often referred to, called Mani Ratnam to discuss this, he was furious. 'Mani got very angry with the suggestion. He asked me a valid question, "How can Shah Rukh Khan hug Manisha Koirala and imagine Malaika Arora?!"'

Mani Ratnam did have a point, and that ending didn't happen. Despite making sparse numbers in India, it became the first Bollywood film to break into the UK top ten charts. Showcased at prestigious festivals such as Era New Horizons and Helsinki International Film Festival, *Dil Se..* garnered international acclaim. The film raked in impressive figures, grossing $975,000 in the US and £537,930 in the UK. The movie's appeal extended to Japan as well, where it was a hit.

The year 1998 was also the year when Karan Johar made his directorial debut with *Kuch Kuch Hota Hai*. He and Shah Rukh had first met on the set of *Karan Arjun* and had become friends on the set of *DDLJ*. Karan's father Yash Johar had also taken him along when he was offering Shah Rukh *Duplicate* in 1994, and they were going to discuss dates and fees. In his memoir *An Unsuitable Boy*, Karan wrote about how he first met Shah Rukh on the set of *Karan Arjun*, where Yash Johar had gone to sign the actor for *Duplicate*.

What Karan remembers from that meeting was that Shah Rukh was wearing this bright orange Levi's shirt. He said in an interview in 2023, 'You know how you build a perception and hear about movie stars and how they are? I had this impression that movie stars were a certain way because my father was a producer, and he'd dealt with many. With Shah Rukh, there was a lot of talk that he was kind of arrogant ... Not arrogant, but like he knew what he was doing because he comes from drama and theatre, but in one minute, I was just swept away by the magic of Shah Rukh Khan. He looks into your eyes and speaks to you, and that is the most beautiful part about Shah Rukh.'[9]

Clearly, the impression of Shah Rukh being arrogant had persisted despite his affable roles, and Karan, too, was taken in by what he had heard. But that was before they worked together. In his memoir, he reflected on his preconceived notion of Shah Rukh as a young, borderline-arrogant figure. However, that perception quickly changed during their first meeting at Film City. Shah Rukh's warmth and friendliness left a lasting impression, especially when he respectfully opened the car door for his father. What was intended to be a brief ten-minute conversation turned into a two-hour discussion, during which Shah Rukh's accessibility and genuine respect for his father won Karan over completely. Having witnessed his father's disillusionment with many in the industry, he was naturally protective and apprehensive about how others treated him. Yet, Shah Rukh, being an outsider and relatively new to the film world, stood out with his different approach. Despite not being his favourite actor at the time—he was a big Aamir Khan fan—he found himself captivated by Shah Rukh's charm, humour and sensitivity.[10]

Shah Rukh and Karan went on to become one of Bollywood's most celebrated actor-director duo. Today they call each other family. But in Shah Rukh, Karan first found the acceptance that his family and friends hadn't been able to provide him until then. On the chat show *Be a Man, Yaar!*, Karan spoke about how Shah Rukh made him feel comfortable in his skin, something that was rare for him back then. That explains the core of their friendship. He said, 'The first person that made me feel I was okay was Shah Rukh Khan. He was born and brought up in a progressive environment. He had done theatre and worked with all kinds of people. My parents were not being able to understand me. My "feminine side" that was coming out strongly was met with laughter and made fun of. When I got older, people got quieter but there was still chitter chatter around. Maybe the way I walked or spoke (I think). Shah Rukh was the first man that didn't make me feel lesser. He made me feel like an equal. He accepted what in those days was considered walking funny, being pansy, being effeminate. He was so cool about it. He had open chats with me. Even when I had to say the biggest things about my personality and sexuality, I spoke to him first. He was the first sense of support I had.'

Their equation explains why Shah Rukh said yes to *Kuch Kuch Hota Hai*, even when there was no script. Karan was supposed to present an idea for his first film to Shah Rukh by January 1996, but had nothing ready. By March–April of that year, while Shah Rukh was shooting for *Chaahat* in Jaipur, he asked Karan to share his concept. Karan, unsure of what to present, remembered an English film he had watched, where a man, after losing his wife during childbirth, eventually bonds with his child and finds a new partner. Inspired by this, Karan envisioned a story where Shah Rukh's character, having lost his wife, had to raise their child and find a new partner to complete the family.

As he travelled to meet Shah Rukh, Karan developed a scene involving a child receiving a note labelled 'Mother', even though her mother was deceased. During their meeting, Karan improvised the scene, describing how a father explains the essence of motherhood to his child. The emotional impact of this scene moved both Karan and Shah Rukh, who was visibly touched, possibly thinking about his own mother.

By the end of their conversation, Shah Rukh had committed to the project, advising Karan to write a love story and to cast Kajol. Returning to Mumbai, Karan discussed the idea with Kajol, who agreed to do it whenever Karan was ready. With both Shah Rukh and Kajol on board and dates set for October 1997, Karan began the process of writing the film.

The film rolled in October 1997. Just before the release of *Kuch Kuch Hota Hai*, Karan's father's film *Duplicate* hit the theatres and unfortunately bombed. Distributors grew wary of *Kuch Kuch Hota Hai*, fearing another loss. This disappointment weighed heavily on Yash Johar during the *Kuch Kuch Hota Hai* shoot in Ooty. Thankfully, Yash Chopra, recognizing the potential of *Kuch Kuch Hota Hai*, intervened when distributors pulled out. Aditya Chopra, too, believed in the film, and Yash Chopra stepped in to distribute it across India and overseas territories. His faith in the project ultimately saved the day, compensating for the losses incurred by *Duplicate* and allowing *Kuch Kuch Hota Hai* to reach audiences.

By 1997, at Aditya's insistence, Yash Chopra had opened a distribution office in the UK. Their first release, *Dil To Pagal Hai*, netted £1 million (Rs 9.3 crore roughly), an unprecedented figure for an Indian film. A year later, they opened an office in the US with Karan's debut film, *Kuch Kuch Hota Hai*. This film surpassed even *DDLJ*'s record, grossing over $7 million worldwide (Rs 57 crore). *Kuch Kuch Hota Hai* also entered the UK top ten charts at number nine.

The world was finally welcoming—and seeing—Bollywood.

The one thing that Shah Rukh never denies is how much he likes money. Almost as much as his ideals. However, his collaborators, from Yash Chopra to Karan Johar, have openly said that he never takes a penny from them until a project is completed. Karan said in an interview to

Mid-Day in 2023, 'Whatever is given [he takes it]. Our contracts with Shah Rukh Khan are about "It's a pleasure to work with you, thank you". We don't have any detailed paperwork. All said and done [it's about what] we expect of each other.'[11]

In fact, Shah Rukh has even shot for two of Karan's films for free: the 2022 film *Brahmastra* (for fourteen days) and his guest appearance in the 2016 film *Ae Dil Hai Mushkil*.

As someone who had had a difficult equation with money in his early years, the money and the early successes were important to him. Even as he allowed his passion to take over and decided to put his own money into finishing films, such as *Kabhi Haan Kabhi Naa*, post-*DDLJ* saw him making more money than he had ever imagined possible. And he didn't shy away from making the most of it. It eventually helped him buy his dream home—Mannat.

In Hindi cinema's trade circuits, it is believed that what separates superstars from legends is their willingness to gamble. Shah Rukh's decision to work for free in films sometimes showed his fiery passion for acting. In an industry often driven by financial gain, it was unthinkable that someone would even forgo payment. Shah Rukh didn't see films as a means to an end—they were a sacred calling that went beyond the mere concept of money. This set him apart and set the stage for a career that inspires young aspirants in Bollywood till date—the willingness to invest in art and bet on themselves without the certainty of a favourable outcome.

In a Huffington Post interview, he spoke about the value of money in his life. 'I come from a very poor background. I have seen my parents eating food with *daal* that had more water than substance. They would make a joke about it—"Today let's have watered-down *daal*." Or my mother would say, "No, I am not hungry today, I had food outside." We were not stupid to know that she hadn't eaten. We knew our constraints. We were a very educated family, very soft-spoken, secular and happy and nuclear. But we were poor. And I did not like it.' He wittily once said that being a philosopher or a teacher was better when one was rich. Shah Rukh attributed his focus on earning well to one advice his mother gave him: You have got to be a little practical.[12]

And he made money. Nearly all his films in the 1990s were big money spinners. But he didn't stop at that. *Kuch Kuch Hota Hai* was the start of Bollywood's obsession with the idea that great marriages or relationships are always founded on deep friendship: *Pyaar dosti hai … Agar woh meri sab se acchi dost nahin ban sakti, toh main usse kabhi pyaar kar hi nahi sakta, kyunki dosti bina toh pyaar hota hi nahin. Simple, pyaar dosti hai.* [Love is friendship If she can't become my best friend, I can never love her, because without friendship there can be no love. Simple, love is friendship].

This idea, until that point, was alien to Indians. The vocabulary of romance was changing. Karan told us the story of Rahul, a young widower, whose eight-year-old daughter takes it upon herself to reunite him with his long-lost best friend, Anjali, after reading letters from her dead mother. Most of the film's first half is set in a college that looks nothing like the most popular colleges of the country, something that Karan is critiqued for till date. It looked right out of an average American high school movie, complete with lockers and cheerleaders. But then again, even though this Xavier's College looked different, perhaps it was its idealism, coupled with the innate 'coolness' and carefree beats of youth, that resonated with millions of youngsters in India.

Shah Rukh once again played Rahul, the coolest student in college, wearing snug tees and a neckpiece that spelt 'c-o-o-l'. This was an airbrushed world, before Instagram filters were a thing. For Karan, fashion continues to be the key. He wanted to pursue a career in fashion, but it was Aditya Chopra who encouraged him into movies. But in his debut movie, he set new style standards. Before shooting began, Karan and his designer friend Manish Malhotra made special trips to London for costumes.

Although Yash Johar initially thought this shopping spree was excessive, he ultimately agreed to a budget of £5,000 (Rs 35 lakh today), which was

> **In Hindi cinema's trade circuits, it is believed that what separates superstars from legends is their willingness to gamble … Shah Rukh didn't see films as a means to an end—they were a sacred calling that went beyond the mere concept of money.**

later increased to £8,000 (Rs 55 lakh after adjusting for inflation). Karan and Manish deliberately chose clothes with prominent designer labels to ensure the audience recognized the effort and expense involved. Anjali's first scene shows her playing basketball in a DKNY tracksuit, while the sartorially evolved Rahul favoured Polo Sport and GAP.

Despite the film's fantastical settings, it is deeply rooted in Indian emotions—a motif that was successful in Indian films of that time. Karan, known for his emotional storytelling, crafted scenes to evoke maximum emotions. Although the film is set in India, the characters, much like in *DDLJ*, are hybrids—modern, articulate individuals who, beneath their trendy Western facades, proudly maintain their Indian identity. Rahul visits the temple every week, and Pooja, played by a young Rani Mukerji, raised in London and educated at Oxford University, dresses like a Western fashion model but sings a Hindu hymn when asked to perform publicly. She tells Rahul, 'Living in London and studying there has not made me forget my roots—and don't you ever forget that.' On the film's twenty-first anniversary, Karan pointed out Rahul's flaws in an interview. If he had to reimagine him, he'd perhaps make the character more self-assured and strong. 'I'd give him a spine and more EQ [emotional quotient]. I'd also introduce more confrontation. Rahul, today, would be able to have an open conversation with Anjali. He'll know that she likes him and he'd address that with her.'[13]

Films such as *DDLJ* and *Kuch Kuch Hota Hai* assured NRIs that they did belong—living in the West did not strip them of their roots. Indian values were adaptable, allowing them to straddle both worlds, just as the characters in these films did. Both movies offered NRIs an idealized version of India, free from poverty, corruption and injustice. Instead, they depicted a nostalgia-filled homeland, full of beautiful homes, large loving families, traditions and rituals, and children who, despite their cool demeanour, remained happily obedient to their parents.

For the approximately twenty million Indians living overseas, Hindi films have always been more than mere entertainment. They serve as a means to unite the community, maintain an emotional connection with their distant motherland and provide an affordable way to introduce

A gleeful cast at the mahurat party of *Baazigar*. Perhaps they knew what a hit they had on their hands!

From *Yes Boss* to Dreamz Unlimited, Juhi and Shah Rukh, partners in reel and real life.

Whether it is Rahul-Pooja in *Dil To Pagal Hai* or Devdas-Paro, Shah Rukh Khan and Madhuri Dixit make a dazzling pair on screen.

Shah Rukh's luscious locks and dimples have their own fan club.

Helping people, whether through the Meer Foundation or on his own, has always been something Shah Rukh believes in. Here he had organized a fundraiser in 1995 for junior artistes.

Two superstars, one epic friendship. Shah Rukh and Salman Khan at a party in the late 1990s.

Shah Rukh and Amitabh Bachchan, the Badshah and the Shahenshah of Bollywood, being spotted together is so rare that the world stops to watch.

When Farah Khan choreographs, Shah Rukh dances his heart out—an association that has lasted for two decades and counting.

Shah Rukh, Rani Mukerji and Aziz Mirza during *Chalte Chalte* promotions.

Shah Rukh and Deepika Padukone have been giving us one hit after another since *Om Shanti Om*.

The King of Romance (Yash Chopra) and the King of Bollywood (Shah Rukh), with the Nawab of Pataudi (Saif Ali Khan) thrown into the mix.

Shah Rukh, Subhash Ghai, Sanjay Dutt and Jackie Shroff at a party in the 1990s.

Behind the scenes: Kajol and Shah Rukh's *'Jaati Hoon Main'* moments with Rakesh Roshan on the set of *Karan Arjun*.

Shah Rukh and Sanjay Leela Bhansali during the shooting of *Devdas*, turning their inherent swag into timeless art.

On the *Swades* set, Shah Rukh and Ashutosh Gowariker prove that great films start with great teamwork!

The 1990s' dream team—and best friends. Shah Rukh, Gauri and Karan Johar looking effortlessly stylish!

Dilip Kumar and Shah Rukh shared a father–son bond.

A BTS shot of when Shah Rukh's Raj took down Parmeet Sethi's Kuljeet in Aditya Chopra's cult film *Dilwale Dulhania Le Jayenge*.

A BTS peek at how Shah Rukh became Shanker in Rakesh Roshan's *Koyla*.

Jackie Shroff and Shah Rukh turn goon patrol into a high-octane showdown in *One 2 Ka 4*!

Left: Twinkle Khanna shows Shah Rukh that even in *Badshah*, she's the one with the real power.

Right: Producing and acting together for the first time. Shah Rukh as Ajay Bakshi in *Phir Bhi Dil Hai Hindustani*.

Dancing through life: Shah Rukh and Gauri show young love's got rhythm.

Lala Rukh makes a rare Eid appearance, completing the family photo, with Suhana, Shah Rukh, Gauri and Aryan.

Did someone say 'Rab Ne Bana Di Jodi'?

Holding his heart in his arms. Shah Rukh and his favourite girl, daughter Suhana.

Indian culture to second-generation children growing up as hybrids between two cultures.

For some, Shah Rukh is their only reference to India. Parveen Banderkar, who was born in Cape Town, South Africa, and has lived there her entire life, discovered Shah Rukh from the 1990s' movies that played on their local television. 'I have no family in India. So for me, Shah Rukh became a doorway to a world and a life I wasn't destined to live,' she said, during a late-night phone call. 'How do I, as a South African woman who has never been to India, connect to cinema and also a language I don't speak? I learnt Hindi by watching his movies. I have never studied Hindi. My understanding of Hindi is at a filmy level. I don't converse in Hindi, but I watch movies without subtitles because I learnt an entire language by just watching films. When I went to India in 2015 for a vacation, I could have conversations with taxi drivers, hotel staff and shopkeepers in Hindi.'

Parveen's first trip to Mumbai was in 2010. 'My grandmother wanted to see her village because she was getting old. It eventually became a family trip when my brother, my cousins and a few other family members joined in. There was just one thing I wanted to do—go to Maratha Mandir to watch *DDLJ* and see Mannat. I was a teenager throwing a tantrum. I couldn't explain to anyone why I wanted to watch a movie I have watched every few days for all my life. I regret that I couldn't go to watch *DDLJ*, but I was adamant that I wanted to see Mannat. My father was exasperated. I couldn't explain to him why it was so important for me to stop there for a minute, to just see the place. Everyone kept telling me, "No one is going to ask you to come in for tea." I cried and cried, and swore that I wouldn't get back on the plane till I saw his house. So the next day, my father was forced to take a detour and ask the tour guide to stop outside Mannat. I jumped out of the car, crossed the road, stood there for a minute and ran back across the road. Shah Rukh is a language for me—a tool for me to connect with people and mostly with my roots. If it weren't for him, I wouldn't have known where I come from.'

It is for fans such as Parveen that, in 2004, Shah Rukh decided to travel the world with his Temptation tour. At a time when Bollywood was a global rage, Shah Rukh wanted to take the stars across the world and make them a global sensation. It was a classic Bollywood spectacle featuring actors lip-syncing to popular songs and performing dance routines, interspersed with comedy acts and fan interactions. Film archivist Nasreen Munni Kabir even chronicled the journey of this tour in her three-part documentary series *The Inner and Outer World of Shah Rukh Khan*. A year later, while talking to writer Aseem Chhabra, she talked about Shah Rukh's reaction when she went to him for the documentary. 'His first reaction was "Why me?", and "Am I important enough to make any difference?" Shah Rukh is definitely a man who has taken Indian cinema to the next level.'[14]

Temptation 2004 was a stage show with a star-studded line-up. The show wasn't just about music—it was a full-fledged entertainment package, with singing, dancing and even skits performed by the stars. At the end of the two-month tour, Temptation 2004 was a global success, touring twenty-two venues around the world. The scale of the show was massive, attracting crowds of 15,000 at Dubai's Festival City Arena, just one example of the enthusiastic response it garnered. This marked the beginning of Shah Rukh's involvement with the Temptation series, which took place four times over the next few years—2004, 2005, 2006 and 2008.

> 'I sell dreams, and I peddle love to millions of people ... Humanity is a lot like me. It's an ageing movie star, grappling with all the newness around it, wondering whether it got it right in the first place and still trying to find a way to keep on shining regardless.'

The 2004 show boasted six leading stars, each representing a different temptation, with Shah Rukh being the lead attraction—representing love, wearing the colour red. The tour sold out in sixteen cities across Europe, including in the UK, and in the US and Canada, with venue capacities ranging from 7,000 to 20,000 seats. Despite ticket prices between $300 and $400 (between Rs 42,000 and Rs 50,000 today), each venue was spilling at the seams on the day of the shows. In Toronto, the overwhelming demand at the 19,800-seat Scotiabank Arena (previously called the Air Canada Centre) led to a second show being added three days later; and in London there were two back-to-back shows.

The phenomenon reached Elvis-level hysteria. Fans with thick American accents kept vigil in hotel lobbies at 2 a.m., hoping to catch a glimpse of their favourite star. At the shows, tearful girls screamed, 'We love you, Shah Rukh Khan!' Local organizers reported turning down $2,000 offers for backstage passes. *Time* magazine's Asian edition, which featured Shah Rukh on the cover of its 'Asia's Heroes'[15] special issue the following month, reported that his bodyguard, a burly bald man with two teenage daughters, received so many offers of sex in exchange for access that it had become 'disturbing' for him.[16]

In an article published in *The Globe and Mail*, the journalist who covered the tour reported that despite Temptation 2004 featuring five other top stars of Bollywood as five other temptations—Saif Ali Khan as envy, Rani Mukerji as lust, Arjun Rampal as power, Priyanka Chopra as greed and Preity Zinta as passion—all the audience wanted to see was Shah Rukh, as love.[17]

The scene outside the hotel the cast stayed in was vibrant—Bollywood fans exuded palpable excitement as they eagerly awaited a glimpse of their beloved Shah Rukh Khan and the stars of the Temptation 2004 tour. The crowd began to assemble by early afternoon, with fervent admirers clutching posters and cameras, some even proudly displaying personal mementoes of their encounters with the actor. As the day progressed, the gathering only grew larger, a testament to the immense popularity of the event.

The previous night's performance had been sold out, prompting the decision to extend the tour due to overwhelming demand. In interviews, fans expressed their deep admiration for Shah Rukh. Urveshi Patel, a devoted fan from Montreal, excitedly said, 'We love Shah Rukh Khan for everything he represents—his looks, his acting, his voice. We make it a point to attend every Bollywood show, but this one was unmissable because of Shah Rukh.' Darshna Patel, a mother of two, shared a personal connection, revealing that she named her son Raj after Shah Rukh's character from *DDLJ*. 'I was pregnant when the movie came out, and decided right then to name my son Raj,' she recounted.

The tour hinged on Shah Rukh's superstardom and what had by then become a global fascination for Bollywood. Nasreen Munni Kabir succinctly explained in her documentary that Shah Rukh was at the core of the tour—their sales pitch. 'The man has a certain amount of humility in public situations. He often says, "Oh if I say this, I may sound pompous." He is very aware of how he is projecting himself. He enjoys stardom, but he remembers the days when he did not have the stardom,' she says. 'He excelled in school. He had a humble middle-class life in Delhi. But he always had a charisma, not because of the movies, but because he is who he is.'[18]

In *The Inner and Outer World of Shah Rukh Khan*, the actor recounts a childhood encounter, something that crops up twice in his films. Young and eager, he once approached cricket legend Imran Khan for an autograph, only to be dismissed. This experience left a mark on him, who now, despite his busy schedule, makes himself available for autographs and photos with fans.

A large number of his fans are not even Indians. Long before Korean stars made it into our lives as the epitome of mush and romance, India offered Shah Rukh to the world. Shah Rukh, who knows how to hold on to fans, gave people several stories during the Temptation trip, none of which resembled his Imran Khan story.

Stacey, a Bollywood buff living in San Francisco, wrote in her blog about the time she stalked the star during the tour in 2004 and how gracefully he handled her. 'I could see as I started to walk toward Shah Rukh that he recognized me as a fan about to intrude on his quiet moment. The bodyguard had his back to me. My heart was pounding. I knew this was going to be a peak life experience. No other celebrity encounter had been this momentous, and I've never been as awkward or tongue-tied. Most of the sentences I started I couldn't finish. Shah Rukh was just lovely, though. He may have been annoyed at my intrusion, but he never showed it. He was just finishing his cigarette, and he politely refrained from lighting another one while I was there. He was wearing black with an eye-catching pendant and his hair casually brushed forward. In his films it's usually off his forehead. I'm 5'8" and Shah Rukh is about the same, so we were eye to eye. I was too bashful to gaze into his eyes for any length of time, but he didn't seem smaller or larger than I'd expected. He was definitely better looking. He had a kind of quiet-but-aware stillness that's so different from his energetic screen personality. I walked up and pulled out a mouse pad and the Temptation program, saying something like "Hello, I'm Stacey. My friend called me and told me you were here." Then I asked him to sign two autographs for friends. I didn't ask him for one for myself, because I knew my co-worker already got one for me. Three autographs seemed greedy. Then the bodyguard said, "Where did you come from?" I pointed to the curb and said, "From a cab right there." The bodyguard told me I was going to get him in trouble and he told me to go away. I said, "But this is my guy!" We began to argue, and Shah Rukh didn't say anything. Instead, he signed his photo on the back of the program to me, and it's really special because he wrote something different from his usual "lots of love". It's a good thing Shah Rukh took the time to do this, because the one my co-worker got was written with a brown felt tip pen on a brown bag, and within months, the autograph faded completely. I still have it, but there's nothing to see. I know it's there, though. After the autographs, while I was still arguing with the bodyguard, Shah Rukh must have decided that it was okay for me to be there, or he could tell I wasn't going away. He held up his arms, waved me over with his fingers, and said, "Give me a hug." I was gobsmacked. We hugged, and I was so overwhelmed, I have no memory of what it felt like. I've been telling people ever since that I want to be hypnotised so I can remember it properly.

'I had a brief, halting conversation with Shah Rukh. It went something like this:

Me: Do you get to spend any more time in San Francisco?

SRK: No, we're leaving early tomorrow.

Me: That's too bad, because I have a whole stack of books picked out for your kids at the Borders where I work.

SRK: So, you've seen some Hindi films?

Me: I've seen every single one of yours, even *Fauji*! (His first TV series that was not on DVD in 2004). Right now we're all watching "The Inner World of Shah Rukh Khan". (A new documentary)

SRK: Oh, the filmmaker, she's inside eating ...

'The rest of the party came outside, and I knew my time was up. I hadn't forgotten my camera, but I just couldn't ask for more, and I hate flash photos. I thanked Shah Rukh and said goodbye. He saluted me by touching his hand to his forehead (an aadab), and I walked away in a daze.'[19]

Temptation 2004 was a vision fit for the global stage. From the stage to costume changes to the overall production, the tour was unparalleled. It had cutting-edge sound and lighting technology that was a celebration of Shah Rukh's career, his boundless energy and the power of Bollywood to enthral audiences worldwide. The choreography was a kaleidoscope of styles, mirroring the diversity of Shah Rukh's songs. Imagine the high-octane steps in *'Chaiyya Chaiyya'* from *Dil Se..* interspersed with the delicate sway of a love song from *Kuch Kuch Hota Hai*.

Shah Rukh in many ways is a visionary. He bought an LCD for the stage that cost about a million dollars back then, but changed the way the audiences viewed the performances. The stars involved had to do one free show to pay for it, but in the end it dazzled the audiences.

While for the most part the tour went smoothly, there was one accident in Colombo, Sri Lanka, in September 2004 that alarmed the troupe. The show had received extensive coverage in the local media. On the day of the event, it drew a crowd of approximately 25,000. Priyanka Chopra was performing with Shah Rukh when a bomb exploded in the stands just six feet away from them. The blast resulted in the deaths of at least two people and injured about eighteen others. The concert was taking place in Sri Lanka despite complaints from Buddhist monks who were unhappy that the event coincided with the death anniversary of a popular monk.[20]

After the incident, Priyanka gave an interview to Rediff, saying, 'Shah Rukh and I were dancing onstage for the last song of our show, *Le ja le ja* (*Kabhi Khushi Kabhie Gham*) and the mood was very upbeat. Suddenly, I heard a deafening noise.' Initially mistaking it for a smoke bomb, she soon realized it was something much more dangerous. As she prepared to move backstage, she witnessed bodies on the ground amid the chaos, with police trying to control the situation. Uncertain whether the noise was from a real bomb or a smoke bomb, she was quickly guided to a car with Shah Rukh, Preity Zinta, Celina Jaitly, Zayed Khan and Saif Ali Khan, and they headed for Colombo airport. Priyanka's mother, who usually sits in the front row at her shows, had been backstage that night. Since Rani and Arjun Rampal were unable to perform due to prior commitments, Zayed and Celina had stepped in. Priyanka later reflected on the narrow escape, realizing that she and Shah Rukh had just been six feet from where the blast had occurred. The incident left her deeply shaken. She said the experience was so unsettling that she spent the entire day in bed upon returning to Mumbai.[21]

But nothing held back Temptation. Despite this tragedy, it went on to have subsequent seasons including one in Sydney in 2013, called Temptation Reloaded. But how does one pinpoint why Temptation was leaps and bounds ahead of anything else on the world stage that Bollywood had put together? And what was the secret to this huge success?

In an interview to ABC channel in 2013, Shah Rukh explained the reasons he felt that Bollywood had gone global. 'It's a hundred-year-old industry. I think it's the earliest industry in the world. Somewhere down the line the fantasy and escapism we offer in our cinema is somewhat real, like getting a job or buying a car or settling down with a happy family. It's not like we go and blow up a meteor [threatening to wipe out Earth]. We don't have superheroes yet. Our heroes are superheroes who fight against the system. It's deep rooted of what the society is going through.'[22]

Or was it the fact that Shah Rukh was a seller of dreams? In his 2017 Ted Talk, he had said, 'I sell dreams, and I peddle love to millions of people ... I've learned that whatever moves you, whatever urges you to create, build, whatever keeps you from failing, whatever helps you survive, is perhaps the oldest and the simplest emotion known to mankind, and that is love ... Humanity is a lot like me. It's an ageing movie star, grappling with all the newness around it, wondering whether it got it right in the first place and still trying to find a way to keep on shining regardless.'[23]

> *Pyaar toh bahut log karte hai ... Lekin mere jaisa pyaar koi nahi kar sakta ... Kyunki kisi ke paas tum joh nahi ho*
>
> Kal Ho Naa Ho, 2003

8

SHAH RUKH KHAN: THE MAN EVERYONE LOVES, AND WANTS

Throughout history, men have attempted to crack the code of 'what women want'. From a slapstick exploration in the Hollywood film *What Women Want*, where Mel Gibson's character can literally hear women's thoughts, to the trendsetting female characters in *Sex and the City*, where four Manhattan women, navigating love and careers, tell the world what's on their minds, pop culture has always had this ongoing quest to answer that one question: What do women want?

Famous film critic Roger Ebert wrote in his review of the Mel Gibson-starrer, 'What women want is very simple: A man willing to listen when they're speaking to him. They also want a lot of other things, but that will do for starters. This we learn from *What Women Want*—a comedy about a man who is jolted by electricity and develops the ability to read women's minds.'[1]

Now you'll wonder why I am bringing this up in a book about Shah Rukh Khan. Well, read on, because this will all make sense.

Growing up in the 1990s, and having lived through the dot-com boom, with Hotmail and Yahoo chat rooms, Orkut and Facebook, all the way to the rise of dating apps and the addiction to Instagram, my answer to what women want has remained constant. And as I was researching for this book, and spoke to women all over the world, I realized something that I knew all along.

Women want a man like Shah Rukh Khan.

I don't mean Rahul or Raj or Samar, I mean the man who plays and embodies all of them. The guy who will pick up the trail of his wife's dress at a social event, the man who will be able to bond with our mothers while doing kitchen chores, who will hold the door open for others, who will spoil his daughter, who will choose love even when it's impossible, who will give his all to change the world and who isn't too 'macho' to show affection. The innumerable pictures of him giving bear hugs and genuine kisses to people reminds you how beautiful a genuine display of physical affection really is.

During my research for this book, I have spoken to several fans of Shah Rukh across the world—men, women, queer, South Asian, American, British, European, across ages. The one thing that is common is their love for Shah Rukh—not just for his films or his characters, but for the person.

In a world where we are surrounded by actors—now they are on our Instagram feeds, every step documented by the paparazzi, their inner lives intimately known to us—what sets Shah Rukh apart? What makes him like no other?

The first person who mentioned to me that they loved Shah Rukh was my childhood friend Titaas Mitra. She was all of five, couldn't decide what she wanted for lunch that day—but she knew she loved Shah Rukh Khan.

She was spending the afternoon at my home in our quaint little town of Singrauli in Madhya Pradesh. That week my father had bought us audio cassettes from the Symphony audio store in Calcutta (now Kolkata). In 1996, small towns such as Singrauli didn't have much beyond bare essentials—a handful of grocery stores, some medical stores, the weekly mandi and a hospital with basic facilities.

Every month when one of our parents went to the big city—Calcutta, Benares (now Varanasi) or Delhi—we'd give them a list of audio cassettes to get for us. I remember Titaas excitedly grabbing the audio cassette of *Pardes* and kissing Shah Rukh's face, before playing it on our big old stereo. We even danced to *'Ye Dil … Deewana'*, not knowing it was a song about heartbreak.

When I now tell her this story on a call, she laughs. 'I don't even know why I started loving Shah Rukh. I was five. I didn't know much about love, but I definitely knew I loved *him*. It started with *Baazigar*. I kept rooting for Ajay Sharma. I still hate Madan Chopra. I cried when his character died. What happened to him was wrong. I now know it was a negative character, but back then I understood his rage because his father and sister had died. It was after that film that I got on his team. I cannot stand him being wronged. And I have stayed on Team Shah Rukh ever since. There is no other celebrity I love or will ever love as much as Shah Rukh. I have a certain loyalty towards him. Even if I don't like a film of his, I will never say anything bad about it. *Mere bachpan ka pyaar hai, Rifat bi.*' She laughs as she quotes the iconic *Kuch Kuch Hota Hai* dialogue.

Years later, in college, I heard a truth that hit home like no other—from another die-hard fan, my friend Prerona Sanyal. It had been a decade of loving Shah Rukh by then, and we were able to approach his public persona and movies from a more mature perspective. Having gone through the phase of our first crush, first love and first heartbreak, Shah Rukh became even more relatable.

We were strolling down Park Street in Calcutta one December evening. One of us was going through a break-up and we were discussing what was wrong with the men we were dating. This was a conversation that could have gone on for hours, days, weeks, months, even years. I don't remember much of what Prerona said, except that at one point she looked at me with the utmost certainty and announced, 'There isn't a '90s kid in India who hasn't been in love with Shah Rukh at some point in their life … that's who we are looking for.'

It's been so many years since that conversation. While writing this chapter, I called her to ask why she had said that. She quotes Shah Rukh's interview from the launch of Ted Talks India in 2017. 'I am not the best lover in the world (as my films have shown), I am love itself.' She then adds, 'Salman did a lot of romantic movies, but he wasn't a romance boy, because his movies had a lot more about the other relationships. For instance, in *Hum Aapke Hain Koun..!* Madhuri Dixit and Renuka Shahane, or him and Mohnish Bahl. It wasn't like *DDLJ*, where the focus was solely on what Raj could do or the extent he could go to for Simran. The madness Shah Rukh embodied was unseen. Salman, too, went all the way in *Maine Pyar Kiya*, but the madness with which Shah Rukh made sure that he got the girl he was in love with, with the blessings of her father, was rare. Men were perceived to be aloof back then and women wanted that kind of passion from a man. Kids in the '90s have seen two sorts of men—those who are nothing like Shah Rukh, or those who are exactly like Shah Rukh. The sort of investment he makes emotionally in the lives of others is what became our epitome. After *DDLJ*, most of his films dedicated an entire half to showcasing the process of Shah Rukh falling in love with a woman. Like, one of my problems with *K3G* [*Kabhi Khushi Kabhie Gham...*] is that I wanted to see more of Shah Rukh and Kajol. What happens to you when you bear the repercussions of going against the world for love? Also, so much of his love is transformative. We see what it does for the woman with him. It changes her—not in an imposing way, but in a way that nudges her to become her own person.'[2]

My aunt, Debjani Mitra, objects to how '90s' kids have sort of laid claim to Shah Rukh. She calls herself the OG Shah Rukh fan from the '80s. 'You guys haven't even watched his early works. Have you watched *Doosra Keval*? Have you watched *Fauji*? Have you watched *Circus*?' she asked me, almost miffed. 'I remember when *Deewana* was released ... My girls and I from college [in Bhagalpur, Bihar] got together to catch the first day, first show. We are his early cheerleaders ... You all have merely joined the force.'

The fact that this love spans generations has been pointed out by several people. I read a piece by Pakistani journalist Muzhira Amin, who wrote in *Dawn*, during *Jawan*'s release, 'I come from a line of women who have loved Shah Rukh Khan for decades. It was *Darr* for my grandmother, *Dilwale Dulhania Le Jayenge* for my mother and *My Name Is Khan* for me. So my admiration for King Khan, irrespective of his movies, is perpetual.'[3]

Shah Rukh is no longer simply a star—he is an emotion on which women connect with each other.

I gave Amin a call to understand the common theme running through this unanimous love. 'For the three of us, it was about a man who offered us space. We are all women who haven't had very good relationships with men. It is wholesome to see men who are respectful. His movies feel like home and give us what we don't have. My naani and I have watched marathons of *Veer-Zara*. My mother loves *DDLJ*. My mom was married by the time she was seventeen. She grew up with me. When I was eight, my father had a rule that we had to go to bed by eleven at night. My mother and I would sneak out and put on an SRK film and watch it together. My father wouldn't allow us to watch *Kabhi Alvida Naa Kehna* because of the kind of film it was. We both got out late in the night and watched the movie until three, and cried through it. I almost skipped school the next day. But *DDLJ* is what cemented this love we have for him. It is that fantasy we all want to live—go on one last vacation before our freedom is taken away from us and meet this man in a foreign land, someone so unlike anyone you've ever known or seen. He drops everything to follow you to your country and win your family's approval. I blame Shah Rukh for the fact that I am single. My expectations are so high. It's not about romance alone. The fact that I can be an equal in a relationship is important. When I had a fight with the last person I dated, I wanted him to show up on my door with cards. It never happened. Shah Rukh would do it, so why can't these guys? I need my man to match up to the bar set by him,' Amin said.

What she said was perfectly explained in an article by *Vogue India*, where the writer notes, 'Khan looks at women not with the quintessential male gaze, as if they are the objects of his desire, but with soft glances that speak volumes. He doesn't wish to conquer them, as most men in films and reality do; instead, he wants to be conquered by them. There's a sense of feverish devotion in his eyes which is attractive to women who've been told all their lives that they must surrender to the whims of men. In contrast, Khan is always prepared to fully submit to the women he loves, a gesture that is uncharacteristically romantic in a patriarchal society like the one we live in.'[4]

This love that women have for the star is often passed down the generations like an heirloom. Like Manoj Desai of Maratha Mandir said, mothers and daughters come together to watch *DDLJ* at his theatre.

Sanju Guptoo, a housewife in Asansol, West Bengal, says that her daughter has inherited her love for Shah Rukh. 'It's almost like saying, here is something that's dear to me and I hope you show it as much affection as I did. That's how love for Shah Rukh is passed. Women, as they grow older, are often shoved into lonely, domestic spaces. When my daughter was born, I felt like I had created for myself a forever date to watch Shah Rukh's movies with. I remember how thrilled my daughter was when she saw Taapsee Pannu in *Dunki* say, "*Banda hai tu mera ...*" He is our banda [boy], before anyone else. I saw in her eyes the same reverence for him that I, too, have.'

> **'Just the other day, we put on "*Ladki Badi Anjaani Hai*" and I was dancing in front of the TV. She was looking at the screen and I pointed to the screen and told her, "That's your uncle Shah Rukh Khan." My brother was so mad at me, and said, "Please don't make my daughter a mad fan like you." Too late!'**

It's not very different for Parveen Banderkar, the producer of documentaries and commercials from South Africa we mentioned earlier. Parveen tells us that she will ensure the little girls in her family are well acquainted with the most special person in her life. 'We all have our comfort films and the ones that make us cry. My niece is now nine months old, and I have made sure she knows him. Just the other day, we put on "*Ladki Badi Anjaani Hai*" and I was dancing in front of the TV. She was looking at the screen and I pointed to the screen and told her, "That's your uncle Shah Rukh Khan." My brother was so mad at me, and said, "Please don't make my daughter a mad fan like you." Too late! She is going to grow up with the knowledge of who her Uncle Shah Rukh Khan is, even though she was born in 2024. But by the time she is in her teens, she will be quoting *DDLJ*, make no mistake.'

The little one can't miss it because her Aunt Parveen has a giant cut-out of Shah Rukh from *Chak De! India* in her bedroom that she insisted on bringing back from a local theatre. And now every time someone enters her room, Shah Rukh greets them before she does.

Shah Rukh has often been at a loss for words when asked to explain the adulation he receives from his female fans. He has often said to the press, 'I know I am known for my portrayals of Raj and Rahuls, but I am not a romantic at all.'[5] But when someone has been loved by women across the globe, across ages, for decades, there has to be something he is doing right.

While giving an interview during the promotions of *When Harry Met Sejal*, he explained, 'I know how to respect a woman, how to dignify a woman …'[6]

In his films, he strives to show women with freedom and respect, empowering their emotions. This respect, he believes, is the true essence of romance, beyond conventional gestures such as dinner dates, sunset walks or poetic expressions. His iconic open-arm gesture is a symbolic acceptance of them and the deep respect that he has for the emotions of women. This, he feels, is the core of his romantic appeal on screen. 'I love a woman with complete freedom to do what she wants. At least in my movies, that's what we have shown in most of them. Empower the emotions of a woman completely. That's what makes me look romantic. I think the real romance comes from the fact that you dignify and respect a woman's emotions. My hands (spread out) is a gesture of me saying *aapki jitni bhi emotions hai woh sab mujhe acceptable hai, aur main unki bohot izzat karta hoon* [All your emotions are acceptable to me, and I respect all of them].'[7]

In 2014, *Filmfare* spoke to some of his actresses to ask them what about Shah Rukh makes him so special. For some, such as Kajol, he is a forever friend. 'The nicest part about Shah Rukh is that whenever we meet, there is always so much warmth. We pick up where we'd left off,' she said.[8]

To others, Shah Rukh Khan is that dependable colleague who ensures that others shine alongside him. Karisma Kapoor recalled an incident during the filming of a *DTPH* scene in Baden-Baden, Germany, where she had to have a long monologue, in which Shah Rukh's role was to just maintain a steady silence. Despite numerous takes and interruptions due to unexpected rain, every time director Yash Chopra called action, Shah Rukh remained supportive. As Karisma grew increasingly frustrated, he reassured her that things would eventually work out. 'He kept saying, "*Ho jaayega, yaar* [It'll happen]."'

Shilpa Shetty, for whom Shah Rukh was the first co-star, said he taught people the tricks of the trade. During the filming of the song *'Aye Mere Humsafar'* in *Baazigar*, he advised her to treat the camera as the audience, a lesson she continues to apply in her performances even to this day.

Madhuri Dixit said, 'Today, I want to say he's the best man in the film industry.' She praised him for his hard work, determination and dedication, calling him a self-made man who had achieved remarkable success. She described him as a true gentleman, noting that he never left a film set without ensuring the actress was safely dropped off after a shoot. Madhuri appreciated his easygoing nature, his superb sense of humour and the fun they had working together on films such as *Anjaam*, *Koyla* and *DTPH*. She recalled how, during a challenging shoot for *Koyla* in Tawang's extreme cold, Shah Rukh, dressed only in a vest and dhoti, presented her with a card acknowledging their efforts. This gesture deeply touched her.

Women love these little gestures—a thank you note, opening the car door for them, a simple pep talk—and each of his female co-actors has had these stories to tell about him. The stories have remained uniform over the years. It only adds to his 'rizz' (as they call it now) that he smells divine. His co-actors—be it Anushka Sharma or Mahira Khan—have spoken about how good he smells. Mahira said, 'There's one thing about Shah Rukh—he smells, like, amazing. Amazing!'⁹

'I think the real romance comes from the fact that you dignify and respect a woman's emotions. My hands (spread out) is a gesture of me saying *aapki jitni bhi emotions hai woh sab mujhe acceptable hai, aur main unki bohot izzat karta hoon* [All your emotions are acceptable to me, and I respect all of them].'

Shah Rukh spilt his secret in an interview with the *GQ* magazine, 'It's very important for me to smell good. I mix two fragrances—a Dunhill scent that's only available at their London store and a Diptyque one.'¹⁰

My fifty-two-year-old friend Neha Pandey (name changed), who recently went through a divorce with her husband of three decades, was the first to tell me about Shah Rukh smelling good. She had met him at a fan event in Delhi in 2014. 'Most Indian wives are married to men who don't care much about personal hygiene … This idea that sweaty men are sexy is such balderdash. Sporty men, as they call themselves, should smell sweaty and soiled. It's apparently the smell of victory. I reject that idea,' she told me, adding that personal hygiene had been a major point of discord between her and her ex-husband. 'I know people think it's a small problem, but when there are a lot of other issues between two people, these small nagging problems become bigger. I often joke to my friends that Shah Rukh should start coaching classes on how to be a man. More than half of the country's women would get their partners enrolled!'

But there have been bigger things that Shah Rukh has used his public persona for. One of them is Bollywood's inherent sexism. In a BBC interview a few years ago, a British anchor deemed Bollywood sexist and asked him if he had done anything to address it. 'Personally, when I am making films or even working in films, I am very clear about the attitude towards women. Even the smallest aspects of their names coming in the title first.' But he added, 'No one dare misbehave with women on my set. I am very clear on that. I am very close to the women I have worked with. I have just been with women all my life—my mother, sister, daughter, my co-stars. In my films, everything revolves around women—I revolve around women in every film.'[11]

In another interview, he acknowledged the female movie stars he has worked with in his career. '[Women] work harder than I do. They come in four to five hours before I even land on the set. They are somehow considered secondary in the scheme of things of this film world. It's a man's world. And at the end I take all the credit and become the biggest superstar in the world. The beauty of it is that knowing how unfair it is, they have not reduced themselves and gone into victimhood,' he said.

He added, 'They have the courage, the bravery, the strength to realize, "You know what, this is how it is going right now. I do work harder than Shah Rukh. I am better than Shah Rukh. And it's all right if he's sitting now in Davos giving the speech." They know they are the real strength.' He signed off with, 'I tell my two sons that I want to be a woman when I grow up.'[12]

Women in the workforce would kill to have a male colleague like Shah Rukh. I spoke to P.S. (anonymity requested), a journalist who sought respite in Shah Rukh when she was going through a dark phase in her life. 'I remember that interview and I remember thinking that someday I could have it too … a safe workplace or a boss like him.'

She had been working with a male editor for four years, during which he had indicated to her over and over that if she were to give him sexual favours, she would rise through the ranks of the job very quickly. 'I was giving up hope that men can be good. I couldn't leave that job and I couldn't stand my life. It was awful. For the eight hours I was at work, my heart would be in my mouth. So it had become a routine of going home and watching a movie every night. India doesn't make great romantic films any more, so I had to go back to the 1990s and the early 2000s. Sometimes I would watch the same film every night for a week, even two weeks. I eventually got over that time by finding another job and bringing the HR in to tackle the boss. But Shah Rukh's films made sure I didn't become hateful, bitter or hopeless. I found faith in the fact that not every man was the same and that, someday, I would have colleagues who would be better. Right now, my workplace has more women than men, and the men in my team are feminists. Every woman deserves a workplace where her colleague is a professional and not a creep.'

P.S. added that the root cause of sexual harassment is the fact that men are designed to cheat and hunt. 'Men see themselves as some sort of man-eater, and women as their prey. And they are a hunting tribe, which we call the "big boys' club". They will make jokes about women who can't take jokes, they will say we are hormonal if we call their bullshit, they will label us problematic when we aren't "spontaneous" enough. The problem isn't one man—it's this culture of harassment and coercion. The first step to breaking out of it is to acknowledge this is wrong,' she told me.

She reminded me that Shah Rukh has always been very clear he isn't a 'boy's boy'—he is a woman's man. Right from the start, he rejected the idea that actors on set philander in the name of fun. 'Imagine how difficult it would have been for him. They called him pansy for being committed,' she added.

The '90s' magazines were filled with stories of stars and their raging affairs. Shah Rukh was too obviously and publicly besotted with his wife and too respectful of his female colleagues to trigger such rumours. The one time it happened, he made sure it was the last time such a story appeared about him. When his male peers were infamously having a good time, Shah Rukh was eager to go home to his wife. He made a statement on Twitter in 2010, 'Been loyal to my family cos of a simple gumpism. whenever given a choice between a piece of ass or peace of mind...i choose the latter.'[13]

Perhaps it comes from how he sees women. 'I have never thought of women as objects. I have never thought, "Hey, I have met a woman, she is really attractive, let's go to bed with her." My first thought about a woman is how beautiful she is even when she doesn't bed me. My kids ask me, "Did you really kiss the girl in the film? Do you really love Rani Aunty and Kajal Aunty and Juhi Aunty?" Yes, I love them. My children will always be able to say, yes my dad loves this lady. But my dad has never ever belittled our mother,' said Shah Rukh.[14]

That's one aspect of Shah Rukh's appeal. Another is that he is so secure in his masculinity that he doesn't feel the need to impose on others how manly he is. He doesn't go out of his way to butch himself up and indulge in the 'men will be men' banter. He is comfortable getting into a bathtub and being covered in bubbles next to Hindi cinema's most gorgeous leading ladies—Hema Malini, Juhi Chawla, Kareena Kapoor and Sridevi. A Lux commercial cashed in on his metrosexual appeal. 'I wanted to get into the tub and not just stand outside watching a lady get into it or something ... I guess that would've been a more predictable male perception of how the ad should've been done. I wanted to do it the proper way,' he was quoted as saying to *The Times of India*. He was the second male actor to be the face of Lux after Paul Newman in 1995.[15]

Men don't find it manly to jump into a tub and talk about 'the secret behind their beauty', as the Lux punchline goes. Aastha Saxena, a real estate broker in Mumbai, says, 'I don't get why men are so horridly insecure of their manliness. The one time I suggested to my boyfriend that he join me in the tub, he said he would rather watch football. Somehow a man in a tub becomes about their sexuality. Shah Rukh himself was deemed girly after this commercial. I hate the fact that men can't openly pamper themselves till date. Imagine what a dismal life it is that men can't allow themselves a day of sipping some wine, covered in bubbles and listening to nice jazz music.'

Shah Rukh is aware of his sex appeal. 'I'm too sexy to lust. I think people who don't feel sexy from within are the ones who lust. I genuinely believe that I am a very, very sexy guy,' he said in a 2006 interview.[16]

And in true global superstar style, this sex appeal of Shah Rukh goes beyond borders. Maedhbh Keating-Fitzpatrick, an Irish woman who lives in London, first discovered Bollywood when Salman Khan and Katrina Kaif were shooting in Trinity College, Dublin, for a song sequence in *Ek Tha Tiger*. This led her to watch a Shah Rukh Khan film—and there was no going back. 'I was charmed. My friend Jameela took it upon herself to show me more movies and they were all '90s Shah Rukh Khan ones. I started watching them, and I love them. I have watched *DDLJ*, *Dilwale*, *K3G*, *Kuch Kuch Hota Hai* and *Jab Tak Hai Jaan*. I have watched the *Don* movies. I still have a few left, but the ones with Kajol are lovely. I have liked other movies of other actors, so one would wonder why him, or what about him. What makes me put on a movie in a language I don't know, with subtitles, to see this man? Women appreciate kindness and sweetness. Traditionally masculine guys can't show softness as beautifully. When I watch him, that's what I pick up. Men are patriarchal—they are rough and tough. He is a man who feels like an ally. Mothers feel like he is a guy they could have raised. There is a willingness to be vulnerable, and the ability to be silly. He feels like an ally even though his movies could be dated today. He is the man who is willing to be in your quarter.

> 'Women appreciate kindness and sweetness. Traditionally masculine guys can't show softness as beautifully. When I watch him, that's what I pick up ... He is a man who feels like an ally. Mothers feel like he is a guy they could have raised. There is a willingness to be vulnerable, and the ability to be silly.'

Most people in my life don't know Shah Rukh, but he is the face they recognize because he is massively popular. But what sets apart his love from anyone else's is that he is one of us and is absolutely okay with that.'

But what's the most amazing part is that despite being considered such a sexy man, the emotion women feel for him is not that of just lust. Rehana Khan (name changed), a shopkeeper I met in the main market of Aqaba in Jordan, got talking about Shah Rukh when she heard I was from India. The same morning, a group of boat owners at the Aqaba bay played *'Bole Chudiyaan'* from *K3G* for me and my friend when they found out that we were Indians. In my experience while travelling internationally, Shah Rukh is a great conversation starter. In Germany they discovered Shah Rukh after the release of *K3G* in 2006 and then he shot *Don* there. An article about his global appeal in the BBC quoted a staff from a movie theatre, who said, 'If you are talking about Bollywood in Germany, you are talking about Shah Rukh Khan.'

And often Shah Rukh is a great way to get handsome discounts. Like Rehana gave me after our chat. She asked me if I had ever met Shah Rukh. I told her I had. She said she wanted to meet him someday. 'You know, we women never look at Shah Rukh and say, "Oh I want to sleep with him." Women are built differently, I believe. We love him. And by love, I mean I want to have a conversation with him for an hour—ask him how he is feeling, what bothered him that day. It's not lust. He evokes pure love. So when I see him with his wife, I feel very happy. He is so adorable with his daughter,' she said.

Would you believe that as one of the most loved male superstars in the world, he has actually never had a woman make a pass at him? 'Women love me! I am sure they do, and I love them back. I think somewhere there's a line, the way I am, it has never crossed anybody's mind to really propose to me. I think only my wife got stuck. I've never had a woman make a pass at me. Unfortunately. And I am too shy to make a pass at a woman.'[17] He said that despite his on-screen persona as a romantic hero, he has always struggled with romantic interactions in real life. Although he has many female friends and enjoys spending time with their children, he has never been comfortable initiating romantic or flirtatious conversations, and nor has he ever received such advances from women.

'I play with their kids. But I've never been able to go up to a woman and say anything to her ... nice, kind, romantic, interesting, wild, or, you know, sexy. And I've never had women do the same to me either.'

He gets the same respect from his female fans that he gives them. This one time, a user on Twitter asked him tips on wooing women. He shut them down, saying, 'Start with not using the word "Patana" for a girl. Try with more gentleness and respect.'[18]

Shah Rukh has always credited the women in his life for raising him right. In 2018, at the Annual Crystal Award at the World Economic Forum Annual Meeting in Davos, he said, 'How do I say this without sounding wrong? I don't spend time in the company of men. I am naturally inclined towards women. My mother was very strong. I am a movie star, which is a difficult business for any lady to handle. My wife does that with amazing aplomb and platitude. She is extremely strong. I thank my sister, wife and daughter for bringing me up well. They taught me the value of requesting and imploring a "yes" from a woman instead of forcing it upon them.'[19]

The kind of father he is has often seemed attractive to women. In an old interview for *Femina* magazine, he listed out his expectations of the man Suhana would date. 'She's my princess, not your conquest,' he said.[20] But he is also the 'chill' father. Later he confessed, 'It's false bravado. I know that when it comes down to it, when my daughter likes somebody, I'll not be able to say anything and just accept it. Before it happens, I thought I'll just put this out, just in case somebody reads it and thinks they should respect me a little more than they can, and take it seriously. But I don't think it's serious at all.'[21]

In the last episode of *The Fabulous Lives of Bollywood Wives* season 1, Maheep Kapoor, wife of actor Sanjay Kapoor, says, 'SRK used to be the babysitter (when Gauri partied with her girls). We dumped our children on him. I remember we were coming back and Shanaya was crying because we had to leave one day earlier. He used to shop for them and come back with track pants. He took Shanaya to Hamleys and asked her, "What do you want?" Shanaya wanted a particular doll.' The actor found that doll, and when they got back to Mumbai, he sent it to her.

His persona as a father is what adds to his charm. Bela Raman, a housewife in Hyderabad, explains this beautifully. 'The metrics on which men fall in love are very different from what women love in a man. This also translates to how we love our celebrities. Most men, including my husband, love Sridevi. They are charmed by her beauty, her innocence, her doe-eyed look. When I, or for that matter other women, discuss how they love Shah Rukh, we'll never talk about his physical attributes. We will tell you about his ability to respect women. Like, I admire how he is a good father. I remember I had watched an interview on UTV Stars, where his manager said Shah Rukh is invested in his kids' day-to-day studies. My husband had trouble remembering which class our children were in! In the documentary about his inner life, we see him play football with Aryan, give Suhana a kiss. I have never been kissed by my father. My son has never played any sport with his father. Every Sunday, my husband would plonk himself in front of the TV and not want to talk to any of us. He wanted his alone time because he had a long, busy, hard week. I didn't bring this up during one of our fights, but I was thinking that he couldn't be busier than Shah Rukh, surely. He didn't mend his ways, but there were ample jokes about how Shah Rukh is not man enough. Or that he is gay. Apparently, doing just these basic things makes a man feel less of a man.'

Now that's another thing. Shah Rukh has, from the start of his career, fielded questions about his sexual orientation. He was unlike other men. In his memoir *A Rude Life*, Vir Sanghvi wrote about the time he asked Shah Rukh about his sexuality. 'I pushed the envelope by asking if he was gay or bisexual, as was rumoured in film circles. It was not a question anyone had asked him to his face before but he was unfazed, dismissed it with aplomb and we moved on to the next subject. Though I thought the whole interview went very well, the only bit people remembered was the gay question. Shahrukh was asked about it for months afterwards, usually by film journalists who had never had the guts to confront him with the question before. He was super cool. To one journalist who demanded to know why I had asked him if he was gay, Shahrukh responded: "I don't know. Maybe if I had said yes, he would have asked me out to dinner."'[22]

He finds the question as silly as his fans do. But he had set the record straight: 'I am sensitive, so that makes me a little effeminate. I am neither gay, nor bisexual. I do not like to clarify this because if someone of my stature says I am not gay, does that mean being gay is bad?'[23]

The rumours persisted when, in another *Filmfare* interview, he said, 'That's rubbish. I don't do men. I don't do women. I am happily in love with my wife.' And then he joked, 'Hey, I like that line from *Sex and the City*, "I'm try-sexual. I try anything that's sexual." Okay, I'm try-sexual (*laughs*). No, hey, cut that out!'[24]

Iram Rizvi (name changed), a young fan all of seventeen, feels that Gen Z girls, too, adore Shah Rukh. 'I think he was born at the wrong time. If he grew up around Gen Z, people would call him a green flag and not gay! Women who are my mom's friends think of him as a package. He is chivalrous. He will protect his family. And he is sensitive. Boys really need to break out of their patterns and address their shortcomings instead of attacking good people,' she says.

This week Iram and her friends Rishita and Junie will be hosting a sleepover at her Bengaluru house for a movie-marathon night. There is *Kal Ho Naa Ho* on the list. 'Two of our guy friends will be coming as well. We want to see what they think of Rohit and Aman. It is packed with innuendos alluding to their sexuality. But I want our male friends to learn right away that caring for each other has no bearing on their sexuality. They can become good boys and not hyper masculine men—it's a clear choice. The latter is not attractive at all, and I can't imagine any girl around me falling for it.'

> 'I think he was born at the wrong time. If he grew up around Gen Z, people would call him a green flag ... Women who are my mom's friends think of him as a package. He is chivalrous. He will protect his family. And he is sensitive.'

During the course of this book, every person I spoke to introduced me to more fans of Shah Rukh. By the end of it, I had created a whole network of his fans categorized by age, ethnicity and work profiles.

Maedhbh got me in touch with her Pakistani friend Jameela Khan in London. As an expat living in the UK, the library of Shah Rukh's films is what keeps her close to home. 'I started watching his movies as a habit when I went to university. I was away from home and wanted comfort,' she tells me. During that period she understood why Shah Rukh is such a fantasy for women—it was his ability to say sorry and mean it, an idea that extends from his movies to his persona. She saw that men quite often have trouble being sincerely apologetic. It is something she cannot get on board with and recommends that women accept apologies from men only when they go beyond being a stray word and are backed by action. 'I introduced everyone around me to his movies because the easiest way for someone to emotionally access me is through his movies. When he cries, the world cries. Shah Rukh has this persistence to want to prove himself to someone. There are times when female characters are pissed at him, and he doesn't give up until they believe in how sorry he is. In a lot of ways, women crave wanting to know that a man is always trying to make amends and win you back. A lot of his characters go to lengths to make sure the woman knows she is loved, wanted and the guy is willing to do anything to make up. Effort is beautiful. A lot of men don't know what they want. We also live in a world where there is no dearth of options for men and women. There is a lack of commitment and people yearn for people who know how to stay committed. He signifies that. If you watch *Main Hoon Na*, he goes in disguise to meet his brother. He would go through fire to make sure the people he loves know that they are loved.'

Similarly, Stacey, the fan from San Francisco who wrote about her experience from the Temptation tour, connected me to Carolyn Honig, who lives in Bay Area, California. She and Stacey have been friends for decades now. The reason: Shah Rukh Khan. It always intrigues me when a non-Indian, or a non-South Asian, falls for Bollywood. When I spoke to Carolyn, that's what I asked her. She said she loved the song and dance. She was drawn to Bollywood when *Lagaan* was shortlisted at the 2002 Academy Awards. And then she continued to watch—for Shah Rukh. 'The first Shah Rukh film I saw was *Asoka*. In fact, Stacey and I were the only two light-skinned people in the queue at a Hindi movie theatre (Freemont)

> 'We also live in a world where there is no dearth of options for men and women. There is a lack of commitment and people yearn for people who know how to stay committed. He signifies that.'

to watch an Indian film, *Paheli*. There was an instant kinship. I drove her home, and here we are, so many years later. We have been living together for a decade. Then I went on a spree, catching up on all his films. I found a video store in Berkeley, California. I used to drive over and the man at the store would give me five videos at a time. It became a weekly ritual. When I watched *Devdas* with a non-fan, they were so depressed by the film and its ending. *Devdas* was the first DVD I bought. I own *K3G*, *Kal Ho Naa Ho*, *Kabhi Alvida Naa Kehna* and *Dil Se*. Now I watch it all on Netflix. I would be lying if I said Shah Rukh was an instant love. He wasn't. I kept thinking he was strange-looking. But he is so charming that he grew on me. I didn't realize when he became my favourite. He became my guide to a culture I didn't know anything about. At the time, I seriously considered writing an Americans' guide to Bollywood. It would be like a guide book, segregated by directors, actors, timeline and anecdotes, and cross-referenced. I had all the data but the computer broke down. Now I am a fifty-two-year-old American woman who loves Bollywood and Shah Rukh. Bollywood became my channel to Indian food—I started eating at Indian restaurants, trying out different curries, biryanis. My favourite is gulab jamun, kheer, jalebi and laddoos. All the Hindi I know is from Bollywood. I couldn't get myself to learn the script. There was an Indian restaurant near my house that sold desserts by the pound and I would buy my weekly stock from them. I have gone for a Bollywood cruise—it left from Miami and docked at New York. When I went to the terminal, they thought I was in the wrong line. I loved that cruise. I did dandiya on it and shared a room with the dancers. They tried to keep offering me coffee, and I had to tell them I loved my chai, like a desi girl.'

Not to break anyone's heart, but I keep reminding women that Shah Rukh says he isn't a prototype they should be chasing at all. He makes it a point to remind people of his flaws. Like every human being, he has some too. He isn't perfect. And he says he is bad with relationships. He calls himself detached yet emotional—demotional—closeted and reclusive.

Shreshtha Iyer told me, 'It's exactly what Shah Rukh says about his film *Paheli*. The perfect man—who admires, adores and loves—is an illusion. That's exactly what *Paheli* reflects. The desires, cravings, love of a woman cannot be fulfilled by a man. All Shah Rukh fans are aware of his shortcomings, because he is very open about who he is as a person. What we admire is his self-awareness and his effort to rectify the problems he sees in himself. *Paheli* is a prime example of how he perceives the shortcomings of masculinity and knows the importance of emancipating a woman. "Demotional", perhaps, but the desire to create systemic changes as an artiste is admirable.'

Shah Rukh says he finds it easy to pretend and project on screen what he is not in life. 'I don't have to believe in it, I have to make you believe in it and that's a challenge, always. An actor always goes for something that he is not. It's a vent. I want to be a Batman, a Spider-Man, a firefighter, an evil conniving don and I want to be the greatest lover in the world. And I am not any of these. That's why it turns me on.'[25] He even takes potshots at his iconic train sequence. 'I am not telling you to run after a train and climb it. In real life, I would stop the train, or say let's meet at the next station. I would never do it in real life, putting my hand out, beating her would-be-husband. In *Kuch Kuch Hota Hai*, the girl is getting married to a guy downstairs, [and] I walk up to her and say "I love you". Now that's extremely weird.'[26]

Desiring someone like Shah Rukh is not a realistic expectation. A lot of his persona is exaggerated because of the nature of Bollywood films. And his fans must have that reality check in place. Camiel Hu, who lives in Singapore and calls herself a realistic and measured fan of Shah Rukh, tells me, 'I am not blind to who he is. I can believe he is detached. Success can be very lonely. It can make you lose out on people. And when the world loves you so much and you are so powerful, you can lose sight of reality. It is very real. Fandom by design is cut out to place people on pedestals. I have often wondered why Shah Rukh doesn't fall from there. Because whoever he is, whatever he is, he isn't pretending. He is this person. He is a little pompous when he says he is the last of the stars. But the reason he is the last of the stars is because Shah Rukh isn't faking this. There is no dishonesty. You can't fake for thirty years every day, day after day, in every conversation and public appearance. Your reality will be exposed at some point. Shah Rukh is out there, being real, wearing his scars, head held high, despite everything he has gone through in 2023. He stands tall, undefeated and won't back down—and that's why people love him so much. Women, more than anything else, love a man with a spine.'

It is our short-sightedness, or should I say lack of awareness, that we assume only women fall for Shah Rukh. I had this realization while interviewing Shivangi Johri, the travel influencer quoted earlier. I remember asking her, 'Are you a big fan of Shah Rukh?' And she said, 'My husband, more than me.' I was pleasantly surprised when I realized that there was a man out there who loved Shah Rukh more than his wife did.

However, men admire Shah Rukh for entirely different things. Some are inspired by his never-give-up spirit, some are in awe of how a middle-class boy from Delhi built an empire from scratch, and some see him as the one who paved the way for others by breaking toxic stereotypes of masculinity.

'Fandom by design is cut out to place people on pedestals. I have often wondered why Shah Rukh doesn't fall from there. Because whoever he is, whatever he is, he isn't pretending. He is this person. He is a little pompous when he says he is the last of the stars. But the reason he is the last of the stars is because Shah Rukh isn't faking this.'

My friend Abhimanyu Sureka tells me that Shah Rukh, for men too, is the definition of what an ideal man should be like. 'A man from humble beginnings who made it so big that today he is the face of India internationally. People will come and go, but no one will beat Shah Rukh. But his success is only an aspect of why he is an ideal man even for men. There is a video of him at Dilip Kumar's funeral where he greets the guards from Mumbai Police who were there for crowd control. He didn't need to do that, but he did. He is humble. He will be at a party and bump into an industry veteran—like Amitabh Bachchan—and do pranaam. He can even make Jaya Bachchan laugh. He is chivalrous. All the women I know think of him as the modern-day benchmark of chivalry. He is that man every parent wants their son to be like. I was told as a kid, "*Shah Rukh jaise tameezdaar bano, bado ki izzat karo, auraton ka samman karo, bachcho se sneh karo* [Be as courteous as Shah Rukh, respect your elders, honour women and be affectionate towards children]." Look at how he protects his family and kids. It's tremendous. Especially after what the family went through, the fact that the head of the family stands rock-solid by them and will not let anything bad happen to them is just so aspirational for men of my generation. He will protect but never impose. He is that ideal prototype of a man seeped in Indian values.'

Just like the female fans, male fans have their own dreamy stories of what Shah Rukh does for them. The most dreamy story of a male Shah Rukh fan—perhaps the biggest I know—is Nayandeep Rakshit's. He is a chat show host and a well-known movie influencer, but I met him as an eighteen-year-old when we were both cub reporters in Calcutta. We went for several cups of tea at Flury's in Park Street and chatted about our love for films. But the one thing I learnt from our first meeting was that if there was anything he loved more than films, it was Shah Rukh Khan. Many years later I met him in Mumbai to interview him for this book. We were at the coffee shop below Shah Rukh's office in Khar. He told me his story all over again. 'I started working with TTIS [The Telegraph in Schools] with the desire to meet him. I had met him on stage once in Kolkata, and then I met him at the airport. It was 17 April 2011, and I was waiting for him at the Dum Dum airport [now Netaji Subhas Chandra Bose airport]. Back then, he used to attend matches in the city. I saw him and walked towards him to click a picture. One of the policemen guarding him pushed me away. I almost hit a wall. He sent his bodyguard to check on me. I vividly remember him shouting at the cop and saying, "How can you push somebody like that?" He called me and said, "Come here, beta." He checked whether I was okay and then clicked a picture with me. Today, I thank Shah Sir for a lot of good that has come into my life. I thank him for Mumbai, and my career.'

Nayandeep always wanted to move to Mumbai to meet Shah Rukh. 'When I moved, I told my family that the day Shah Sir knows me by my name, I will come back.'

I remember Nayandeep's first few months in the city. To put it mildly, they were tempestuous. Homesick, stuck with roommates he did not like and bosses who were harsh, kicking the nest and becoming an adult was taking a toll on him. Every few days, he would tell me, 'I want to go back. *Aar parchi na* [Can't take this any more].' On a rainy evening in 2014, I remember standing at the same coffee shop, dissuading him from returning to Kolkata. I told him, 'Look where you are standing, Nayan. This is Shah Rukh's building. You are already here. Do you really want to go back now?' He stayed. 'Someday Shah Sir will know me,' he vowed that evening.

On 13 October 2014, he did his first interview with Shah Rukh. 'I met Shah Sir for a *Happy New Year* interview. I had a book about Shah Rukh Sir with me [*Shah Rukh Can*]. He autographed it and wrote: Stay well and always keep beaming. Everything he has ever told me is so precious to me. He had messaged me once, "Keep your innocence intact. Don't let the harshness of the world get to you." Any word he tells anyone is not in passing. He means it. He speaks to *you*. You are not one of the many fans he has. You matter to him.'

> 'Shah Rukh is out there, being real, wearing his scars, head held high despite everything he has gone through in 2023. He stands tall, undefeated and wouldn't back down—and that's why people love him so much. Women, more than anything else, love a man with a spine.'

In the past few years, Shah Rukh has visibly pulled the plug on his press interactions. This year, Nayandeep met him again after five years. 'I was hosting the Zee Cine Awards red carpet and the first thing he asked when he saw me was, "How are you, beta?" I got so emotional. I barely met him for a few minutes. I asked him about his health. He asked me, "Are you happy?" It's very basic, but most people forget to ask you that. His heart will never shut down for his fans. He really is an emotion. Fans can never explain why. It's like magic. I connect with the humanity he shows every time to everyone. Love for him always starts with his on-screen persona, but then you meet the man and you realize why he is who he is. If he wasn't a good person, I wouldn't have stayed in love for so long. As journalists, you meet stars so often. Eventually, the on-screen persona takes a backseat and you see the person they really are. And I saw the person Shah Rukh is—warm, kind-hearted, a gentleman to men, women, kids and animals. The true definition of a real man is that. He will love you regardless of who you are, where you come from and what you become. He talked to me with the same love when I was just another fan, when I was a rookie reporter, and today when people know me and I have some sort of a standing. His respect has stayed the same for me. Not many people have that. When I was a kid, I used to cry when someone hit Shah Rukh in a film, but even after all these years, when it comes to him, I am that child who can't stand anything against Shah Sir.'

Nayandeep brings to the fore a vital question: Who is a real man?

In the context of Shah Rukh, this has often been discussed. His appearance is at odds with what the world feels an attractive man should be. Mills & Boon has made us believe that only a tall, dark, handsome man is attractive. Bollywood in the 1990s told us only macho, muscular men, such as Sanjay Dutt, are attractive. And then came Shah Rukh and proved to everyone that there's no single definition of what makes 'a real man'. A former model from the late 1990s says Shah Rukh broke the mould even for men like him. He and Shah Rukh are contemporaries from Delhi's theatre circles. He requests us to not name him as he has today made a career in a different industry. He said, 'I was told by many agents that I was too short to be a model. I was considered too thin. Contemporaries such as Milind Soman were built differently. They were conventionally good-looking. My physicality led me to several internal conflicts. I battle with such conflicts even today. I hate a man who looks like Hrithik Roshan or Fawad Khan almost naturally, like a reflex. But what Shah Rukh did was change the definition of beauty in a man. He wasn't conventionally good-looking. He proved that personality was more important than your face. Your face is not something over which you have control. Personality is something that is self-built. I am glad that the industry widened and so did the idea of beauty. Shah Rukh's popularity and success have a huge role to play in making men comfortable in their skin.'

He connected me with another model who also benefited from Shah Rukh's success. 'In 2005, I did my first mainstream show after a conventionally good-looking supermodel dropped out at the last minute. The designer looked at me and said, "While you are not an obvious choice for me as a model, I guess you'll work. Look at Shah Rukh winning hearts. He is romancing Sushmita Sen, so I guess you'll do!" *Main Hoon Na* was a rage then, and he played one of the film's songs for the show too. I used to be wildly insecure of the fact that I wasn't muscular. I was lean, but fit. Over the years, I realized none of it matters if I can work the crowd.'

After the show, he bought himself a shimmery golden shirt, much like the one Shah Rukh wore in *'Tumse Milke Dil Ka'* in *Main Hoon Na*. 'Models are never a hundred per cent comfortable about their bodies or their looks. At least I am not. If I feel out of sorts, I wear that golden shirt and watch *Main Hoon Na* to get through the bad day.'

A lot of Shah Rukh's fans derive strength from his ability to smash toxic patriarchal norms. Cisgender heterosexual men are frequently inspired by his positive masculinity on screen. Chat-show host and producer Nikhil Taneja wrote in one of his Instagram posts, 'One of my favourite moments in an SRK film is a scene in *Kuch Kuch Hota Hai*. Rahul and Tina are outside the temple and he says, I worship three women in my life: The Goddess, my own mother—and the third is the woman standing in front of him, the women he loves. From then till now SRK has repeatedly shown that masculinity can very well be about "worshipping" the person you love, in a wholesome, positive way. It's not that there haven't been problematic moments in SRK films, but even in his interviews, he speaks and stands for always being respectful of women.'[27]

On his show *Be A Man, Yaar!*, several celebrity guests have 'simped on' Shah Rukh. Vicky Kaushal said Shah Rukh has the 'best rizz game'.[28]

This love for Shah Rukh goes beyond just actors in India. When asked about his favourite Indian actor, *Harry Potter* star Daniel Radcliffe, now a Tony Award winner, said in a 2010 *DNA* interview, 'Shah Rukh Khan is really famous in Britain and I'm really fond of him. He is definitely an epitome of style and class!'[29]

While Nayandeep's experience gives us a glimpse of the human side of the star, for most men it's his drive that's so alluring. My friend

Ashish Aggarwala tells me that as a boy from a middle-class family in Kolkata, he has always been impressed by Shah Rukh's ambition. He quotes Shah Rukh's interview from *The Los Angeles Times* in 2011, 'I was driving down a small lane in India recently, and I remembered that 20 years ago I was driving down the same lane, and I had maybe $10 or $20 in my pocket. I couldn't believe all that had happened to me. I feel lucky and even guilty to have this much.'[30] Ashish tells me, 'I come from a family of businessmen. I am Marwari. This is the spirit I aspired for. This idea—*chaand taare tod lau, saari duniya par main chhau, bas itna sa khwab hai* [I want to pluck the moon and the stars from the sky, and spread myself across the entire world, that's my only dream] ... I wanted to live that. And the beauty of Shah Rukh is that there is genuine hard work in his journey—and that shows. It is not manufactured or manipulated. He drove me to work hard. I have believed that if you work hard, you'll get what you want. My work ethics, my idea of hard work, my idea of honestly doing whatever I do comes from him. I know I can never be Shah Rukh. In fact, I don't aspire to be him either, but I want to work as hard as Shah Rukh and be the best at the work I do.'

Ashish asks me if I can get him an autograph from Shah Rukh to keep on his work desk. 'If there is ever a creative block, I want inspiration right in front of me. Nothing much, something basic: "Never stop working hard ... With love, SRK." I know it's the good juju I need.'

In 2011 BBC interviewed Shah Rukh to understand what makes him 'the most popular movie star in the world'. Legions of fans call him the King of Bollywood. He, true to his humble self, said, 'I get amazed they call me that (King or Badshah)—and I think maybe deep down inside my heart I don't deserve all of this. I feel very grateful and very odd. I don't even know why people like me so much.'[31]

He said he acts to cover up his awkwardness. He loves acting but can never watch his own films because he is too embarrassed. He dreams of making movies that sell the joy of India to the world, those that will cross over and satisfy audiences even in the West. 'I'll keep tirelessly working towards that ... I don't want to sell the poverty and the snake charmers of India. I want to sell the educated middle class of India. I want to tell them there's a lot of intelligence here, intellect here, richness here, happiness here, colourful culture here, and with due respect, we are not just some country, a Third World country. I don't want to sell the sadness of this country. I want to sell the happiness of the country.'[32]

How does a man who means so much to so many people across the world continue to do it consistently over three decades? Shah Rukh has a simple answer, 'I feel very happy that I'm allowed by God to come and be someone else. That's all I need to do, and I just keep doing it every morning I get up. My family keeps asking, "How do you do this?" I said, "I just love it. I'm just very happy doing acting."'[33]

> '**People will come and go, but no one will beat Shah Rukh. But his success is only an aspect of why he is an ideal man even for men.**'

Shah Rukh never sees himself as the superstar he is. He calls himself an employee of the myth of Shah Rukh. And the audience is his boss. He will be fired if he can't make his boss happy. He was fired for a bit, until he won them over again in 2023 with some exceptional performances.

How does such a loved man determine his legacy to someone who has never heard of him? He describes himself as 'an actor somewhere in India who has tried, and is still trying very hard'.[34] The word 'legacy' doesn't sit right with him. 'You don't leave a legacy. Legacies are made.'[35] But what he wants to leave for the younger generation is this thought: 'If I can pass on the culture of immense hard work with a lot of humour. Wear your success like a T-shirt, not a tuxedo. You work hard, enjoy yourself, give a few laughs and if it makes you a star, wear it on your sleeve. If it doesn't make you a star, at least you tried. You worked hard, so enjoy yourself.'[36]

But he doesn't make false promises to anyone. You'd assume that once you get to the top, it's a feeling so wholesome and absolute that you want nothing more. But that's not true of Shah Rukh. While spreading joy across the world to people who have never met him and perhaps never will in their lifetime, he admits it is lonely being him. 'I can come across as a user, manipulator, disinterested, weird, reclusive, strange, arrogant from the outside. But the people involved know the truth ... there are days I feel lonely on the inside. I guess that's the way I am.'[37]

Why is it lonely, someone asked him another time, and he said, 'It's lonely not because it's sad, it's just that the work takes a lot of time. Your life gets dedicated to others. I have to do so much in a day. I would like to go and sit with my friends, but when I go somewhere, there are 40 people who want to meet me. So I have to dedicate that private time to public.'[38]

But for a man who has loved his fans so much and for whom his fans mean the world, he goes to sleep every night with the awareness that his stardom will change, even diminish. And he knew this early on in his life. He said in a 1997 interview, 'I think I know somewhere this is very transitory. But I am just enjoying the fact that people are screaming and there are so many flowers coming and I am the King Khan ... I think of my mom and all the good things which will remain with me except my stardom.'[39]

As I typed out that last sentence, I stared at the word 'stardom'. Memories from his fiftieth birthday celebrations outside Mannat flashed before my eyes. Scores of people chanting his name, shedding tears of joy. I have seen mass hysteria of disproportionate measures in the past decade—be it for Amitabh Bachchan or for Salman Khan, even Fawad Khan and Varun Dhawan. But something about Shah Rukh's fandom strikes different. In that one year of lockdown when the lane outside Mannat was empty, you could tell something was really wrong with the world. For everyone who comes to the city, Mannat is the symbol that dreams do come true. It's an affirmation of the fact that Mumbai is rightly called the City of Dreams. People standing outside Mannat and Shah Rukh greeting them from the ramp are visuals as inevitable in Bandstand as the setting sun.

This year on Eid, I was stranded without a rickshaw near Mannat and was witness to the mass hysteria all over again. Someone shouted, '*Khan sa'ab aa gaye hai* [Mr Khan has arrived]!' And people in pristine white clothes ran towards his house. The joy was evident on their faces. I don't see the crowds outside Mannat ever dwindling, at least not in my lifetime.

This chapter can go on forever, because every fan knows more fans and insist that they are bigger fans than the ones I have already interviewed. Shah Rukh's words played in my ears: I think of all the good things that will remain ... Now that's the thing about stardom. All good things do remain ...

> *Darrne mein koi burai nahi hai. Bas apne darr ko itna badaa mat bana do ki tumhe aage badhne se rok le*
>
> — *My Name Is Khan*, 2010

9

DOOM OF Y2K

The classic design flaw in a superstar's life is that they get cast into a mould. But Shah Rukh didn't want to become an actor to swim with the tide. Being typecast is something he rebels strongly against and something he understands is the pitfall of superstardom. He said in an interview to Huffington Post India, 'Cast me because I am talented. Cast me because I can play ugly or handsome when I want. I am an actor. Wherever my arms can reach out, wherever my breath can reach out, that is my space.' He spoke about how he could move effortlessly between the worlds of Mani Ratnam's cinema, discussions with top global figures such as Tim Cook and casual interactions with everyday people, such as his son AbRam's nanny. Shah Rukh insists that no director, writer or film-maker should limit him to a specific role or genre. He proudly lists his diverse body of works, from *Kabhi Haan Kabhi Naa* and *Chak De! India* to *RA.One* and *Chennai Express*, to highlight his capability to take on varied roles and stories. He said, 'I am Shah Rukh Khan and I can do everything.'[1]

It is perhaps with that very confidence that Shah Rukh ventured into production—to make movies for himself that no one else would give him the chance to make. Shah Rukh was the first leading man of his generation to make the leap to production.

In 1999, Shah Rukh, Juhi Chawla and Aziz Mirza formed a small production company. At the time it seemed like a brilliant idea. What better than converting friendship into professional bond? Aziz was one of Shah Rukh's first directors (*Circus*). He and his wife, Nirmala, had been gracious hosts to Shah Rukh when he had first moved to Mumbai. Both had made their feature-film debuts with *Raju Ban Gaya Gentleman*, where Juhi had played the female lead. In an industry where relationships often fluctuate with box office success, Shah Rukh, Juhi and Aziz maintained a lasting friendship. They enjoyed telling clean, simple stories with a social message. The trio believed that having their own production house would grant them creative freedom and they would be able to produce the kind of films they wanted, without any compromises. Shah Rukh called himself 'the poor man's Raj Kapoor'.[2] It was also an opportune time to get into production as the market was thriving. Beyond theatrical revenues, music, satellite and overseas markets were also generating substantial income.

The idea for the company emerged from a casual conversation. Aziz wanted to make a film with Shah Rukh, but did not want to exploit their friendship by underpaying him. He insisted that Shah Rukh take his market rate and a percentage of the profits. Shah Rukh suggested they become partners instead. What started with Shah Rukh soon became a trend, with stars such as Ajay Devgn and Aamir Khan also starting their own companies.

After *Raju Ban Gaya Gentleman*, their second collaboration, this time as a team, was a quirky film titled *Yes Boss* in 1997, in which Shah Rukh played an ambitious employee who occasionally scouted women for his boss to win his favour. However, the film did moderate business, leaving the trio feeling that their unique brand of stories may not be lucrative enough for them as producers.

His venture into production was serendipitous. During a conversation with Ratan Jain and a non-industry friend, the idea of producing a film such as *Yes Boss* emerged. This casual discussion ignited Shah Rukh's belief in the potential that he believed he, Juhi and Aziz had as a trio, emphasizing that if an outsider could invest in their vision, they should have faith in themselves too. When Aziz considered launching a production company, he saw the opportunity to involve Shah Rukh and Juhi as partners, marking the beginning of their company.

The name 'Dreamz Unlimited' came about during an informal brainstorming session. They initially considered 'Dreams', but Shah Rukh suggested adding a twist by spelling it with a 'z', leading to the name 'Dreamz Unlimited'. Each of the trio invested Rs 500,000 to kickstart the venture with *Yes Boss*. Yash Johar joined to oversee production, while Juhi's husband Jay Mehta took care of the documentation. Contributions from friends such as Karan Johar and Manish Malhotra were invaluable, with Aditya Chopra and Jatin-Lalit crafting the title song. Sony acquired the music rights, and Kishore Lulla secured the overseas rights, offering not just financial backing but also a boost of confidence.

Shah Rukh reflected on his unexpected path to becoming a producer with a sense of pride. He described the company as a close-knit family rather than a conventional business and hoped it would mirror the success of his acting career. Despite the demands of balancing production with his acting roles—such as deferring projects with Aditya Chopra and David Dhawan—he remained eager and ready for new challenges, embracing the role of a producer with enthusiasm and flair. 'I've worked the hardest in my stint as a producer. We all have worked very hard. But Juhi and I had to also take care of our appearances because after the hard work, we had to face the camera for some other films. I postponed Adi's and David (Dhawan)'s film for some months because of my film. But the hard work notwithstanding, I'm ready for the next one.'[3]

They purchased a four-storey building and set up a stylish office. The nameplate on Shah Rukh's office door read 'Superstar'. The company had grand plans to produce not only films but also television shows and advertisements. Shah Rukh, always the technology enthusiast, wanted his team to have the best equipment, believing that superior technique would lead to better films. Thus, a sister company was established and state-of-the-art equipment was imported. The ultimate vision was to combine all these ventures into a mega studio complex housing post-production facilities, equipment storage, creative offices, a five-star hotel, a multiplex and a bowling alley. Shah Rukh has always had a dream of bringing

Bollywood on a par with Hollywood when it came to technology. 'I want to earn enough money to be able to buy new equipment, besides the ones we bought for *Phir Bhi*... [I want] new technology and someday [hope to] make a film of international standards in India. I dream of the day when Shekhar Kapur does not have to go to Hollywood to make his films, he can jolly well make them here,' he said.[4]

None of the partners knew anything about the logistics of starting and running a business. Jai Mehta, who had a corporate background, assisted them in registering the company and creating an operational blueprint. Yash Johar, with fifty years of experience in the unpredictable world of film-making, managed production. Juhi's brother Sanjiv was hired as a production executive and apprenticed with Yash Johar. Although Shah Rukh, Juhi, Aziz and most of their twenty-odd employees were inexperienced in production, they hoped that Shah Rukh's star power and their collective goodwill within the industry would help them sail through. Only if that is ever enough, especially in a tempestuous industry like film-making.

> **It is perhaps with that very confidence that Shah Rukh ventured into production—to make movies for himself that no one else would give him the chance to make. Shah Rukh was the first leading man of his generation to make the leap to production.**

Phir Bhi Dil Hai Hindustani (*PBDHH*) was made by Aziz as the Indian equivalent of Billy Wilder's classic, *The Front Page*. It tells the story of two television journalists working for rival channels, both willing to stop at nothing to win the ratings war. Inspired by the famous sting operations of Tehelka around that time, there was one woven into the film's story as well. It was an ambitious outing that exposed systemic discrepancies. The two journalists took on their greedy employers, corrupt politicians and the police. The film had the right amount of righteous rage and showcased why it was essential to use the media to expose the truth.

In a 1999 interview, Shah Rukh spoke about their maiden production venture. 'Even as an actor, I've never been scared of a release. Frankly, the release of a film means that it's on air. After that, a film is beyond anyone's control ... but yes, I'm a little more numb now as a producer than I've ever been as an actor. I've been taking a keen interest in the film's post-production work and the publicity. I believe in the American style of lavish publicity. I'm not going to tell the world that it's the greatest film ever made, but I'm surely going to publicise the film as the greatest film.'[5]

Through the 1990s, satellite television transformed the Indian media landscape. By 1999, viewers who were once limited to two monotonous channels now had more than fifty exciting options. The dot-com boom had happened, and Aziz believed that a film addressing the commercialization of the media would provide a meaningful commentary on the increasingly materialistic post-liberalization India.

Neither Karan nor Aditya was convinced. For them cinema meant commercial success, and they both found the theme of *PBDHH* perplexing. People come to the movies to escape their realities, not come face to face with it. Why make an eccentric movie that people might not resonate with?

But the partners proceeded undeterred. While Aziz and Juhi were cautious with spending, Shah Rukh was a generous producer. He wanted his debut production to exude style and sophistication. Thus, he instructed Sanjiv to ensure that 'anything anybody required' was available. The budget was set at an impressive Rs 3 crore ($3 million). Top-tier technicians were brought on board, including renowned cinematographer Santosh Sivan. Shah Rukh's close friend and favourite choreographer Farah Khan also joined the team. Farah, who had worked with Shah Rukh since his early films, even created his signature move—sweeping his hand through his hair—that made female fans swoon.

The production involved creating twenty-four sets, one of which, the interior of Shah Rukh's house, went unused. *PBDHH* premiered on 21 January 2000, drawing Bollywood's biggest stars. Veteran actors Dilip Kumar, Rekha and Jaya Bachchan attended to see Shah Rukh's creation. The after-party was held at the trendy nightclub called Fire and Ice in Mumbai.

Within a week of its release, critics had ripped the film apart and box office collections were conspicuously lower than expected. In 2018, Shah Rukh tweeted, 'This one was special. It was a complete disaster and completely written off. Our failure made us and me stronger. Love PBDHH ...'

For those of us whose career is observing the business of films, there was perhaps another reason why this film didn't work. In the week prior to the release of *PBDHH*, another film was released—*Kaho Naa... Pyaar Hai*—which launched one of the most gorgeous actors Bollywood has ever seen. Director Rakesh Roshan fashioned a typical debut vehicle for son Hrithik. With his first film Hrithik made the leap from being just a newcomer to a full-fledged heart-throb overnight. He possessed the unique combination of boyish charm and a sculpted physique, thanks to his rigorous pre-film training. This chiselled look, a novelty at the time, was a refreshing change from the more traditional Bollywood leading men.

But Hrithik wasn't just a pretty face. He had impressive dancing skills, as particularly seen in the iconic song 'Ek Pal Ka Jeena'. His smooth moves and undeniable stage presence left audiences, especially young women, mesmerized. But the film itself played to the audiences. *Kaho Naa... Pyaar Hai* was a classic romantic drama with a twist. Hrithik played a double role, showcasing his versatility as an actor. The characters, one a brooding musician and the other a charming playboy, offered something to everyone. The soundtrack was another major contributing factor to its raging success. Catchy tunes and heartfelt lyrics resonated with the audiences. Hrithik's Rohit–Raj, his double roles in the film, became the new idealized romantic-hero icons.

Critics did point out the somewhat clichéd storyline, but the fresh faces, the high-energy music and the overall entertainment package proved irresistible. *Kaho Naa... Pyaar Hai* became a record-breaking blockbuster, cementing Hrithik's place in Bollywood and igniting the 'Hrithik Mania'.

You'd ask the most natural next question: Why can't two superstars coexist in an ecosystem? They surely can. The Khans coexisted in harmony, and through the 1990s there was success for actors such as Ajay Devgn and Akshay Kumar as well. But the dawn of the new millennium brought about a change in outlook within India—the rise of extremism's ugly head. In the March 2000 edition of *India Today*, a cover story about Hrithik went up with the headline: 'In a Bollywood dominated by the Khans, Hrithik Roshan suddenly becomes a national craze.'[6]

The headline seemed innocent enough, but as other publications picked it up and the reactions started flowing through the country, the unpleasantness made itself apparent.

The piece quoted Sriniwas Sadani, twenty-nine, proprietor of the Hallmark store in Elgin Road, Kolkata. 'No one, no cricketer, film star or pop musician has sold so many posters,' he said, adding, 'People have forgotten Shah Rukh Khan.' The piece got even more personal when it ran a section about Shah Rukh, Aamir and Salman.

'SHAH RUKH KHAN: Great energy and sheer mannerism with flashes of histrionic ability ... But HRITHIK is more sophisticated. Finally you have an actor who is also a star.

'AAMIR KHAN: He is a very intense actor besides being a heartthrob ... But HRITHIK has intelligence and charisma. He can do complex roles and has nuances.

'SALMAN KHAN: He can be good. But what sets him apart is his great body and amazing narcissism ... But HRITHIK's honesty comes through to all people. The camera loves him.'

In *King of Bollywood*, Anupama Chopra vividly describes a turbulent period in Shah Rukh's life. While he was in London recovering from a knee surgery, an *India Today* cover that questioned his relevance hit the stands. Gauri, deeply concerned, tried to keep the magazine from him, but Shah Rukh was infuriated by the sudden dismissal of a decade's worth of his hard work, feeling as though he was being unceremoniously cast aside as irrelevant. The constant barrage of comparisons to Hrithik and the relentless scrutiny left him feeling exposed and deeply hurt, as if the world was brazenly undermining his achievements.

Shah Rukh internalized the anger and disappointment. He became uncharacteristically quiet. He hunkered down at home, playing out comforting rituals in his garden with Aryan. 'Who is the best?' Shah Rukh would ask. 'Papa, you are the best,' Aryan would reply. He was only three and did not understand what his father was asking or why he needed the encouragement.[7] But Shah Rukh clung to the reassuring knowledge that at least one person in the world, without reservation or hesitation, still thought that Shah Rukh Khan was unsurpassed. Although Aamir's film *Mela* had collapsed with a din equal to Shah Rukh's, Aamir didn't become a target. Hrithik was specifically positioned as the first star in a decade to edge Shah Rukh unceremoniously off his King Khan throne. The backlash against Shah Rukh, compounded by the theme of *PBDHH*, which sharply criticized the media, became venomous. The film press, especially *Stardust*, devoted reams of newsprint to the story.

Amid the storm surrounding Shah Rukh, Gauri emerged as a fierce supporter, publicly standing beside him. In a powerful interview, she spoke about Shah Rukh's remarkable rise from humble beginnings—starting from television and theatre, with no film industry connections, to becoming a celebrated star. She said that such a journey was inherently fraught with challenges, and that criticism, a natural by-product of fame, was inevitable. She reassured Shah Rukh that enduring such rough patches were part of the universal experience of being in the limelight. 'Criticism has to come with stardom and you have to learn how to deal with it. Everybody goes through these phases in life,' she was quoted as saying.[8]

Of course, Gauri had seen the industry closely by then and knew this situation of pitting two actors against each other wasn't something new. She dismissed the comparisons between Shah Rukh and Hrithik as both absurd and reductive. She lauded Hrithik's talent, acknowledging that he was a promising new entrant in the industry. Yet, she found the comparisons nonsensical, pointing out that Hrithik was a decade younger and not yet comparable to Shah Rukh's established legacy. She recalled how Shah Rukh had once been compared to Amitabh Bachchan, a measure she deemed equally unfair. She said, 'How can you compare Amitabh to Shah Rukh? Amitabh was brilliant. They are two different people who have achieved success in their own ways and in different periods of time.'

Shah Rukh has never thought of himself as an insecure actor. In fact, right before the release of *PBDHH*, he said that the number one position was a fallacy. 'I would have been (insecure) if I lived in a shell or in an ivory tower. But I don't go into a shell, I don't live in an ivory tower,' he said, adding that he was grounded and not detached from his surroundings.[9]

Shah Rukh is confident that any decline in his career would be gradual and not sudden. He doesn't lose sleep over his status or fret about his popularity. Instead, he finds reassurance in his ongoing work and the consistent support of his audience. The idea of losing public recognition or not seeing smiles on people's faces concerns him, but he is certain that his continued work will prevent such scenarios. He does not measure his success by the accolades he receives or his position on charts, maintaining a sense of security and focus on his craft.[10]

But the media frenzy against Shah Rukh continued to intensify, and perhaps eventually the insecurity did creep in. Shah Rukh was a king, but he was also only human. In May 2000 he appeared in a cheeky Pepsi commercial. A blog, India FM, wrote that Shah Rukh had stirred up a buzz with a cheeky Pepsi commercial that added a new twist to the prevalent cola wars. The commercial, which spoofed a Hrithik Coke ad, featured a lookalike of the Bollywood heart-throb being humorously outshone by Shah Rukh.[11]

The ad shows a game of spin the bottle and has Shah Rukh telling a beautiful girl (Tara Sharma) in a bowling alley that she would have to kiss the person towards whom the bottle points. When he spins the bottle, it points towards the Hrithik clone and Shah Rukh tells him, '*Ek smile ho jaye* [Give us a smile].' As the clone obliges, his braces sparkle and glint, leading to an 'ugh' moment from the girl. Needless to say, she doesn't kiss him, but does end up kissing Shah Rukh by the time the ad ends.

The reaction was swift and intense. Rakesh Roshan, Hrithik's father, was reportedly incensed upon seeing the ad, which he perceived as an unfair slight. Hrithik himself was furious and fired off angry letters to Pepsi, decrying the ad as distasteful and a slight to his burgeoning career. He argued that seasoned stars should offer support rather than ridiculing newcomers.

Prahlad Kakkar, the ad's director, attempted to defuse the situation by assuring Hrithik that the ad was meant to be taken light-heartedly. Kakkar even said he had sent a tape of the commercial to Hrithik, although the actor claimed he had never received it.

Panchjanya, the mouthpiece magazine of the right-wing Hindu organization Rashtriya Swayamsevak Sangh (RSS), published a cover story claiming that Hrithik was the Hindu answer to the Muslim Khan dominance in Bollywood.[12] They wrote that the Pepsi ad was a malicious attempt to undermine Hrithik's popularity because he was challenging the Khans. *The Times of India* published a lead editorial in response to the 'bizarre cover story'. The saffron publication had depicted Bollywood's top three Khans—Shah Rukh, Aamir and Salman—as 'henchmen of Dawood Ibrahim', alleging that they formed a gang dominating Bollywood through intimidation, forcing producers to sign them, while blocking Hindu actors as part of an 'international conspiracy'. *Panchjanya* even suggested that Muslims exclusively drank Pepsi because Shah Rukh Khan endorsed it, unlike Coke, promoted by the Hindu Hrithik Roshan. *The Times of India* noted that the star value of any actor was determined by millions of cinema fans across the country and not by producers, directors or financiers in Mumbai or Dubai.[13]

However, it wasn't just *Panchjanya* and the RSS that saw a Khan conspiracy. Around the same time, Shiv Sena chief Bal Thackeray also voiced his displeasure to his followers in Mumbai, declaring, 'We have tolerated the Khans of the film industry for too long. How long are we going to tolerate them?'[14]

Panchjanya editor Tarun Vijay defended the article. He denied any communal bias, asserting that the controversy stemmed from a leftist journalist from Jawaharlal Nehru University who had misinterpreted the piece. This misrepresentation, he argued, shifted the focus away from the article's original concern—mafia influence in the film industry—to unnecessary discussions involving the RSS and its chief, K.S. Sudarshan. Vijay explained that the article's headline, 'MNCs and Mafia of Gulf Sow the Seeds of Disharmony', was intended to address the dangers posed by external forces that threatened societal harmony, and not focus on personal rivalries among actors such as Hrithik Roshan. The article had initially suggested that conflicts involving Hrithik might be driven by other stars' jealousy. Vijay further clarified that the article warned against the spread of communalism and criticized the absurd notion that consumer choices influenced by celebrity endorsements could be seen as a serious issue. Ultimately, the article aimed to caution against the divisive tactics employed by mafias and multinational corporations. He said, 'If someone drinks Coke or Pepsi just because Shah Rukh or Hrithik are campaigning for the drinks, that would be ridiculous. In fact the entire story warns against falling prey to the designs of the mafia's and the MNCs' dividing game.'[15]

Eventually, like every controversy, this, too, died down. And Dreamz Unlimited went back to dreaming again. And this time it dreamt bigger. But Aziz, Shah Rukh and Juhi experienced a period of emotional turbulence, taking turns to comfort and support each other. Aziz, in particular, felt a profound sense of responsibility for the setback. Having guided Shah Rukh and Juhi both professionally and personally, he felt that he had let them down for the first time in their long collaboration. Overwhelmed by the persistent gloom, the trio decided to leave Mumbai to escape the relentless pressure.

Despite this setback, they decided to place their bets on a period film about a legendary third-century pacifist emperor, and titled it *Asoka*.

Asoka was directed by Santosh Sivan, the cinematographer for *PBDHH*. Sivan was affectionately called 'Santa' by Shah Rukh, who had been friends with him since they had worked together in *Dil Se..* in 1997. Sivan felt Shah Rukh had the elegance to play Asoka and would be great in the role. At its core, this was a film about the futility of war. The story followed the romantic Asoka, who in his quest for the throne turned into a killing machine only to find himself drawn to peace after a bloody victory. The film was mounted on a budget of Rs 12.5 crore. The production agreed to everything the film-maker asked for—a 700-person crew, six cameras set up and every modern-day equipment filming might need.

Asoka premiered at the Venice Film Festival on 7 September 2001. It also featured at the Toronto Film Festival on 13 September. The film opened to rave reviews, but the box office results did not live up to the hype. In the UK, *Asoka* initially made it to the top ten charts, but quickly fell. In India, it performed well in Mumbai and south India, but did not fare well in other states such as Delhi, Rajasthan and Uttar Pradesh. Dreamz Unlimited took a hit of over Rs 4 crore—the decision to act as overseas distributors proved catastrophic.

However, the company persevered, and this time decided to play it safe. The result was the box office hit *Chalte Chalte* in 2003. Directed by Aziz, it featured Shah Rukh as the classic rom-com hero, paired with Rani Mukerji, whom he had worked with earlier. The classic story of the estranged husband and wife who find their way back to each other was safe and helped the company float. Shah Rukh described it as a 'once-bitten-twice-shy kind of film'.

However, the film led to tensions within the company. The original choice for the female lead was Aishwarya Rai, but Rani Mukerji replaced her after Salman Khan interrupted the film's mahurat shot and created a scene, accusing Shah Rukh of getting too friendly with his (then former) girlfriend.[16] The casting of Rani also seems to have been a bone of contention with Juhi, who was displeased with the choice but 'understood' that she was too old to play the female romantic lead. She was focused on marriage and motherhood by then.

Addressing the closure of the company, Juhi told *The Times of India* in an interview that the ambitious project didn't go as planned and the lessons learnt were hard-earned. She noted that managing a production company was far more complex than simply acting in films. The company's success with *Chalte Chalte* was overshadowed by tragedy when Aziz lost his wife, and Shah Rukh's shift to pursuing his own projects meant Juhi realized she again needed to focus solely on acting. She decided to step away from production to regain her freedom and return to her primary passion.[17]

In the same interview, she said, 'I'd jump to do a film with Aamir Khan. Aamir thinks through things before starting a project. But I don't meet Aamir or Shah Rukh so often now. But we continue to share a good rapport when we meet. Besides, I am older now and they are working with younger heroines.'

Admitting to the discord in *King of Bollywood*, Shah Rukh said, 'We enjoyed our failure more than our success, because I think in our success we hurt each other a lot.'

By March 2001, the company's accumulated losses had reached millions, forcing Shah Rukh to close the business. When he informed his thirty-two employees, he broke down in tears. But perhaps as a testimony to his resilience, Shah Rukh didn't give up on production. He merely strategized his next move.

In 2002, Shah Rukh founded Red Chillies Entertainment with his wife Gauri, which went on to become one of the most successful ventures in Bollywood. Red Chillies has since been responsible for producing many of Shah Rukh's films, along with numerous other successful projects.

The studio is involved in various aspects of the film industry, including creative development, production, marketing, distribution, licensing, merchandising and syndication, both domestically and internationally. Additionally, it boasts a state-of-the-art VFX studio.

The first film under that banner was Farah Khan's directorial debut *Main Hoon Na*. The film was that year's first overseas blockbuster. It had numerous sold-out screenings in the US, Canada and Britain, generating an estimated $1.3 million in revenue over a single weekend across 120 screens.[18]

Even as the distributor, Eros, tabulated the total gross for Canada and the US on Monday, it became apparent that the film was already attracting repeat viewers. The film debuted on seventy-nine screens in the US and Canada, setting a record for an Indian film, only to set another by adding five more screens the following week.[19] 'Typically, we reduce the number of screens in the second week, but the response to this film has been phenomenal,' said Lokesh Dhar, a studio representative of Eros.

In the US and Canada, the film earned approximately $704,651 on opening day, with most Saturday-evening screenings selling out nationwide. With an average of $9,000 per screen, it reportedly ranked as the fifteenth-highest-grossing film in the US, where *Mean Girls* topped the box office with a $24-million haul.

In the UK, *Main Hoon Na* secured the seventh spot in weekend grosses, according to trade publications. It garnered about $600,000 across roughly forty screens, boasting the highest per-screen average of $15,000 nationwide. The highest-grossing film in England was *Kill Bill Vol. 2*, raking in $2 million in its second weekend.[20]

Main Hoon Na became one of the top ten openings in England since Mani Ratnam's *Dil Se..* Additionally, the film set a record for highest grosser at the box office by a female director in India—no other Indian female director has been able to match Farah Khan's success yet.

Farah and Shah Rukh both knew what worked about the film—it was the desi potboiler that audiences expected a Hindi film to be. She said at the film's launch, 'This film has everything. It is a 1970s Hindi commercial film—mother, dying father, obedient son, romance, comedy, and a lot of action. In short, doses of everything that you see in a Hindi film.'[21]

Shah Rukh as producer fully backed her vision. He always let his directors go wild with the story, and supported it whole-heartedly. This was a hat tip to the glorious storytelling of 1970s' cinema. Shah Rukh didn't mind going back in time and repackaging some of that goodness for his audience. At the film's music launch event, he said, 'These aspects were present in the films that were made in the 1970s. I mean … the kind of films that Manmohan Desai made. But let me make it clear, I am not comparing Farah Khan with the great Manmohan*ji*. The film has all those elements that are not found in today's films.'

Main Hoon Na was finally that warm hug of success for his production dreams that he was waiting for. After some ups and many downs as a producer, this film had hit the jackpot. Shah Rukh had found his rhythm, that perfect blend of story and heart that worked with the audiences. More than just the numbers, the film brought Shah Rukh a sense of accomplishment that he had sorely been missing for some time. Before this film, Shah Rukh's production ventures had been a mixed bag, but this film was different. Shah Rukh gained a new perspective when he turned producer, which opened doors for him within the industry. Apart from being a superstar actor, he was being seen as someone who could take projects from script to screen. This success created a stronger bargaining position for him, something that upped his clout as a heavyweight in the industry.

But more than anything else, Shah Rukh wasn't just acting in other people's stories any more—he was taking control and telling his own.

> "Har team mein sirf ek hi gunda ho sakta hai ... Aur iss team ka gunda main hoon"
>
> **Chak De! India, 2007**

10

RISK HAI TOH ISHQ HAI, BABY

'Why make *Psycho* again? Why make *The Sound of Music* again? Why commit hara-kiri?' Shah Rukh had said in an interview about *Devdas* during the US leg of the film's promotions. Self-aware and intuitive, Shah Rukh possesses the rare quality of reading his interviewer's mind and taking charge of the conversation. That explains why he is the one celebrity journalists love to interview. When *Devdas* was being made, he knew that the world considered his casting a blasphemy. He wasn't wrong—he was so unlike the last Devdas of Hindi cinema, Dilip Kumar. The thespian let his silences speak; Shah Rukh was larger-than-life and strikingly flamboyant. Moreover, the casting was in sharp contrast to the expectations of the audience. How will the man who is known to deliver happy stories play the king of tragedy?

Sarat Chandra Chattopadhyay's *Devdas* is a timeless tale of love, loss and self-destruction. Set against the backdrop of rural Bengal, the story unfolds the tragic life of Devdas, a young aristocrat whose deep love for his childhood companion, Parvati (Paro), is thwarted by rigid societal norms and family pride. Unable to marry Paro, Devdas descends into a path of alcoholism and despair, seeking solace in the company of Chandramukhi, a courtesan. His emotional struggle and refusal to confront his emotions take him on a downward spiral, culminating in his heart-rending death. Through its exploration of unfulfilled love and the devastating consequences of societal constraints, *Devdas* is a story that continues to resonate with readers and audiences, arguably making it one of the most iconic tales India has ever seen.

Shah Rukh wasn't Sanjay Leela Bhansali's first choice. He initially wanted to cast his *Hum Dil De Chuke Sanam* lead Ajay Devgn. In an interview in early 2024, Bhansali admitted, 'Ajay's character (in *Hum Dil De Chuke Sanam*) was my starting point to make *Devdas*. I slowly moved towards this film from there. But having gone through the process with Ajay, there was no challenge or excitement in casting him again in a similar role. It would have been a process of continuation instead of creation. With Shah Rukh, it was a completely new experience. I wanted my Devdas to be a simple, volatile, boy-man, who is angry and mean and yet has a sad streak that shimmers in his eyes.'[1]

Bhansali gave everything he had to *Devdas*. While he had already made great films such as *Khamoshi* and *Hum Dil De Chuke Sanam*, this was the movie he made to scale up and show the world what his true voice as an artiste was. 'I knew I would never make a better love story, because there is none,' he said on the eve of its release.

But the world was baffled by his decision to revisit the film. Imagine if someone were to suggest a do-over of *Mughal-E-Azam*. Just like K. Asif had set the bar high with *Mughal-E-Azam*, so had Bimal Roy in the 1955 *Devdas*. It is difficult, if not impossible, to retell these stories.

There was another aspect that was working against the movie. This was the new millennium. Films such as *Dil Chahta Hai* had released the year before and changed the vocabulary of Hindi cinema. The films then were sharp and contemporary, in a way speaking of the times they were being made in. They could no longer afford the luxury of moving at a languid pace, and modern-day romances, as defined in *Dil Chahta Hai*, were just '*aaj Pooja, kal koi dooja* [today it's Pooja, tomorrow it's someone else]'. At such a time, how could a lover drinking himself to death and marinating in the pain from his heartbreak be a relatable story for anyone? Nabendhu Ghosh, scriptwriter for Bimal Roy's *Devdas* (1955), even said ahead of Bhansali's release, 'You see, Saratbabu placed Devdas on a pedestal. He is a unique character. People are attracted to Devdas because of his intensity of love. The language, the dialogues he utters—they are wonderful. He could have done wonderful things if he had won Paro. He did not. He lost everything, but he did not mind. And he did it convincingly. Today, people cry, ruminate and grieve. Then they forget. But Devdas was all about *sadhana*, *tapasya* (devotion, penance).'[2]

However, Bhansali knew a story as powerful as *Devdas* could be reinterpreted for generations. He wasn't wrong. Seven years later, Anurag Kashyap made his own version of it, *Dev.D*, with a little bit of rock and roll thrown in.

Ahead of *Devdas*'s release, Bhansali explained, 'Many people ask me why I chose to remake *Devdas*. I wanted to make a film that celebrated grandeur and grace. Gandhi*ji* (Mahatma Gandhi) was a very frail man. When he walked on the road everyone turned around to look at him. Why does everyone stand up the minute Lata*ji* (Mangeshkar) enters a room? It's her aura which commands respect. It's what is inherent in her that makes people worship her. Likewise the qualities in Sarat Babu (Sarat Chandra Chatterjee)'s novel are timeless. Also, love can never be outdated!'[3]

Bhansali went wild with the cinematography and set design. It was grand, emotionally dramatic and visually opulent. It was this film that served as the blueprint for all his future films. The film was expensive and lavish, and that became his trademark style of film-making henceforth. The visuals he had in mind for his *Devdas* were something 1980s' and 1990s' storytelling couldn't fathom. In Bhansali's *Devdas*, Chandramukhi's kotha is transformed into an ornate palace, with a budget of Rs 12 crore ($2.6 million). Madhuri Dixit, who played Chandramukhi, donned a 30-kg lehenga for the song '*Kaahe Chhed Mohe*'. Paro's house, done up in 157,000 pieces of stained-glass artefacts symbolizing her delicate beauty, cost Rs 3 crore ($650,000). Every song in the film was a spectacular set piece, requiring extensive rehearsals and dozens of dancers. The final budget reached Rs 50 crore ($11 million). Bhansali himself admitted that the costs were exorbitant, around Rs 60 crore ($13 million) at that time, as were the sets, designed by Nitin Desai, and the costumes, by Neeta Lulla for Aishwarya Rai, and Abu Jani and Sandeep Khosla for Madhuri Dixit and Shah Rukh. Production stretched over 275 days, significantly adding to the expenses. Each song required thirteen to fifteen days of shoot, with hours dedicated to lighting up each frame. Despite the high costs, the team remained enthusiastic and committed. 'The biggest investment that we have made in the film is of human effort. My team has put in a lot of hard work in the film. And that is the biggest cost, one that cannot be valued.'[4]

The risk of unravelling a classic in the times of masala potboilers did not deter Bhansali. 'Our primary purpose wasn't profit. It was to create something we believed in. Even a minor musical piece has been treated elaborately with a huge orchestra and chorus. Some songs are so lavishly mounted they will leave the audience spellbound. I feel this kind of conviction and honesty cannot go to waste.'[5]

Devdas's exorbitant budget became the talking point in those days. A portion of the set caught fire, and producer Bharat Shah was arrested for alleged ties to the underworld. With the many problems that the film faced during its shoot, naysayers started talking about the film's 'bad luck'. In an interview to Wild Films India, Bhansali said, 'People said this film is jinxed, this film brings bad vibes, you should shut down this film, this will be in losses. The set caught fire, Bharat bhai (producer Bharat Shah) was also in trouble, I was in a problem, Shah Rukh Khan was in a problem. We were all suffering. You don't get anything in life easily. You have to work hard. Maybe it was bad timing, or perhaps it was a test to see how long we could sustain our passion.'[6]

Bhansali was often told that *Devdas* was the story of a loser, but for him, the way the film was made and what it achieved made them all winners. 'It is no more a story of a loser. It is a story of all of us being winners.'[7]

And as Shah Rukh himself had said about *DDLJ*, great films are not planned—they are just made. *Devdas* turned out to be a blockbuster, earning Rs 70 crore.

Bhansali first took the film to Shah Rukh after *Phir Bhi Dil Hai Hindustani* had been released. Over the years, Shah Rukh had become the nation's poster boy for young love. Somewhere he had got himself stuck in the Rahul–Raj mould. His films and roles were beginning to feel similar, often blending into one another. The great thing was that it was working. The bad thing also was that it was working.

Why change what's not broken?

Shah Rukh's attempts to break away from this romantic image with *PBDHH* and *One 2 Ka 4* had been unsuccessful. Up until Bhansali's offer, Shah Rukh had neither done a period film nor attempted a character as tormented as Devdas. Initially, he wasn't particularly enthusiastic. But Bhansali, whimsical even then, was sure that he would only make the film if Shah Rukh played the titular role. He continues to do this till date, shelving projects until he is convinced of his cast. We saw it with *Inshallah*, starring Salman Khan and Alia Bhatt, and *Baiju Bawra*, with Ranbir Kapoor and Ranveer Singh—if his casting falls through, he abandons the project, at least for the foreseeable future. This was the passion that reeled Shah Rukh in, and he agreed. 'For me, *Devdas* is the greatest story ever told, the greatest film ever made,' he said.

Shah Rukh was enticed by the possessive cruelty of the young man Bhansali saw in Devdas. Though he struggled to connect with Devdas's self-destructive instincts, Shah Rukh approached the character with a modern perspective—as a man unable to commit. Devdas had the defiance of a petulant child, who would do exactly what he had been asked not to. Shah Rukh aimed to infuse his portrayal of Devdas with what he feels is the quintessential contradiction in a man's mind. 'A man is never in love with just one woman. Men are confused about what they want. They desire ownership of a woman, but also grow bored of her,' he said. Shah Rukh's Devdas was meaner and more modern than previous versions. His passion had a polished viciousness to it. For him, Devdas became 'the story of three people who loved each other so very, very much that they hurt each other and themselves'.

Shah Rukh did not even attempt watching Dilip Kumar's *Devdas* before filming. He approached the role with the calm understanding that he was not competing with one of India's greatest actors. 'If you are running with

Carl Lewis, you are relaxed because you know you won't beat him. There is no competition,' he said.

Once the looming expectation of matching up to Dilip Kumar was out of the way, he started having fun. His prep involved a fair amount of drinking. He joked with some journalists, 'One thing I did—I normally never drink—but for this film, I drank. I tell you, life can be very hard. Imagine, it is two in the morning and I have to drink Bacardi and have Madhuri [Dixit] fawn all over me on one side, while Ash [Rai] is dancing for me on the other. I tell you, life sucks!'⁹

But as soon as he got into character, the laughs dried up. The role and the performance wrung him completely. He didn't sign anything else immediately. Usually, Shah Rukh likes the relentless pace of his life and work, but he believed *Devdas* put him in touch with his inner artiste. In an interview, he explained the aftermath of the film. He talked about how Dilip Kumar had also had a similar experience when he did *Devdas*, to the extent that he had to undergo psychiatric treatment and take more than a year to recover.

Shah Rukh did not even attempt watching Dilip Kumar's *Devdas* before filming. He approached the role with the calm understanding that he was not competing with one of India's greatest actors. 'If you are running with Carl Lewis, you are relaxed because you know you won't beat him. There is no competition.'

Shah Rukh reminisced about the final day of shooting, when he was perched in the branches of a tree, holding Aishwarya Rai's hand. He recalled that he continued to hold her hand even after the shot was completed, realizing that he would miss the feeling of sadness that had pervaded his experience for an entire year. He acknowledged that sadness can bring out the best in art, and after wrapping up the film, he took a six-month break to savour the profound emotion of being sad. He explained, 'It is a very beautiful emotion to be in. We stars live in this bubble where everyone is smiling at you, where everyone loves you.

Somehow, you lose touch with real, deep-down sadness. Working on this film put us in touch with that emotion.'[10]

The film was made over two years, but it was a labour of love. Bhansali described it as 'going through a nightmare to fulfil a dream'. *Devdas* was screened at the Cannes Film Festival in 2002 in the 'Out of Competition' section. The reception was fantastic. International audiences loved the film's grandeur, story and music. This screening was a big moment for Indian cinema at Cannes. It showcased Bollywood's ability to tell stories that had global resonance. The lead actors, Shah Rukh and Aishwarya, made a memorable entrance in a horse-drawn carriage. Aishwarya's debut at Cannes with *Devdas* is still well remembered by festival regulars.

Shah Rukh Khan was cautious about declaring *Devdas* a defining moment in Indian cinema. Despite Indian film-makers in the 1950s and the 1960s such as Satyajit Ray and Raj Kapoor garnering international acclaim, over the decades the excitement around Indian films had dwindled and they had begun to be seen as 'Third World' cinema. Shah Rukh acknowledged the progress being made, mentioning milestones such as Aamir Khan's *Lagaan* being nominated for the Oscars, the international appreciation *Asoka* had received and the success of Mira Nair's *Monsoon Wedding*. Shah Rukh emphasized that these developments represented a trend in Hindi and Asian cinema, and believed that this momentum should be built upon rather than allowed to fade. 'We have been offered a platform. The road is there; the gate is in sight. We should now work towards opening it.'[11]

Rumours started doing the rounds that Indian actors were being wooed by Hollywood film-makers. But Shah Rukh maintained that the role had to justify his presence—he wasn't chasing Hollywood. Right after Cannes, he spoke in an interview about his excitement upon meeting film-maker Martin Scorsese, stating that he was thrilled just to shake his hand. He acknowledged that while he had been approached by many in the UK who were interested in having him work in their films, he had no desire to chase those opportunities. At Cannes, where everyone had their own dreams, Shah Rukh made it clear that he wanted to continue working in Hindi films. His aspiration was to see an Indian film, made in traditional Indian style, be appreciated globally, much like Roberto Benigni's

Life Is Beautiful. Although he had not received any concrete offers, he was content with his career path and was not overly concerned if such international opportunities did not materialize.[12]

Devdas proved to be a box office juggernaut, reigning supreme as the highest-grossing Indian film of its year. It raked in a staggering $35 million worldwide. The film's domestic performance was particularly impressive. It shattered opening-day records, pulling in a whopping Rs 20.9 million, the highest for an Indian film at the time. This momentum continued throughout its theatrical run, amassing a total domestic gross of around Rs 41.66 crore (Rs 57.86 crore). *Devdas* didn't disappoint overseas either, captivating international audiences and earning an estimated Rs 31.6 crore. It's worth noting that Box Office Mojo reported a worldwide collection of $5,428,774, with nearly equal contributions from domestic and international markets. However, this figure might be lower than the actual total, say desi trade pundits. The film was India's official entry for the Oscars and received a BAFTA nomination for Best Foreign Film and swept all major awards at home.[13]

But that's not why the film was crucial to Shah Rukh's career. Prior to *Devdas*, he had built a massive fan base playing the charming, heroic lead in countless Bollywood romances. *Devdas*, however, offered a dramatic shift. Here, he took on the role of a deeply flawed character (not usually associated with him after *Darr*) consumed by alcoholism and unrequited love. A previously unseen depth and versatility in his acting shone through, proving he could master roles beyond the quintessential Bollywood hero.

When the film was showcased at the Locarno Film Festival earlier this year, I stumbled upon an unusual social media page by one of Shah Rukh's fans. Close to a year of research on the book has taught me that Shah Rukh's fans can be distinctly categorized—those who are militant in their love for him and will slam any word of critique about him; female fans who repost videos of Shah Rukh that cater purely to their gender; and those who host routine 'How well do you know Shah Rukh' quizzes. Roohi, an assistant professor at an institute in Delhi, didn't fit any of these types and so I sent her a direct message on X to chat with her. For her the fan-club page was an escape from her day-to-day life, a space to be nostalgic in an unhindered way.

'I am thirty-four years old. I am in academia. Life is serious and all we talk about, even with friends, is "What is next in your career? When are you having kids?". Movies give you joy and transport you to a dreamland. This handle is very different from my real life. I have been a Shah Rukh fan since I was four. The first film I loved was *Darr* and I don't know what I loved about him in that film, but I remember asking my parents if he would come over for dinner someday. The beauty of Shah Rukh's career is that it has kept getting better over the years. Many of my childhood favourites don't match the image I have of them in my mind. But that's not the case with Shah Rukh.'

> 'It is a very beautiful emotion to be in. We stars live in this bubble where everyone is smiling at you, where everyone loves you. Somehow, you lose touch with real, deep-down sadness. Working on this film put us in touch with that emotion.'

We got talking about *Devdas*, which was a prominent conversation that week. During a discussion about the film at the festival, Shah Rukh expressed his discomfort with playing characters that demeaned women, which influenced his view of his role in *Devdas*. 'I don't want the audience to like my Devdas character, who disses a woman. In fact, I wanted it to come across as a spineless person who shouldn't be looked up to by anybody,' he said.[14]

Roohi tells me that this statement stayed with her all day. 'The film is really loud initially, but once the actors enter the frame, the drama takes over. Shah Rukh is phenomenal in the film … There is nothing to like about this man. He is saying these long dialogues that are so flowery, but the film is so well made that you enjoy it. When we see Shah Rukh play Veer or Mohan [in *Veer-Zaara* and *Swades*, respectively], we forget those men don't exist. But Devdas actually does, in different forms among us.'

Devdas wasn't just a showcase of Shah Rukh's acting chops, it also garnered him critical acclaim. He was always a mass favourite, but bowling over critics wasn't always his thing. You'd believe he didn't care much for it either, but with *Devdas*, the game had been upped. It opened doors to a wider range of roles, allowing him to explore complex characters beyond the earmarked purview of classic romantic heroes

Devdas was also a declaration of intent. Shah Rukh set his sights on a new challenge—embodying characters earlier played by Hindi-film legends. This would be a daunting task for an industry such as ours, where heroes are worshipped and stories are elevated to mythical mantles. But who else to conquer this Olympus but Shah Rukh?

In 2006 Shah Rukh followed up on his new hunger for iconic roles by playing the charismatic underworld don in Farhan Akhtar's remake of the 1978 cult classic *Don*, originally starring Amitabh Bachchan. It was a bold move, to say the least. Bachchan's portrayal of the underworld kingpin was nothing short of magnificent. Everything from the original *Don*—the character, the dialogues, the songs—was etched in the mind of every cinema-going Indian across generations. Stepping into those shoes meant facing inevitable comparisons and even the possibility of leaving his fans disappointed. With this remake, Shah Rukh was walking a tightrope—honouring Bachchan's legacy while carving his own path.

The risk wasn't limited to comparisons. Remakes are often met with a healthy dose of scepticism from the audience, who might question the need for a remake in the first place. There was a real possibility that Shah Rukh's *Don* wouldn't resonate as strongly with audiences as the original, potentially jeopardizing his own reputation. He wasn't simply picking up a role—he was attempting to redefine a beloved character for a new generation, much like what he did with *Devdas*. It was a high-stakes gamble. But Shah Rukh was willing to risk it. He would have been happy to do *Sholay* as well, but lost out on the chance. 'I would have done *Sholay*, but somebody's beaten us to it (Ram Gopal Varma is remaking the Ramesh Sippy classic, with Amitabh Bachchan playing Gabbar Singh). I am okay. I mean, I don't decide. It is the director who has to take a call. I think Sanjay Leela Bhansali was very keen to make *Devdas* and Farhan Akhtar was very keen to make *Don*. There's nothing really wonderful in remaking a film, unless the director and the actor feel it was a special film to them when they were growing up. And *Devdas* and *Don* were both very special to me. My parents used to love *Devdas* and Dilip sa'ab. And I loved *Don* when I was growing up. It was great, sort of reliving that.'[15]

Despite the inherent risks, the gamble with *Don* paid off in spectacular fashion. Director Farhan Akhtar masterfully navigated the tightrope walk of honouring the original while injecting the film with a fresh perspective. It retained the core elements that made the first *Don* a classic—the thrilling action sequences, the charismatic anti-hero, the gorgeous moll and the catchy music. However, Akhtar gave it a contemporary edge, updating the narrative for a modern audience. Shah Rukh delivered a nuanced performance, capturing the swagger and menace of Don while adding a layer of vulnerability not present in the original. *Don*'s success stemmed from a combination of factors—a director who understood the delicate balance between nostalgia and innovation, a stellar performance by the leading man and a script that resonated with both fans of the original and new audiences.

Wybhav Jaireth, a teacher and game developer based in Amsterdam, labels it his favourite Shah Rukh film. 'I love the older *Don*, but I don't think there's anything common between the two films except the names. And that's the beauty of an adaptation. To copy something beat by beat shows a lack of inventive thinking. Farhan [Akhtar] and Shah Rukh gave fans something new despite staying loyal to the original. Shah Rukh's badass swag is what makes *Don* so crackling. He has fun with the dark shades of a character, and that shows on screen.'

After 2002, Shah Rukh changed as an artiste. He was still the undisputed king of romance in Bollywood, but post *Devdas*, he experienced a metamorphosis. The artiste now had a voice. Films such as *Veer-Zaara* and *Swades* (both 2004) showed his willingness to blend the familiar with the socially conscious, using his immense popularity to deliver powerful messages.

For instance, *Veer-Zaara*, which on the surface might appear to be another love story—a charming protagonist (Veer, played by Shah Rukh), a beautiful love interest (Zaara, played by Preity Zinta) and a story that spans decades—was really about making love the one religion that bound everyone and preached the oneness of people on both sides of the India–Pakistan border.

Yash Chopra first thought of calling it 'Yeh Kahaan Aa Gaye Hum', but 'Veer-Zaara' went better with the mood of the film. 'The film's lovers are not bothered with the strife around them. For them, love is the only religion. I had finalised another script. Even the casting was done. Then, Aditya came up with this idea. He told me he could not direct this subject, that I had to do it. He narrated a few scenes, and I was hooked. Though it is a film about cross-border love, there is not a word of politics in it. Forget politics, there isn't even a slap or raised voices in *Veer-Zaara*. It is a very intense, humane and emotional story. *Veer-Zaara* is a humble tribute to my home in Punjab,' said Yash Chopra.[16]

> 'Every religion preaches peace. Then why the bloodshed for the sake of religion? Why are we destroying each other?'
> —Yash Chopra on *Veer-Zaara*

Chopra was a product of a tumultuous period in Indian history. The Partition of India in 1947 deeply impacted his life and artistic vision. Born in Lahore, then part of undivided India, Chopra's world was violently upended by the Partition. He, along with millions of others, was forced to flee his home and migrate to a new land. This displacement, a defining characteristic of his experience, undoubtedly left an emotional scar on him. The familiar streets of Lahore, the comfort of his community and the security of his childhood home were all ripped away, replaced by the uncertainty and hardship of starting anew in a foreign land.

His first film, *Dharmputra* (1961), delved into this experience and tackled themes of religious animosity and the human cost of political upheaval. The echoes of his childhood scars found closure in *Veer-Zaara*. 'Every religion preaches peace. Then why the bloodshed for the sake of religion? Why are we destroying each other?' the film-maker said in an interview.[17]

By this time, Shah Rukh had figured his way around the vocabulary of a romantic film. He knew their beats, he knew the charm of the romantic leads and he knew how to woo the ladies. He famously said during the promotions of *Veer-Zaara* that he could sleepwalk his way through a romantic movie. But that's not what this film was about. '*Veer-Zaara* is not just a romantic role. It also has a lot of pain and emotion. Though it shows a Pakistani girl, the film does not indulge in country bashing. I have never done films which indulged in country bashing. It's good for peace and mankind that there is no tension between India and Pakistan,' he said.[18]

The film also made a significant departure from tradition by featuring music composed by Madan Mohan, who had passed away in 1975. Chopra had some of the maestro's unused compositions re-recorded, with the project overseen by Madan Mohan's son, Sanjeev Kohli.

A feature in Pakistani newspaper *Dawn* in December 2004 lauded Shah Rukh for participating in films that didn't indulge in Pakistan bashing. The piece read, '*Veer-Zaara* was a second attempt to highlight the growing relations between the two nations. The first was "Main Hoon Naa" released in early 2004, which depicts an Indian military officer fighting militants from his own country attempting to derail peace moves with Pakistan. The movie has been one of the biggest hits of 2004, with critics claiming it is a true reflection of improved relations between the two countries. Khan is not alone in his stance: a series of concerts from Bollywood are being organised across the border, Pakistani stars are bagging roles in Bollywood films and vice-versa, and Indian films are being screened at Pakistani festivals.'[19]

The tide of hate was turning, and Hindi films and leading stars such as Shah Rukh had an active role to play in it.

Veer-Zaara proved to be a box office success. Estimates suggest the film grossed around Rs 95.39 crore worldwide, with a strong performance both domestically in India and internationally. Domestically the film collected an estimated net amount of Rs 41.86 crore and a gross of Rs 58.14 crore. The overseas market also contributed significantly, bringing in a gross collection of approximately Rs 37.25 crore.

However, many found the story implausible. Two lovers waiting on either side of the border to be united after twenty years just wasn't believable to many people. But three years later, the world discovered a real-life Zaara in Paramjit Kaur, an elderly woman from Hoshiarpur. Her only treasure was a photo of herself with her husband, Kashmir Singh, taken shortly after their marriage in 1964. Singh, a soldier in the Indian Army's military intelligence, was arrested in Pakistan and imprisoned in Mianwali Central Jail for over thirty years. Just when his family in India had assumed he was dead, he sent a letter home. The letter, written in Hindi and Urdu, was addressed to their son, Shashipal Singh. Despite the joy that Singh was alive, the letter's mention of a 'death sentence' worried his family. Paramjit and Shashipal pleaded with the Indian government to secure Singh's release, hoping for a reunion after decades of separation. Paramjit said in a news report, 'The Prime Minister, I believe, is flagging off a bus to Nankana Sahib on Friday from Amritsar. I want to ask Manmohan Saheb to please get his countrymen back from across the border.' However, the real-life Veer did not have the happy ending that the on-screen Veer did.[20]

Shah Rukh's next film cemented his acting prowess. We saw him in a role that saw the actor completely shorn of the persona of Shah Rukh Khan. In its place was a simple man, Mohan Bhargava, a NASA scientist who returns to a neglected village in India to meet his old nanny.

Swades, directed by his *Kabhi Haan Kabhi Naa* co-star Ashutosh Gowariker, was a radical departure from the romantic genre Shah Rukh had mastered by then. The film's first posters were unusual. Shah Rukh, dressed in simple attire and seemingly out of place, was foregrounded against a backdrop of villagers.

The film delved into themes of social disparity, the brain drain plaguing developing nations and the importance of giving back to one's country. Mohan grapples with the stark contrast between his comfortable life in the US and the hardships faced by his fellow villagers. The film was a far cry from the charismatic lover boy he usually played. He embodied the internal conflict of a man caught between two worlds, ultimately choosing to use his skills to uplift the villagers in India.

The beauty of the film was that it ideologically adopted a liberal stance while delivering a potent nationalist message. Using the village as a microcosm of contemporary Indian society, the film delved into the cultural and traditional failures to embrace the 'new'. It examined the fear and reluctance in developing nations to adopt newer technology, the abandonment of responsibilities by the young Western-educated crowd in favour of materialism, and the need for self-sustaining independence. The inspiring sequence where Mohan helps the village generate its own electricity from a stream in the surrounding hills remains memorable for this very reason.

Unlike mainstream Hollywood films that typically focused on the individual—a hallmark of Western capitalism—*Swades* showed the power and integrity of the collective. It suggested that to thrive, there must be a dismantling of social barriers and a capacity for self-criticism. While Mohan may not be a revolutionary on a broader political scale, he was someone who sought purpose and direction in a world that labelled itself a post-modern global village. *Swades* became a powerful message for educated Indians abroad, most of his NRI fan base, urging them to consider the impact they can have on their homeland.

With this newer clutch of films, Shah Rukh had started making his audiences think. It had been nearly a decade since *DDLJ* hit home with the desi crowd, and now he nudged them to do more than just reminisce through rose-tinted glasses about the home they had left behind. Shah Rukh said in an interview, 'This generation of the educated middle class is the future of our country. That is what *Swades* highlights. We want to show that the educated people from our country can bring about change, if they want to. If you have achieved everything in life and believe in genuine patriotism, you should not just say we are Indians and we're Bharatiya. Instead, you should help the illiterate.'[21]

According to him, true patriotism of the current era lies in making tangible contributions to society. Shah Rukh's character, Mohan Bhargava, is portrayed as a complex individual with strong convictions, embodying the heroism of someone who abandons a prestigious position in the US to confront his internal struggles and contribute to his homeland. This narrative of personal growth and discovery underscores the essence of the film.

Whether it was showcasing unwavering devotion in *Veer-Zaara* or social awakening in *Swades*, his films became a canvas for his evolving voice as an artiste. Aware of his immense fan base, he put the power of cinema to use. By weaving relevant messages into stories that resonated with the audiences, he sparked conversations about critical issues. At thirty-nine years of age, he became the voice for a generation, using his stardom to inspire and provoke thought.

But the numbers told a different story. *Swades* was made on a budget of Rs 22 crore but grossed only Rs 16 crore in India. Its rights were sold for Rs 15.5 crore, yet its share was barely Rs 9 crore, resulting in a loss of around Rs 6.5 crore, roughly 40 per cent.[22]

Despite this, in 2004, *Swades* had the fourth-highest opening after *Veer-Zaara*, *Main Hoon Na* and *Mujhse Shaadi Karogi*. Upon its release, however, its viewership declined. A report on Rediff read, 'It is a Rs 300 million, three-and-half-hour long moral science lesson.'[23]

The film was too sophisticated for the average audience, who preferred more action-packed entertainment. Cinema had to help them escape into a world that was grander than theirs. The audience didn't wish to ruminate or see on screen the hardships of their day-to-day lives—the film was thus deemed boring.

The year 2004, however, belonged to Shah Rukh—there was acclaim for *Swades*, and commercial success for *Veer-Zaara* and *Main Hoon Na*. Everyone expected him to win the National Award that year, but he lost out to Saif Ali Khan for *Hum Tum*. Shah Rukh later made a jab at an award function when he told *Hum Tum* director Kunal Kohli, '*Hum Tum* was very nice. … I should have got it but that's another story.'[24]

Shah Rukh got what he wanted from *Swades*. He didn't do the film for the money, the acclaim or even the awards. History has been kinder to *Swades* than audiences and critics the year of its release. Shah Rukh perhaps knew that. He said, 'If one is looking for a deeper meaning in life, money gets a secondary or incidental status. What's really important is to

> **'If one is looking for a deeper meaning in life, money gets a secondary or incidental status. What's really important is to pursue our dreams and desires. I desire to make a film that truly entertains. If it makes a lot of money, great, but I can't do a movie only for money's sake.'**

pursue our dreams and desires. I desire to make a film that truly entertains. If it makes a lot of money, great, but I can't do a movie only for money's sake. The objective is the film and the creativity that goes into making it. The money is peripheral. If it were otherwise, it would be like passing off the side dishes as the main course!'[25]

I spoke to Zehan Motlekar, who moved back to rural Maharashtra after spending over a decade in the US. A techie by profession, his job had driven him to the point of burnout. He talked about how *Swades* inspired him to make the change. 'I was watching *Swades* one evening when I decided that if I had to change something about my life, I had to do it immediately. *Swades* wasn't just a film, it was a wake-up call for many of us. We all eventually decided to reject the relentless American life and return home. Not all of us are capable of great changes, but like Shah Rukh Khan says, one should be a man who tries their best. I am not Mohan Bhargava, but my life should benefit my country first. *Swades* inspired a whole generation to rethink their responsibilities and the meaning of true patriotism. Scenes such as when Mohan drinks water from a village boy's pot, or when he lights up a bulb with sheer ingenuity are more than cinematic moments on a 70-mm screen. They are reflections of the real challenges that India faces and the quiet heroes who work to overcome them.'

He spoke about how this role by his favourite actor made an entire generation want to make a difference. 'As a fan, Shah Rukh's portrayal in *Swades* showed me that being a hero isn't about grand gestures, but about making a difference in whatever capacity you can. It raised our expectations of cinema and of ourselves. Shah Rukh set the bar higher—not just in terms of acting, but in his choice of stories that matter. In *Swades*, he didn't just play a role—he became the voice for a generation that believes in change, and for that, we'll always hold him in the highest regard.'

With *Swades* began a wave of conscientious cinema. *Lagaan* had elements of patriotic fervour, but it was a period piece. *Swades* was contemporary and spoke to global audiences in a more intimate fashion. What started with *Swades* gave way to Rakeysh Omprakash Mehra's *Rang De Basanti* (2006) and then Shah Rukh's own *Chak De! India* (2007).

In his career, Shah Rukh was deeply affected by the failure of three films—*Dil Se..*, *Swades* and *Zero*. We'll discuss the last one in a later chapter, because that's a story that needs to be told at length—every time you beat Shah Rukh to the ground, he bounces back more gloriously than before.

> **BANIYE KA DIMAAG, AUR MIYA BHAI KI DARING**
>
> Raees, 2017

11

THE KHAN STOOD TALL

'It's a non-Shah Rukh Khan film with sixteen actresses and no love angle,' said Shah Rukh while promoting *Chak De! India*. Who would have thought the superstar would break the very mould that made him, to go on to make India's most loved sports film. But it was no easy shift, even for him. He admitted that he was scared of being so brave with his choices. 'My wife tells me I should keep experimenting. She thinks if I fail it wouldn't affect my status or me. But inside I am scared ... I am scared of *Chak De*. Over the years, my audience has seen me doing the usual song and dance stuff. Suddenly, I am doing a film where I am surrounded by sixteen girls and I don't even have a single song. I can't do this kind of film as I am not a big actor. I mean I am a big star but not a big actor to keep experimenting. I'm aware of that and it scares me. As a student, I have prepared for the exam but some last-minute jitters are still there.'[1]

Chak De! India, directed by Shimit Amin, follows a classic underdog narrative, where a struggling women's hockey team, under the guidance of a disgraced coach, overcomes challenges and achieves victory. Shah Rukh's portrayal of Kabir Khan, a fallen hero seeking redemption, is the focal conflict point.

But writer Jaideep Sahni and director Shimit Amin didn't start with Shah Rukh in mind. 'By the time the first draft was over I started feeling that it would be good if Shah Rukh Khan comes on board for this. Of course, now when you see the film, SRK brought a much-needed combination of talent, credibility, and charisma to it which you can only admire and not explain,' said Sahni in an interview in 2020.[2]

For the director, the film was eye-opening. Amin said, 'When I'd go out on Sunday mornings searching for female athletes, every single green patch that I passed had boys playing cricket. No hockey anywhere—forget female hockey players. I couldn't even see a female cricketer anywhere.'[3] It wasn't something anyone had stopped to ponder about until they read the script. It was one of those life-altering experiences.

The casting process wasn't typical. The film-maker needed women with natural athleticism. They opted for semi-athletic individuals, and then faced the challenge of transforming them into both hockey stars and believable actors. For three gruelling months, the cast and crew embarked upon an intense training regime. Rising before dawn at 4.30 a.m., they spent five hours honing their hockey skills, followed by physiotherapy sessions to recoup. Despite the uncertainty, a spirit of community emerged. Actors, both experienced and those learning the ropes, supported each other through the demanding training. This created a sense of easy camaraderie that was visible on screen as well—they weren't just playing a team, they were becoming one.

They lucked out with their leading man, who turned out to be deft at hockey. 'Shooting a match with him was easy because of the way he took to it. He knew the drill really well. As for why Shah Rukh Khan, we were just lucky. It was a huge coincidence that he turned out to be a hockey player,' Amin said in an interview.[4]

For Shah Rukh, other than being a departure from the usual after so many years, and getting to live his dream of doing a sports film, there was another conversation Kabir Khan sparked. It was a post-9/11 world and Islamophobia was rampant. The film, rather deftly, started conversations about being Muslim—and for me, this film was Shah Rukh, in turn, owning his own identity as a Muslim man.

A column on this appeared in 2007 that discussed how, in his career spanning two decades, Shah Rukh Khan has rarely played an explicitly Muslim character—aside from a fleeting appearance in Kamal Haasan's *Hey! Ram*. Even in *Chak De! India*, his character Kabir Khan's faith is subtly woven into the narrative. The script offers only hints—a name, a scruffy beard and a courteous 'aadab' as his greeting. Kabir Khan is never shown performing namaz, wearing traditional attire or verbally affirming his faith. Despite this, the underlying tension of being a Muslim in modern India quietly pulses through his journey—a subtlety that seems deliberate and in tune with Shah Rukh's nuanced approach to the role. The column explained it, 'But, much as the script overtly downplays any mention of Kabir Khan's faith, it is Khan's dilemma as a Muslim in today's India that courses through the narrative. And that's the way Shah Rukh would have wanted it, I am sure. Unlike the other two Khans who share the mantle with him.'[5]

It was a prominent conversation in those days. In an interview a few years before the release of *Chak De! India*, Shah Rukh spoke candidly about the idea of jihad. 'If some person is using the name of Islam and confusing it with jihad, I think one needs to understand the meaning of jihad. And jihad means overcoming your own frailties, your own streak of violence, and I wanted to understand all that. I've read the Quran, I've read the Bhagavad Gita, I've read the Mahabharata. But I've understood the essence that jihad is not about killing other people, jihad is about killing the badness in you. It's an emotional war, and when people use it for a physical or material war then it's a wrong use of the term. The earlier the world understands that, the better.'[6]

The shadow of the 9/11 attacks in 2001 hung heavy upon the world and led to a shift in global attitudes. Islamophobia grew in many parts of the world in the years that followed, and some political leaders used rhetoric that played on these fears, further dividing communities and stoking suspicion of Muslims. Terms such as 'clash of civilizations' and the need for a 'war on terror' were fuelling fear and hatred for Muslims across the world. This involved scapegoating Muslim minorities for social and economic problems, or using anxieties about terrorism to justify discriminatory policies.

A Rediff post describes how this shift in world dynamics affecting the average Indian Muslim led to Shah Rukh stepping up and making a statement through his films. Being a Muslim in India, particularly in the current climate, is undoubtedly challenging. Moderate Muslims, who form the vast majority of the population in India, constantly grapple with two burdens—the historical shadow of Partition and their perceived stance on Pakistan, and the present-day stigma of Muslims constantly being blamed for orchestrating terrorist activities within the country. The silence of the superstars often mirrors the broader, collective silence of society—a silence that many are complicit in, yet it is the silence of Muslims that is relentlessly scrutinized.[7] As the writer of the post said, 'I am sure SRK himself has had to face this dilemma, this doubt over his commitment to India. And it comes out in a searing line in the movie: "*Aise logo ko Partition ke time mein hi Pakistan jaana chahiye tha* [These people should have gone to Pakistan at the time of Partition]." It is a line, a charge, that must trouble SRK no end, as it does no doubt millions of other Indians, for it returns to haunt him during the movie.'[8]

The truth is that the film, though a fictional story, is deeply inspired by the life of Mir Ranjan Negi, a former Indian hockey goalkeeper, who faced severe backlash following the 7-1 defeat against Pakistan in the 1982 Asian Games final. This devastating loss led to intense personal scrutiny and blame on Negi. Despite the fact that the defeat was a collective team failure, Negi became the scapegoat. This harsh criticism forced him into seclusion, and he even faced hostility during his wedding, where unruly elements cut off the power supply to the venue. Disheartened, Negi quit the sport. However, sixteen years later, he reluctantly returned to hockey as a coach. His return saw success when India won the gold medal at the 1998 Asian Games. Determined to contribute to the game, Negi then turned his focus to training the women's team. His expertise as a goalkeeping coach helped India secure a gold medal in the 2002 Commonwealth Games in women's hockey.

In a 2021 interview, Negi recounted how *Chak De! India* came about. The film started off as a documentary, but writer Jaideep Sahni couldn't pool in the money for it. He said, 'Back then, no one talked about women's hockey. The Indian Women's Hockey Team had won the gold medal at the 2002 Commonwealth Games. A small article appeared in the newspapers, and the rest of the sports page was dedicated to cricket. One man saw this and felt really bad. He thought about doing something for women's hockey, but even with his best efforts, he couldn't go beyond collecting Rs 10,000 for them. The man in question was Jaideep Sahni, who conceptualised and wrote *Chak De! India*. He thought of writing the film in order to get the spotlight on women's hockey and get them sponsors and everything else they deserved. He travelled to Bengaluru and met the real players and got to know about me and the rest is history.'[9]

Negi helped train the team of girls in the film. 'When they (producers) were writing the screenplay, they faced some technical problems regarding hockey. Then they approached me and appointed me as the technical director of the movie. Almost 35-40 per cent of the movie was about hockey and I had to teach the girls the game so that it looked real on the screen. It was real fun working with them as some of them had never touched a hockey stick in their life,' Negi said in another interview to *Hindustan Times*.[10]

This was perhaps the first Shah Rukh Khan film that didn't have an ounce of romance surrounding his role. But how do you justify sixteen women and a film about hockey with him leading from the front? It was a risky move, as audiences strongly associated him with romantic leads.

Every artiste craves a platform to express their worldview, and for actors that platform often comes through the characters they inhabit. It is a conscious choice they are making to tell a certain sort of story, well knowing the impact of it all.

As an article published at the time observed, the movie grapples with a profound question: Can a Muslim maintain their identity while being loyal to India? Or, more pointedly, how should a Muslim respond when their loyalty is questioned? This theme resonates deeply, as Shah Rukh's character subtly conveys that, unlike others, Muslims are not afforded a second chance. When a friend advocating for him as the coach of the national women's team tries to console him with the idea that everyone deserves one mistake—'*Hum sab ki ek galati maaf*'—Kabir Khan's response is telling: '*Sabki nahi, sabki nahi* [Not everyone].' He never explicitly mentions the word 'Muslim', but the implication is unmistakable—

an Indian Muslim is not forgiven. As he reiterates later, the weight of failure is immense and not everyone can endure it. But Kabir Khan is different. After disappearing for seven years, he returns to reclaim his honour and restore public confidence in his patriotism. While training his team, he emphasizes one thing above all: India, the nation, the tricolour. Kabir Khan venerates the tricolour and embodies Indian pride. But when it comes to his personal life, he firmly closes the door in the final scene, sending a clear message: Whatever he is at home, in the public sphere, he stands as a proud Indian. The writer of a Rediff article sums up the feeling with, 'For someone like me searching for the kind of Muslim SRK will play, and I daresay the kind of Muslim SRK is, Kabir Khan is the answer. For Muslims caught in the pincer between extremism and majority scepticism, Kabir Khan provides the answer.'[11]

While actors serve the film-making process, Shah Rukh, with his immense popularity, wielded a different kind of power. He understood his influence as a kind of 'soft power', and stepping outside the familiar bubble of romance allowed him to champion causes he believed in, using his stardom to spark conversations and challenge perspectives. This shift became a way for him to overpower the limitations of playing a character and become a true thinking man's hero.

Sahni vehemently disagrees that *Chak De! India* isn't a love story. He said, 'A lot of people say that in *Chak De...* there is no love story but I would say that, of course, there is a love story, between Shah Rukh and his country.'[12] Perhaps that is accurate.

In 2007, when India won the T-20 World Cup, everyone in every city was out on the roads singing the film's title track. It became a celebratory anthem for Indians. The film's worldwide gross was in the range of Rs 102 crore (approximately $27.05 million at the time). It made Rs 66.54 crore (which is approximately $17.6 million at the time), but the film's moral victory triumphs the mathematics of it.[13]

The film cast a much-needed spotlight on women's sports in India, a previously unexplored territory, not just in mainstream cinema but also in mainstream discourse. Sahni recounted on Netflix's *The Romantics* how the bathrooms for female hockey players in their training-camp dorms didn't even have lightbulbs. Two of the female players would hold up a jersey and another player would change behind it. Such conversations about the lack of facilities in India came up in public consciousness. Why do we care so much about cricket and so little about our national sport? *Chak De! India* brought the struggles and triumphs of female athletes to the forefront, sparking national conversations and inspiring young girls to pursue their dreams of becoming sportswomen.

My friend Akanksha Bhatli, who works for Meta India, told me that she fell for Shah Rukh because of *DDLJ*, but *Chak De! India* inspired her. 'When I first came to Mumbai from Lucknow in 2013, one of the first things I did was watch *DDLJ* at Maratha Mandir. I must have seen it at least seventy times. I fall back on that film for hope, for the fact the women deserve agency in their lives. But *Chak De!* legitimized women's love for sports. It can no longer remain a male bastion when a mainstream film legitimizes women's role in it. I have loved sports since I was a kid. I have trained at Sania Mirza's academy in Hyderabad. I play squash. I swim. I have always felt women in sports aren't taken seriously. Their love for sports is not adequately prioritized. So when we spoke of district matches, it was always the boys' teams that were given the push and stature. I didn't fight for it as a kid, but the discrimination became more apparent over the years. When I watched Shah Rukh in *Chak De!*, I saw a man who led a bunch of great sportswomen to victory. I was in eleventh standard then and clueless about life, but the film was hugely inspiring for me. Women have dreams—their dreams are legitimate and their dreams deserve to win.' When India won the T20 World Cup in 2024, she played the title song on full volume for us as she celebrated the big win.

The film is even more rousing when Shah Rukh says, '*Mujhe states ke naam na sunai dete hai, na dikhai dete hai. Sirf ek mulk ka naam sunai deta hai* [Neither do I see nor hear the names of states. I just hear the name of one country]. I-N-D-I-A !' You know a film has hit its mark when its title track is treated like a second national anthem, especially during sports events!

Once he started, Shah Rukh didn't stop. He followed up *Swades* and *Chak De! India* with another powerful film, *My Name Is Khan* (2010), this time helmed by Karan Johar. This film was as personal to him as it was political.

As one of the chapters in Bhaichand Patel's *Bollywood's Top 20: Superstars of Indian Cinema* mentions, the film was a manifestation of Shah Rukh rebelling against the popular idea of what it means to be a Muslim post-9/11.[14]

The author talks about how in the library of his home, Shah Rukh keeps both 'Om' and 'Allah' symbols, reflecting his inclusive approach to faith. He has shared that his children, Aryan and Suhana, recite both the Gayatri Mantra and Bismillah with him, though their favourite celebration is Christmas. 'I am a believer ... I need to be clearly standing for the goodness of Islam ... I think I truly am [an ambassador of Islam]. I follow the tenets of Islam—peace, goodness, kindness to mankind ... I read namaz when I feel like it.' In a March 2007 interview with *Tehelka*, he emphasized his desire to reshape misconceptions about Islam, saying that he would want people to understand that Islam is not just about fanaticism or radicalism, anger or jihad in the commonly misunderstood sense. 'I'd like people to know that the actual meaning of jihad is to overcome one's own violence and weakness,' he said.[15]

Racism in the US was at its peak through the decade after the 9/11 attacks. A 2012 article in *The New York Times* wrote about how Muslim Indian artistes have been subjected to humiliating checks at the airport. 'Aamir Khan was strip-searched at a Chicago airport in 2002. Irrfan Khan, who has acted in Hollywood movies, including the Oscar-scooper *Slumdog Millionaire*, was detained twice in the past. Irrfan is also not related to the other two Khans. Director Kabir Khan was reportedly detained at least three times in 2008 while shooting (a film) in the United States.'[16] The list of those frisked also included the horrific incident when Continental Airlines employees frisked A.P.J. Abdul Kalam, the former President of India, before he boarded a flight to New York. A stand had to be taken.

In *An Unsuitable Boy,* Karan Johar listed out his reasons for making *My Name Is Khan*. A large part of it was that the heightened Islamophobia clashed with his personal values. 'I am one of those people who is very open-minded about religion. I don't have any prejudices. When there's talk about Islam and terrorism, and the association between the two, I believe there are larger political reasons for everything. You can't generalise about a religion. There are millions of people across the world who are Muslim, who are suffering on account of a faulty perception, and I felt very strongly that I wanted to tell that story,' he wrote.[17]

By the time this film was conceptualized, Bollywood was no longer kitsch. Shah Rukh didn't need to flaunt his dimples or have his hair flying stylishly to draw people to the theatres. It was the perfect time to play a Muslim man with Asperger's syndrome, who, after the events of 9/11, is driven to chase down the US President for a meeting. In a *Forrest Gump*-like story, Shah Rukh's character Rizwan, driven by personal reasons, travels across the US to tell the President one thing that needed to be heard more than anything else in those years: 'My name is Khan, and I'm not a terrorist.'

Shah Rukh didn't see the film as a response to terrorism. He said this, too, was a love story, believing that the film was about 'the butterfly effect of an incident like this. That, you know, two people who are actually unrelated to an incident

'Whenever I start feeling too arrogant about myself I always take a trip to America. [US immigration officials] always ask me how tall I am and I always lie and get away with it and say 5 feet 10 inches. Next time I am getting more adventurous. "What colour are you?" I am going to say white.'

somewhere in the world and how their lives and their love changes, and gets completely thwarted.'[18] Ahead of the film's promotions, he said in an interview that he believed in India's secular thinking. 'As far as the public is concerned, India is amazingly secular. I am a Muslim, but I have been a leading star for the last 20 years, so if you just go by that, there is no issue ever. There are vested interests who will always bring that up to provoke people, which I guess keeps happening everywhere. I just thought we should have a message about a film with humanity. Just goodness.'[19]

In a cruel case of irony in 2009, Shah Rukh, promoting *My Name Is Khan*, which deals with the issue of Muslims being stereotyped, was detained by US immigration at Newark Airport for two hours after his name triggered a security alert. A news report in *The Economic Times* read, 'It is not clear why Khan, who is a frequent visitor to the US, and only recently spent a month here shooting for "My Name Is Khan", was subjected to a "secondary inspection", which in itself does not constitute detention. ... He was questioned for nearly two hours, asked what he thought were irrelevant questions, denied the use of his cell phone (which isn't unusual; visitors cannot use mobile phones before clearing immigration) and was finally allowed to make just one phone call under the rules.'[20]

Years later, Shah Rukh uses this incident as part of his self-deprecating humour in speeches. But the incident was repeated in 2012 when he was on his way to Yale University to deliver a lecture. He was held for over two hours by immigration officials at Westchester County Airport in White Plains, New York, after he arrived with Nita Ambani on her private jet. This delay caused him to miss his scheduled appearance at Yale University. He joked about this too when he later addressed the students at Yale. 'Whenever I start feeling too arrogant about myself I always take a trip to America,' he said. Tongue-in-cheek about the US's immigration officials, he said, 'They always ask me how tall I am and I always lie and get away with it and say 5 feet 10 inches. Next time I am getting more adventurous. "What colour are you?" I am going to say white.'[21]

You'd assume that would be the last time this would happen, that lessons would be learnt and such casual racial profiling unlearnt. But in 2016 the pattern was repeated yet again. Shah Rukh was detained at Los Angeles International Airport for the third time in seven years. The reason was possibly the same—a match with a name on one of the numerous US terror watchlists.

Shah Rukh's detainment during *My Name Is Khan* promotions could be deemed a fascinating paradox. It's easy to see how being detained for a film that tackles religious prejudice could be a disillusioning experience. The inconvenience and disruption wouldn't have been pleasant either. However, the film, in its attempt to raise awareness of racial profiling, had a far-reaching impact on the global scale.

In a study titled 'Global Muslim Audiences' Polysemic Reading of "My Name Is Khan": Toward an Emergent Multiculturalism', Priya Kapoor of the Portland State University emphasized that the film made a large section of people feel represented. She wrote, 'MNIK's wrongly imprisoned Rizwan serves as a trigger to recall the many political instances of Muslims who were, and are, locked up illegally in Guantanamo and in other nameless prisons, without legal representation, as well as the atrocities meted [out] to Iraqi prisoners in Abu Ghraib. Many audience members had kept these thoughts to themselves in the years following 9/11, and had never talked to anyone outside their community or close circle of friends about terrorism, religion or identity. I was often thanked for either showing MNIK in class or holding a public screening of the film. This audience response made me aware that this particular act of film screening elicits conversations that most would not easily have [had].'[22]

Not many know that the love story shown in the film was inspired by the book *An Asperger Marriage*. Karan Johar and co-writer Shibani Bhathija did extensive interviews with the co-authors of the book Christopher and Gisela Slater-Walker.

When it came to this film, they needed an actress who could match Shah Rukh's enigma. And who better than Kajol? The first thing she asked Karan was if he really wanted to make this film. She was sure she wanted to do it. 'I knew I had a part that I could sink my teeth into. It is a complex character,' she said in an interview. And she learnt a big life lesson from it: 'It is okay to be imperfect as a human being.'[23]

The gamble paid off. Kajol was perfectly suited to do the role opposite with Shah Rukh, but while working on the film, she met a man very different from the one she had previously worked with in five films. 'On the first day of the shoot itself, it was obvious we were seeing a totally different actor,' she said of Shah Rukh. Though he had always been versatile, some of his mannerisms stood out. 'In this film he had become Rizwan Khan from the very first day. I had never expected how real Shah Rukh would be in this role. I was stunned seeing the transformation. Rizwan Khan is his biggest triumph as an actor,' she said.[24]

The film performed admirably at the box office, though its financial success differed in the domestic and international markets. In India, where the film's themes of religious tolerance likely resonated deeply with the audience, it earned a respectable Rs 82.52 crore (roughly $18.05 million in 2023). This placed it on the list of the five top-grossing films of the year, though some might argue it fell short of expectations considering its high budget of Rs 85 crore. However, the film's true financial triumph came from overseas markets. This initial surge propelled the film's total overseas gross to a staggering Rs 108.83 crore ($23.5 million), pushing the worldwide total to a whopping Rs 223.44 crore (approximately $49.2 million in 2023).[25]

Audiences raved about Shah Rukh's performance. And the message he sent through the film was acknowledged across the globe. A *New York Times* review of the film said, '[This] is one of a handful of Hindi films ("New York", "Kurbaan") about Indians living in a paranoid, post-9/11 America, and there's something fascinating about looking at this country through a Bollywood lens, even when the story is a kind of fairy tale. (Most interesting here is the link made between black Americans and Indians, especially Muslims.) Skillfully directed by Karan Johar and with an evocative score by Shankar, Ehsaan & Loy, "Khan" jerks tears with ease, while teaching lessons about Islam and tolerance.'[26]

My neighbour, who doesn't wish to be named, had a long conversation with me one evening about the film after a society meeting where he was casually fielding jokes about his Muslim identity. He was passive about it, not once getting riled up. I lacked his grace and sternly put a stop to it. I asked him if he was fearful of being assertive—he patiently explained to me that the fact that he came from great privilege meant that on most days he didn't feel threatened. He left off saying, rather kindly, that the world was staring at bigger problems. 'But then there are some days where your identity is something you feel strongly about. I felt like this post-9/11. There was a prevalent wave of hostility against the community. Watching *My Name Is Khan* was a deeply personal experience for me. As a Muslim, seeing a film that portrayed our day-to-day marginalization and struggles with such depth was incredibly validating. The film made me feel seen in a way that was rare and needed. It was as if Shah Rukh Khan and Karan Johar felt motivated to share that story with the world. Today, it would be considered a political statement. A statement against what's happening in

Gaza, what's happening to an average low-income Muslim in India. It feels like we need this message even more now, in 2024. The issues of prejudice and misunderstanding haven't gone away—if anything, they've become more pronounced. *My Name Is Khan* was ahead of its time in highlighting the importance of empathy and understanding, and its relevance today makes me sad that we're still fighting for the same acceptance and respect.'

The biggest praise for Shah Rukh came from *Avatar* director James Cameron, who said in an interview in 2010, 'Shah Rukh Khan is a star. I'm more than happy to sign a poster for him, if he'll sign a poster (of My Name Is Khan) for me!'[27]

You'll often find bestselling author Paulo Coelho recommending *My Name Is Khan* on X. In 2023, he posted, 'King. Legend. Friend. But above all GREAT ACTOR (for those who don't know him in the West, I strongly suggest "My name is Khan—and I am not a terrorist").'[28]

For now, Shah Rukh could peacefully return to his song-and-dance routines—he had said his piece.

'Messages are for the postal service, not for the films. They (films) should be entertaining.'[29] This is something Shah Rukh has maintained. While he did cinema that was incisive and sharp, he ensured his slate had a good mix of what people wanted from him—the feel-good escape of cinema and revenue-generating massy flicks.

In the decade from 2000 to 2010, Shah Rukh achieved a lot, besides experimenting to his heart's content. He did some of his most famous and loved movies, starting with *Mohabbatein*. Aditya Chopra brought back Shah Rukh as the ambassador of love in a film that starred Shah Rukh's favourite actor, Amitabh Bachchan. This is the first time they were facing each other on screen. Shah Rukh played Raj Aryan Malhotra, a music teacher who challenged the strict principal of Gurukul College, Narayan Shankar (played by Bachchan), to accept his message of love. The film explores the conflict between love and discipline, set against the backdrop of college life and the love stories of three young couples. *Mohabbatein* was a box office bonanza! It raked in a whopping Rs 90 crore worldwide (roughly $20 million then). In India alone, the film collected Rs 76.91 crore, with a strong domestic showing of Rs 41.88 crore net and Rs 18.74 crore from overseas markets. The global stardom of Shah Rukh had remained intact even as younger actors had started rising in popularity.

He followed up the success of *Mohabbatein* with *Kabhi Khushi Kabhie Gham*.... It was a tentpole production with superstars across three generations coming together in a Ramayana-like saga. The film, directed by Karan Johar, revolved around a wealthy Indian family with two sons, one biological and one adopted. The drama unfolded when the adopted son (played by Shah Rukh) married a woman from a lower socioeconomic background, against his father's wishes, and was cast out of the family. The younger son (played by Hrithik Roshan) then embarked on a journey to reunite the family. The movie boasted a star-studded cast, which included Amitabh Bachchan, Jaya Bachchan, Kajol and Kareena Kapoor, apart from Shah Rukh and Hrithik.

In his memoir, Karan described his ambition to create a modern version of the Ramayana set in a contemporary world. Inspired by Yash Chopra's *Kabhi Kabhie* and its star-studded ensemble, Karan was fixated on the idea of a grand family saga with six major stars on the poster.

For Shah Rukh, the film was an important one. 'It is a turning point. After all, three superstars are pitted in a row. Never before has such a film been made on such a large scale,' he said in an interview ahead of the film's release.[30] The film's production kicked off at the peak of the alleged Hrithik–Shah Rukh feud, and the latter was determined to maintain his composure despite the strained atmosphere. Karan had signed Hrithik for the role before the release of *Kaho Naa... Pyaar Hai*, but by the time shooting began in September 2000, the film had become a blockbuster, and the comparisons between Shah Rukh and Hrithik were heavily circulating in the media. The resulting negativity on set was unwarranted and unfortunate. Hrithik, Karan observed in his memoir, needed a bit of guidance during this period. The Bachchans did not have a close rapport with him, Shah Rukh remained distant because of the situation and Kajol was on Shah Rukh's side. In such a situation, Karan felt compelled to support Hrithik, leading to a strong friendship developing between the two. He described Hrithik as somewhat lost amid the cast, noting that Hrithik, by nature, was reserved and not the most socially comfortable person.

The film released the same year as *Lagaan* and *Dil Chahta Hai*. The reviews were varied: 'Nowhere close to the magic of *Kuch Kuch Hota Hai*', 'over the top', 'over-opulent', 'not as cool as *Dil Chahta Hai*', 'nowhere close to *Lagaan*' and '*Lagaan* remains the film of the year', among others. It was a cause for grave concern for everyone, especially Karan, that nobody was going to watch or remember *Kabhi Khushi Kabhie Gham*.... But with time, it fared exceedingly well, and endured despite other successes the same year. Karan wrote in his memoir, 'Everyone in the world knows Kabhi Khushi Kabhie Gham . . . as the go-to Bollywood film of this country. It's true. It's got the biggest brand value in Germany, in France, in Ireland. People across the world know this film. It has global love.' And numbers. It is among Dharma Productions' highest-earning films till date.

> '**Sometimes I wonder why I am always picked on. There are other actors who do the same old stuff; nobody writes about them. But if I do it, I'm criticised. Maybe people love me too much. You expect from those you know can deliver. Just like I have expectations from my son.**'

And like a lot of Shah Rukh's films, its pop culture impact was huge. It had quotable dialogues, songs such as *'Suraj Hua Maddham'* and *'Bole Chudiyaan'* and clothes that set a trend. Perhaps the most remarkable aspect of the film's impact on pop culture was its ability to resonate with a generation that wasn't even born when it was released. Even younger movie goers go back to scenes such as the one shot in Chandni Chowk or that of Rahul holding up a photo and declaring *'Aankhein bandh karke apne maa aur baba ka naam lo, phir dekhna har manzil paar ho jaegi* [Close your eyes and utter your parents' names, and you'll be able to achieve any goal]', or the scene where Shah Rukh is running towards the family home and being welcomed by Jaya Bachchan. The film also resonated with NRI audiences. While the character portrayals were considered over-the-top by those living in India, to NRIs it was a reflection of their own struggles to retain their Indian heritage while living in a foreign culture.

The film gave Shah Rukh commercial ground to build his experimental streak on. In an interview a day before the film's release, he said, 'Sometimes I wonder why I am always picked on. There are other actors who do the same old stuff; nobody writes about them. But if I do it, I'm criticised. Maybe people love me too much. You expect from those you know can deliver. Just like I have expectations from my son.'[31]

With *Kal Ho Naa Ho* (2003), directed by Nikhil Advani, Shah Rukh continued to live up to expectations. The film tells the story of Aman Mathur (Shah Rukh), a terminally ill man who enters the lives of Naina Catherine Kapur (Preity Zinta) and Rohit (Saif Ali Khan), and changes it for the better. The film was a critical and commercial success, grossing over Rs 82 crore worldwide. It received numerous accolades, including six Filmfare Awards, and is considered one of the best Bollywood films of the 2000s. *Kal Ho Naa Ho* has become a cult classic and its famous line, '*Haso, gao, muskurao … kya pata kal ho na ho* [Laugh, sing, smile … who knows if there will be a tomorrow]', continues to tell them to seize every day and live life to the fullest.

But then came *Kabhi Alvida Naa Kehna (KANK)*, again directed by Karan Johar. This remains the most polarizing of Shah Rukh's roles till date. In his attempt to continue to experiment, Shah Rukh went a little too far argued critics back then. Shah Rukh played Dev Saran, a former football player married to Rhea (Preity Zinta), a successful fashion editor. Dev's life takes an unexpected turn when he meets Maya Talwar (Rani Mukerji), a kindergarten teacher married to Rishi (Abhishek Bachchan), an outgoing event planner. As Dev and Maya grow closer, they find themselves questioning their own marriages and the meaning of true love. The film takes a close look at intimacy, adultery and sexual chemistry, all along asking what makes for a successful marriage.

His fans refused to believe that Shah Rukh could cheat on his wife, even if it was on-screen. That wasn't the norm, or the image he had built over the years. He perhaps did the film out of his love for Karan. The filmmaker had been writing a sweeping saga, which later became *Kalank*, but in a tragic turn of events, lost his father. Becoming a producer would mean he would need to find his own voice, a creative mind and a film-maker. Karan wanted to go bold and free himself from the moral constraints imposed by society. 'There was so much talk about marriage being a crumbling institution and how divorce was the new marriage and infidelity was a part of every home,' wrote Karan in his memoir. And he knew he needed Shah Rukh by his side if he were to attempt this.

Karan Johar was exasperated, frustrated and furious at the reception of *KANK*. He spoke about how the film became a topic of heated discussions at dining tables across the country. Viewers questioned Shah Rukh's actions in the film and couldn't understand why Rani Mukerji's character left Abhishek Bachchan's, who was the seemingly perfect husband. Karan was irritated by this mass judgement and found himself repeatedly trying to explain the film, saying that perhaps the reason lay in sexual chemistry—or the lack thereof. Despite Rishi being a good man, Maya simply wasn't attracted to him and, instead, found herself drawn to a crabby and irritable Dev. Matters of the heart, you see, he tried to explain. Karan in several interviews over the years has called out the hypocrisy of society, noting that people are quick to judge others without realizing that 'textbook morality' doesn't always apply to real-life situations. He was frustrated, knowing that similar dynamics often played out in people's personal lives, and yet they were quick to criticize the film.

Shah Rukh himself wasn't very convinced about whether he could play Dev. It was incredibly difficult for him to make sense of the character. Karan talked about how the character's motivations—in this case a man having an extramarital affair—were incomprehensible to Shah Rukh. He wrote in his memoir how, after a scene, he had to literally explain it to Shah Rukh: 'Shah Rukh, you are not having an affair. The character is having an affair. Can you not understand this?' Perhaps, for Shah Rukh, Dev was an antithesis of the image he had of himself as an actor, and as a man.

It was incredibly difficult for Shah Rukh to make sense of Dev. The fact that he was the antithesis of his own image played upon his mind. Shah Rukh, in an interview, said, 'In 3 hours you can't convey a message; in fact no movie can. The maximum that you can do is convey a point of view. If you look at my character, he is someone who limps while walking, has a failed career, doesn't have a very happy marriage and finds love outside it. Now KANK tells his point of view based on the circumstances impacting him.' But is it for real, he was asked. He said, 'Okay, so you may not think that this is something from your own life. It may not even be a story about someone whom you know or lives next to your house. But then there are good chances of someone down the street in a remote corner who may have gone through similar circumstances. KANK is a story from that person's point of view!'[32]

Karan was brutally vilified for doing this to Shah Rukh. 'And here I was breaking every conceivable norm. It was as if by making Shah Rukh Khan cheat on his wife on celluloid, I was doing the biggest injustice to cinema,' wrote Karan in *An Unsuitable Boy*.

In the film, Shah Rukh wasn't the typical romantic hero, chaste in his choices and moralities. He wasn't noble and was doing some pretty dishonourable things that came as a rude shock to his female fans. Gone was the charming, self-assured persona. Instead, they met a guy who was disillusioned, trapped in a loveless marriage and teetering on the edge of a mid-life crisis. In a relationship devoid of passion, living with a wife consumed by her career and far more successful, he perfectly captured Dev's rage that stemmed from empty day-to-day affairs and his inability to pursue football. Once a successful player, an accident abruptly ended his career, leaving him unable to live the life he loved. This loss fuelled much of his bitterness, rage and insecurity, especially towards his wife's career achievements. But this is never enough to redeem his character in the eyes of the audience, as it was overshadowed by the narrative of adultery. Shah Rukh plays Dev to perfection with his caustic sarcasm, passive-aggressive behaviour towards his wife and crushing cynicism at the world at large. He bowled over his fans with the sincerity of his performance, even though they didn't like him as Dev. As opposed as they were to seeing him cheating on screen, it was a performance that got the nod of approval from fans and critics alike. They, however, unanimously agreed that Dev Saran would never be their choice of man in real life. They wanted Raj Malhotra over and over again.

While most women are sceptical of Shah Rukh dissociating himself from the idea of monogamy even in films, I spoke to Deeksha Mehta, a researcher in New York who gave me an alternative perspective. She was incidentally watching *KANK* the evening I called her for the interview. 'I absolutely love that *Kabhi Alvida Naa Kehna* dares to explore the nuances of love that society often chooses to ignore or outright reject. It's so disheartening how we live in a world that judges and marginalizes people just because their love doesn't fit the conventional mould, where love is seen as legitimate only if it is within the bounds of marriage. So extramarital affairs are pure lust? That's what you'd like to believe, because in most cultures the idea of marriage is sacrosanct. But *KANK* showed marriages that are flawed and people who are exhausted from fixing it. I think of myself as Rhea. I was married to a Dev and he had a Maya. And that last scene, where Rhea tells Maya, "*Reh ke dekho, pataa chalega* [Stay with him, and then you'll understand]", is something I have said as well. The film is so real, so personal ... even the dialogues have definitely been used in real life by some. If anyone loves in a way that challenges societal norms, they are often met with scorn rather than understanding. The film's portrayal of Dev and Maya's relationship is a beautiful rebellion against this narrow-mindedness. Shah Rukh Khan, Karan Johar and Rani Mukerji created something truly special by showing a love story that doesn't conform to traditional expectations but still finds its own sense of resolution and happiness. What makes it even more powerful is how the film gives them a happy ending, which people feel they didn't deserve—they'd rather seen them punished for cheating. Isn't it better if people who love each other stay together instead of making the world around them unhappy? *KANK* allows the couple to find a sense of peace. It's so refreshing to see a film that says, "Love is complicated, and

> 'Messages are for the postal service, not for the films. They (films) should be entertaining.' This is something Shah Rukh has maintained. While he did cinema that was incisive and sharp, he ensured his slate had a good mix of what people wanted from him—the feel-good escape of cinema and revenue-generating massy flicks.

that's okay." It's not about promoting adultery, but about acknowledging that love isn't always black-and-white. The happy ending for Dev and Maya feels like a triumph, not just for them but for anyone who's ever felt judged for their own unconventional love story. It's a reminder that love, in all its forms, deserves to be honoured.'

Amid professional laurels and risks, Shah Rukh decided to keep his production company flourishing. *Om Shanti Om*, directed by Farah Khan in 2007, was Red Chillies' next. And the film made the bold move of launching a non-star kid at a time when Sanjay Leela Bhansali was putting together the large-scale production of *Saawariya*, which was to launch Rishi Kapoor and Neetu Kapoor's son, Ranbir Kapoor, and Anil Kapoor's daughter, Sonam Kapoor. Having started out as an outsider himself, Shah Rukh saw value in opening doors for new talents and fresh faces. Farah credited him entirely for Deepika's launch. 'To launch a hero is on another level. *Kyunki paisa kaun dega* [Because who will give you the money]? I launched her because of Shah Rukh Khan. He was there. So I could take that risk. ... No one is going to give you a launch unless you are a big star's son. Sorry to say, but that is the truth.'[33]

It was a typical pulpy Bollywood romantic drama that was a mix of reincarnation, romance and intrigue—a hat tip to the world of cinema. The film starred Shah Rukh in a dual role as Om Prakash Makhija, a junior artiste in the 1970s, and Om Kapoor, a superstar in the present day. Om Prakash falls in love with Shantipriya (Deepika Padukone), Bollywood star, but their love is tragically cut short when Shanti is killed in a fire. Decades later, Om Prakash Makhija is reincarnated as Om Kapoor. As he encounters Shanti again in this life, he uncovers the truth about his past and seeks revenge against Shanti's killer, Mukesh Mehra (Arjun Rampal).

Shah Rukh was particularly impressed with Deepika when they were filming. Ahead of the film's release, he said, 'It's a happy film and I think most people want to be happy. We made this film with a lot of happiness. Deepika has done amazingly well. I have been responsible for lots of heroines doing well—that is what people say—but, here, she makes me look good by her radiance.'[34]

Om Shanti Om was a critical and commercial success, grossing over Rs 200 crore worldwide. It received numerous accolades, including eight Filmfare Awards, and is considered one of the highest-grossing Indian films of all time. The film is praised for its grand scale, catchy music and Shah Rukh's over-the-top performance. *Om Shanti Om* has become a cult classic over time.

It was only right that we got an Om to talk about *Om Shanti Om*. Omy Jha, who lives in Arizona, tells me, 'Oh, let me tell you why *Om Shanti Om* is the best Bollywood film ever! It's like the ultimate love letter to all things Bollywood—it has drama, romance and that perfect touch of nostalgia that just warms your heart. Shah Rukh Khan absolutely nails it as Om Prakash Makhija, the dreamy underdog who gets a second shot at life, fame and love. It's like watching a modern-day fairy tale unfold! You can't help but get lost in the vibrant colours, the over-the-top drama and the melodious tracks that make you want to dance along. Plus, the chemistry between Shah Rukh and Deepika Padukone is just off the charts—like, how can anyone not fall in love with them?

'It's not just a movie—it's an experience that makes you laugh, cry and cheer. Whether you're a die-hard fan of Shah Rukh or just love a good Bollywood masala flick, *Om Shanti Om* is that perfect mix of everything we love about the movies. It's like living your own dream on the big screen, full of hope, second chances and a whole lot of heart. What's not to love?'

The Deepika–Shah Rukh chemistry comes a close second to his and Kajol's. The pair was seen recently in *Pathaan* and *Jawan*, after successful collaborations in *Chennai Express* (2013) and *Happy New Year* (2014). She is his lucky charm, they say. But Deepika has a different take. 'We are each other's lucky charm. But, honestly, we are beyond luck. We have a sense of ownership over each other ... I am one of the few people he is vulnerable with. There is so much trust and respect, and I think that luck is just the cherry on the top.'[35] She agreed to do a few scenes in *Jawan* even without reading the script. Her cameo ended up being much longer than she had expected.

There's a reason why Deepika, or for that matter most actors, enjoy working with him. His sets are happy spaces for the cast and crew because as a leading man and a producer, Shah Rukh takes full ownership of the set. His *Kal Ho Naa Ho* co-star Saif calls it 'the responsibility of the main lead'. In some ways, Saif credits Shah Rukh for him growing into the role of a male lead. 'I look up to him and he had influenced a lot of my thoughts on set. I felt Shah Rukh taught me so much—mainly the responsibility of the main lead—but keeping up with him was a real challenge. This role [Rohit in *Kal Ho Naa Ho*] led to me getting my first solo lead [*Hum Tum*].'[36]

Shah Rukh is a natural leader and has always been so. He sets the ambience during a shooting and has been doing so since his days on television. In the 1990s, the hierarchy of film sets was evident. Shah Rukh was the disruptor. Renuka Shahane, who worked with Shah Rukh in *Circus*, said in an interview that the first thing that struck her about him was his confidence.[37] The serial was about a circus falling apart, and Shah Rukh played the owner's US-returned son who tried to save it. Although he was from Delhi and she from Bombay, and their ways of speaking and behaving were different, Shahane felt that he was born to be a star. During one of the shoots, she witnessed around 20,000 people waiting on set just to catch a glimpse of him. This level of adulation was typically reserved for film stars, but Shah Rukh had earned it with his role in *Fauji*.

What impressed her the most was his egalitarian approach—he treated everyone equally, from producers to spot boys. His refusal to believe in hierarchy was refreshing. Despite surviving on a cola and cigarettes throughout the day, he was always full of energy, managing to handle shoots in two shifts—day and night—and still being ready for an extra shift if needed.

Shahane remembered him telling her, 'If the director says jump, you should jump.'

'He is a complete performer, it's in his bones,' she said. 'And, he thrives on appreciation.'

Another thing that she distinctly remembers about him is his respect for women, their contributions and their independence, which she attributed to his close bond with his mother, who was the driving force in his life.

She also remembers how differently he viewed the film industry back then. 'He would find the whole idea of spot boys holding an umbrella for the stars and the different treatment of them very funny. Here with Kundan Shah and Aziz sir, everybody was equal and we would have lunch together,' she said.

His professionalism is something everyone swears by. Kajol described him as having 'infectious energy on set'. She spoke of how his playful personality lightened the mood, even during intense scenes. 'What I don't like and I also find most endearing about him, is the fact that when he comes on the set, he knows all the dialogues of everybody on the set. It doesn't matter if we are doing a three-page scene, he would have memorised all the three pages,' she said.[38]

It's no surprise that he could rope in thirty-one actors in a single song for *Om Shanti Om*. Farah Khan said in a Film Companion interview that Shah Rukh gifted all the stars goodie bags containing watches, phones and more. Actresses were given saris by Manish Malhotra. But in the end they all showed up for Shah Rukh.

To women, Shah Rukh is a special person. Isha Koppikar, his *Don* co-star, spoke about the casting couch in a podcast earlier this year and how starkly different Shah Rukh was from other actors in the industry. 'For actresses, it was never about what you can do. Heroes and actors used to decide. You have heard about #MeToo, and if you had values, it was very difficult. Many actresses left the industry during my time. Either the girls gave in or they gave up. There are very few who are still in the industry and haven't given up, and I am one of them. I was eighteen when a secretary and an actor approached me for a casting couch. They told me that to get work, you have to be "friendly" with actors. I am very friendly, but what does "friendly" mean? I am so friendly that Ekta Kapoor once told me to have some attitude.'[39] But then she worked with Shah Rukh in *Don* and the most lingering bit from the shoot for her was how respectful he was towards women. 'He was such a respectful gentleman and he treated women in such high regard. He made everyone feel special.'[40]

Shah Rukh, even today, is known to ensure the safety of the female actors on his sets. He often arranges for a car full of bodyguards to escort them back to their hotels or homes if the shoot continues into the wee hours of the morning. His *Jawan* co-star Priyamani recalls an instance: 'It was Atlee sir's birthday in Chennai, so all of us were there for the birthday party. So I think this was at about 3 or 4 in the morning. We girls were going back to the hotel. He came and saw us off individually. He came to the car. And he actually had a car of bodyguards follow us up till the hotel because there was a good distance of about 45 minutes to about an hour. So he made the car follow us. We said, "You can go." They said, "No, these are special instructions given by Sir. We have to see you off."'[41]

Perhaps that's what Deepika meant when she said that Shah Rukh is her safe place. In an interview ahead of *Pathaan*, she said, 'I feel at home, I feel safe, I feel secure that he's just the person he is. I think that working with SRK is something I look forward to. He is my safe place ...'[42]

In 2013, Shah Rukh started an unusual trend in Bollywood, an industry known to be male-driven and patriarchal. On International Women's Day he announced that in all his films, the leading actress's name would appear before his in the credits. 'I would request all those who I am working with, starting with *Chennai Express* (to do it). I don't know whether this is going to bring a change but the point needs to be raised.' It was his attempt to achieve gender equality in an industry where even the most popular female stars do not have pay parity. At a press meet, he said, 'They work harder, they look better, they keep the film industry together. I honestly think that they do not get the credit they deserve.'[43]

It's been eleven years, but no other superstar, production house or OTT platform has followed suit. In this, too, Shah Rukh stands alone.

> 'Aaj ... Aaj ek hasi aur baant lo, aaj ek dua aur maang lo, aaj ek ansoon aur pee lo, aaj ek zindagi aur jee lo. Aaj ek sapna aur dekh lo ... Aaj ... Kya pataa, kal ho naa ho'
>
> *Kal Ho Naa Ho*, 2003

12

PICTURE ABHI BAAKI HAI, MERE DOST …

It is a popular industry belief that stars have a shelf life, but actors are evergreen. Once a star has reached their zenith, it is only a matter of time before they fall. And it is not pleasant when the dream factory crashes. In an interview recounting Rajesh Khanna's decline, his wife Dimple Kapadia said, 'It was my first encounter in life with failure. When a successful man goes to pieces, his frustration engulfs the entire surroundings. It was a pathetic sight when Rajesh waited at the end of the week for collection figures but the people didn't have the guts to come and tell him.'[1]

Then how is it that the Khan triumvirate has stayed strong for almost thirty-five years? It is a routine industry conversation about how they have persevered despite everything. Trade gurus believe a superstar is someone who is able to give a bumper opening, bring people to the theatres on the very first day, regardless of the film's quality. But Karan Johar has a whole different definition of what superstardom is. He says, 'The magnetism, the aura, the mystery, I don't think this generation has it. When I was at a party, and Mr Amitabh Bachchan, Mr Dilip Kumar walked in, Mr Shah Rukh Khan walked in, there were heads turning everywhere, I have seen it. That aura, everybody feeling their presence, that was power, that was stardom. That was glory. Today, everybody is much easier, more casual, more accessible, more available. I know which gym you go to, which Pilates class you go to, I know what you eat, I know who you meet, I know everything about you, how can there be any mystery about you?'[2]

You can tell when a superstar is in the vicinity. The aura is palpable. Karan narrates the story of his fiftieth birthday party in an interview: 'When Shah Rukh Khan came to my party, you could feel the thumping energy of the younger generation. You know that SRK is SRK, that kingdom that he has, that feeling that he evokes, it's true. If he walked in right now, you would feel his energy even if you didn't see him. You can sense Shah Rukh. He was the only one who didn't walk the red carpet, and came from the other side at my party. So I could see that from the younger movie actors, maybe from as young as Ananya Panday, right up to his peers, everybody felt that aura.'

And I can say this from experience. I could feel there was a powerful being around me ... it was in the air. Shah Rukh was shooting at YRF Studios, and I was there to meet a friend who was working on *Fan*. She rushed out of the studio to see me. A few minutes later, I sensed something larger-than-life behind me. I turned around and it was Shah Rukh, talking to someone. My friend asked me if I wanted to say hello. But I stood there, smiling, thinking of that five-year-old me who had gone with her mother to watch *DDLJ* at Priya cinema in Calcutta. It was happening. I was seeing Shah Rukh in the flesh. But as a young journalist, you have to learn the art of restraint. The fan child has to take a backseat to the journalist you hope to one day become. So I stood there looking at Shah Rukh for a minute or so, and left. On the rickshaw ride back to my hostel, I wondered what it was about the aura I had felt. Was it magnetism? How did I know there was someone around? A decade later, I think I know the answer. Superstardom is like a superpower—some simply have it, and some don't.

And even in that first experience, I knew Shah Rukh would always have it. Regardless of the fate of his films at the box office. Shah Rukh has gone beyond being an actor or even a star. He is an unattainable dream that people keep going back to. He helps people hope. He is an emotion.

But even for someone like him, the lack of box office success can amount to feeling a little less of that love from fans. After the raging success of the 2000–2010 decade, he could feel the audience's expectations shifting. He couldn't be that dreamy romantic hero any more. People were gravitating towards potboilers and action. The world was still recovering from the economic meltdown of 2008 and romance had become a luxury. The industry needed films that guaranteed sales. Romance is an intimate genre, whereas action and drama have the legs to penetrate the masses. In 2009 Aamir Khan delivered *3 Idiots*, a social comedy that was a takedown of the education system in India. Made on a budget of Rs 55 crore, the film made over Rs 400 crore of lifetime business.[3] Money was crucial in Bollywood at this time and every penny mattered.

> 'The magnetism, the aura, the mystery, I don't think this generation has it. When I was at a party, and Mr Amitabh Bachchan, Mr Dilip Kumar walked in, Mr Shah Rukh Khan walked in, there were heads turning everywhere, I have seen it. That aura, everybody feeling their presence, that was power, that was stardom.'
> —Karan Johar

By 2010, Shah Rukh realized that taking artistic risks solely for personal satisfaction wasn't an option any more. His films carried the weight of hundreds of crores of rupees, and his production house Red Chillies Entertainment depended on financial success. Big-budget films became a necessary safety net for potentially smaller, riskier projects. It was a precarious choice between choosing crowd-pleasers and going against the tide to up the ante.

Shah Rukh chose the latter when, in 2011, he went bigger, grander and gutsier with his choices. He put his might behind *RA.One*. It seemed like a crowd-pleaser—superhero films had proven to be successful. The *Krrish* franchise set up by Rakesh Roshan had shown that India liked its home-grown superheroes. *RA.One* was designed as one.

It was announced amid much fanfare. Trade insiders pegged this as the most expensive movie ever made, with costs crossing the Rs 100-crore mark. From an international crew and Senegalese-American musician Akon recording two songs for them, *'Criminal'* and *'Chhammak Chhallo'*, to grand sets and state-of-the-art technology and visual effects, Shah Rukh gave the film everything. There was even a Rajinikanth cameo thrown in.

This sci-fi thriller was one of its kind in India. During the film's promotions, Shah Rukh said, 'I have made a movie in which nobody can say that it is a second-rated technology. *RA.One* will take Bollywood movies' technology to the world. It is part of my legacy in Bollywood, which has given me so much. I want our cinema to be the best in the world. The movie will leave a mark internationally. I got inspired by a lot of superhero movies but I have made an original movie. It is a family entertainer. Everything is there in the industry but we were not making such films. We have the best theatres in the world, so why could we not make a technology-based movie?'[4]

However, throughout the making of the film, discussions in the media veered towards its budget more than its technological finesse. There was a great deal of talk about how indulgent it was to attempt a film of this nature so soon after the economic meltdown. In an interview, Shah Rukh addressed the chatter, saying he and a lot of important people in the film didn't take a fee. 'Let me put it this way that I have never acted in a more expensive film and I have acted in the most expensive films in the country. I do not know some of the films made down in south like *Robot* and maybe another one or two, they spent a lot of money on the films. But a lot of it has also got to do with the artistic money in it, like the talent money in it. In this film I would be very honest, except me and apart from me also, there is a lot of talent who has not taken money for the film. They have talent and they said that just spend it on the film. I would say, yeah, it is the most expensive film made in India as far as my knowledge goes,' he said.[5]

When the press asked to quote the exact amount that had gone into making the film, director Anubhav Sinha said, 'All I can say is that the amount of money Shah Rukh has pumped into the film is unimaginable. Trust me, it will all show on screen. I can see how passionate Shah Rukh is about this film and he has taken it upon himself to make *RA.One* the biggest of them all.'[6]

After two years of production and crores of money, the film was released on 26 October 2011. It broke box office records and made over Rs 200 crore worldwide. But there were hardly any profits because the film's costs were so high.

The money, the scale, the vision all looked fantastic on the big screen, but the film's storytelling was wobbly. Critics didn't think much of it despite its flawless visuals. Reviews got personal. One went to the extent of branding the film 'Shah Rukh's most expensive midlife crisis'.[7]

Not one to lash out, but neither one to take it lying low, Shah Rukh did respond to the negativity in an interview. Admitting that he was unhappy with the reviews, he agreed that some of the backlash was due to the film's extensive marketing. Despite this, he laid emphasis on the film's commercial success and how it lived up to the idea of him taking the genre forward. What he didn't like were the personal remarks. 'There was this gentleman who wrote in his review that Shah Rukh is going through a midlife crisis. I do not think they have the guts to say it on my face,' he said.[8]

It was one of the rare times he discussed his 'outsider' status in the industry. Shah Rukh said that despite having worked in the industry for two decades, he still felt like an outsider. He said he tends to keep to himself, focus on his work and spend time with his family. He acknowledged that everyone had an opinion on films, and the criticism was bound to come. 'It is there in the air, like you have virus in the air,' he said.

In the end, though, Shah Rukh said he was glad his children enjoyed the film. His reason for making the film was rather simple. Besides giving fans a technologically superior film, he wanted to make the film for his children too. His son Aryan, who was fourteen then, had a preference for action, while his daughter found his 'singing' in films unusual. Understanding the tastes of the younger generation, Shah Rukh wanted to take on roles that were funnier, sweeter or involved action scenes to align with his children's interests.[9]

Anubhav Sinha was devastated with the reviews. He made his next film, *Tum Bin 2*, five years later, and eventually bounced back only in 2018 with the scathing social drama *Mulk*. In an interview to *Variety* in 2023, he lamented, 'Today, *Ra.One* is a hit, but when it was released, they called it a flop. That was a time when the industry wanted Shah Rukh to fail, because they couldn't deal with this size.'[10]

That same year *Don 2* was released. The action thriller, a sequel to the 2006 *Don*, was a hit. Reviewers liked the ingenious thinking, the story, the action sequences and the cast's performances—and they particularly liked Shah Rukh's reprisal of his role as Don. At the time of its release, in December 2011, *Don 2* stood as the third-highest-grossing Hindi film of the year and was considered one of the top-grossing Indian films overall. But Anubhav Sinha was right in that the industry wanted Shah Rukh to fail. Field veterans would tattle to young kids like us about how the stardom of Shah Rukh was bound to dwindle in this decade. It was almost like they were making a prophecy, and hoping it would come true.

That year, before *Don 2*'s release, Shah Rukh also returned to Yash Raj Films to work with Yash Chopra, who was returning to the director's chair after seven years. At that time no one knew that this film, *Jab Tak Hai Jaan*, would be their last together. Yash Chopra was quite tense about directing this time around, something rather uncharacteristic of him. In an interview to *The Telegraph*, he said, 'I have mixed feelings. I am excited. I am nervous. I am very tense. I am scared … In these seven years, the world has gone very, very far. And wonderful film-makers have come into the field. I want to make a small, simple love story … nothing else … I am feeling nervous about it because I don't know what the audience wants today. The audience has changed. I am starting my film with Shah Rukh Khan, Katrina Kaif and Anushka Sharma. I will be releasing the film on Diwali. I pray to God that everything goes well.'[11]

Jab Tak Hai Jaan was a classic Yash Chopra romance. It told the story of Samar Anand, a bomb disposal expert in the Indian Army, played by Shah Rukh. The film unfolds as his diary is discovered by film-maker Akira Rai (Anushka Sharma), which reveals Samar's past as a struggling immigrant in London and how he fell deeply in love with Meera Thapar (Katrina Kaif). However, a tragic event forced them apart, leading Samar to return to India and to a life of danger. Akira is drawn to Samar but also feels compelled to reunite him with his lost love, Meera. The film explores themes of love, destiny and sacrifice, set against the backdrop of breathtaking locations.

The film was Aditya Chopra's idea to bring his father Yash Chopra back to directing. Shah Rukh was their first choice and filming was adjusted around his schedule. Katrina was cast as the leading lady, while Anushka Sharma played the sprightly documentary film-maker determined to uncover the story of the 'Man Who Cannot Die', as Shah Rukh's character was known in the film.

The film was shot in Mumbai and then moved to London for a thirty-five-day shoot, and back to Kashmir and Ladakh.

Yash Chopra might have sensed that this would be the last film he would make. '*Dil kehta hai bohot ho gaya* [My heart says this is enough],' he said on his eightieth birthday in a conversation with Shah Rukh.[12]

Shah Rukh remembers him getting very emotional during the shooting of the film. In *The Romantics*, he talked about the time they were shooting in Ladakh. 'I was doing a shot in Kashmir, but then he came and said, "*Yaar, teri picture khatam ho gayi* [Your film is over]." I said, "*Kya bol rahein ho aap* [What do you mean]?" He said, "*Last shot hain, bas. Ab toh kuch raha nahi. Picture khatam* [This is the last shot. Nothing else is left. The film is over]." He became very emotional. Then he kind of started crying. He said this could be our last shot. I said why last shot? So he said, no, there are no more shots left for you. I said yeah, but we'll make the next one. He said yeah ... *last hain, yaar. Last shot hain* [This is the last shot].'

Nothing had prepared people for Yash Chopra's death. He was finishing the film's edits and had a slight fever. But within a few days, he passed away from multi-organ failure that had started off as dengue.

For Bollywood, it was a bolt from the blue. A legend was gone. And now the road to his film's release was riddled with issues. The edit was yet to be wrapped up. Aditya Chopra had to take the reins of the film and put the finishing touches on it.

Jab Tak Hai Jaan was to have a Diwali release, but clashed with another big-budget film, Ajay Devgn's action-comedy *Son of Sardaar*. Both were aiming for Diwali box office glory, and controversy erupted over alleged unfair practices. Devgn accused Yash Raj Films of using its dominant position to pressure theatres into giving *Jab Tak Hai Jaan* more screens, potentially squeezing out *Son of Sardaar*. Whispers of Yash Raj Films signing contracts with theatres showing *Ek Tha Tiger* that required them to mandatorily screen *Jab Tak Hai Jaan* as well started doing the rounds. The studio, of course, denied these allegations, but Devgn took the matter to the Competition Commission of India. The commission, however, found no evidence of wrongdoing and sided with Yash Raj Films.[13]

The clash took a turn for the personal, with Kajol siding with her husband on the matter. Everyone felt the timing of this made things worse for the film. For Shah Rukh, the passing of Yash Chopra was a profound loss, and it felt to him as though he had lost a father all over again. Reflecting on the events that unfolded around the release of the film, he said it would have been disheartening if this had occurred while Yash Chopra was still alive. He found the situation 'silly and amusing', noting that the release date had been known for a year, suggesting that the makers of *Son of Sardaar* were also aware of it. He believed that concerns about theatre availability should have been addressed earlier, saying. 'If you are worried that you have fewer theatres, then you should have booked them earlier. Because your business house did not and we did, why hold it against us? The onus lies on the buyer. It's a free market, not a monopolistic one, he said.'[14]

He further explained that the star system in the industry thrives because of the free market. 'Is someone going to tell me not to release my film on Friday? It is a personal choice of the exhibitors. They can take whichever film they want. The exhibitors represent the consumers to me,' he said.

It was a strange time for Shah Rukh. He was still coping with Yash Chopra's loss, while promoting their last film together. 'No one is immortal. No matter how big a man is, no one can escape death. It makes you realize that even good people have to pass away. He passed away without any pain. If it were my father, I would wish him the same.'[15]

Jab Tak Hai Jaan was released as scheduled and proved to be a major box office success. The film raked in over Rs 2.36 billion globally, translating to roughly $28 million based on 2012 exchange rates. Domestically, the Indian audience contributed significantly, with the film netting over Rs 1.2 billion (gross figures can be even higher). It was Yash Chopra's final love letter to cinema and the last time we saw our favourite hero romance with his trademark all-consuming passion.

After the year he had had, Shah Rukh wanted to do a light film. Around the same time, Rohit Shetty approached him with a remake of *Angoor*. Though that didn't work out, they went on to do *Chennai Express* together, which, incidentally, Shetty had originally planned on doing with Ajay Devgn. The film clashed with Devgn's dates for other projects, and Shah Rukh was finalized for the role.

Deepika Padukone was cast as the female lead, making *Chennai Express* their second film together after the massive success of *Om Shanti Om*. The film, a commercial entertainer with a romantic storyline, followed Rahul's (Shah Rukh's) journey from Mumbai to Rameshwaram. Notable cast members included southern stars Sathyaraj (of *Baahubali* fame), making this his Bollywood debut, and Priyamani, who performed a hit item number in the film.

Chennai Express was a money churner, even though critics were disappointed by the quality of the film. 'The audience is impressionable; they ask, "tell me what am I coming to watch". I needed to tell them that it's not a *Chak De* (a serious drama), nor is it an action film or a Southern remake. It is a comedic film and a clean and straight-forward family entertainer that is easy on the eye. It is not [Pedro] Almodovar, but it is not *Iron Man* either,' Shah Rukh said.[16]

This was a time Bollywood was obsessing over box office returns. The reviews weren't flattering, but the film was fun. It wasn't what was expected of Shah Rukh, but his fans let it pass. Every male star was betting their reputation on the ability to generate impressive numbers. Shah Rukh had his touch. 'Much as I would like to deny it, it is a monkey off my back and a donkey off my mind,' he told *Mint Lounge* about the Rs 100-crore mania. 'If I knew why the film clicked, I would make another one.'[17]

Hindustan Times' supplement *Brunch* claims to have coined the term '100-crore club'. Trade pundit Komal Nahata in his column wrote, 'It only admits stars whose films have made the biggest bucks. Welcome to the 100-crore club, a term used by the film industry segregating the more successful stars from the rest: only those actors whose films net Rs 100 crore or more are approved for membership.'[18] Every top star in the country was gunning for this club. It was a chase, a rat race—and the one thing that suffers the most when this happens is quality.

This was reflected in Shah Rukh's next movie, which turned out to be the dance-themed comedy *Happy New Year* (*HNY*), helmed by Farah Khan. The duo took a few months to find a co-producer. As Shah Rukh said jokingly, 'I am not going to put the pressure of too many wedding dances on myself.' Someone as sharp as Shah Rukh knows exactly what he is doing and why.

It was a heist comedy with an ensemble cast. The story revolved around a team of six amateur dancers who enter a prestigious dance competition in Dubai as a cover to pull off a heist and avenge a personal betrayal.

The film made money. *Happy New Year* grossed approximately Rs 385 crore ($56 million) worldwide. It performed exceptionally well in both domestic and international markets. But Shah Rukh's reputation took a hit. Again, it was not what one expected of him. Jaya Bachchan slammed the film at an event she was attending. '*HNY* is the most nonsensical film I've seen in recent years. I said that to the film's lead actor as well. I watched it only because Abhishek was part of it. I told him he's a great actor if he can act stupid in front of the camera like that. I can't be part of what is being done in films these days and hence I don't do films any more. Unfortunately cinema today is about business, not art. We call good films art house cinema. What does that even mean? All cinema is art.'[19]

Perhaps, like many, even Shah Rukh fell prey to the thrill of box office numbers. After all, the fabled multi-crore clubs had been established and headlines were always bandying about numbers. Directors such as Farah Khan and Rohit Shetty guaranteed those numbers.

Shah Rukh's next was *Dilwale*. It was a tentpole film, helmed by Rohit Shetty, bringing him and Kajol back on screen as a couple.

In 2014, Shah Rukh extended an olive branch to Devgn. As per a news report, while driving past Mehboob Studio in Bandra, Shah Rukh noticed Subhash, Rohit Shetty's trusted assistant, who informed him that the *Singham Returns* team was shooting nearby. Instead of going home, Shah Rukh made a spontaneous detour to the set. He walked up to Devgn and embraced him warmly, leaving everyone present stunned.[20] 'We are not good friends as we don't meet often. We are very casual. Whenever we meet we are like colleagues ... It is all normal between us,' Devgn told the press in 2015 when asked about the rivalry.[21]

Dilwale also starred Varun Dhawan and Kriti Sanon. It was a mix of romance and action, and received mixed reviews from critics. Critics felt that Shah Rukh's films were consistently not meeting the expectations set by his early career and that he was being driven in his choices mainly by commercial success and not pushing creative boundaries. Fans, on the other hand, were upset that Shah Rukh was being wasted in these roles.

Shah Rukh was adapting to the times, but his efforts weren't working with the people who loved him.

He was sure that the film would reinvent him and Kajol. He told *Forbes* that he believed new directors were bringing their unique film-making styles to the table; Rohit Shetty wanted to revisit Shah Rukh and Kajol's iconic romantic chemistry on-screen but through a fresh lens that aligned with his own sensibilities.

Shetty envisioned a version of Shah Rukh and Kajol that was distinct from their past roles. Initially, Shah Rukh and Kajol were uncertain about some scenes, feeling they were unfamiliar. However, after Shetty showed them a rough cut, they were both genuinely impressed by how it felt both new and reminiscent of their earlier work.

At the box office, this time Shah Rukh's film clashed with Sanjay Leela Bhansali's epic romance *Bajirao Mastani*, starring Ranveer Singh, Deepika Padukone and Priyanka Chopra. The fact that the fight was such a close one was baffling.

As a reporter with *The Times of India* then, I was put on the job of covering *Bajirao Mastani* extensively. I travelled with Ranveer and Deepika to Ahmedabad for one of their events, interviewed the stars and saw the drama about the clash unfold from close quarters. Ranveer was visibly nervous, not because he wasn't sure of his performance or worried Shah Rukh's film would beat his. He was happy to be beaten by Shah Rukh. But he was worried about the film not working at all. It is not uncommon for such clashes to harm the business or scope of a good movie. For instance, the charming little *Meri Pyaari Bindu*, which later achieved cult status with cinephiles, went unnoticed at the box office because it was released around the same time as *Baahubali*.

Two days before the film's release, we were doing a release-day piece with Ranveer and Deepika at the Mumbai suburban hotel Sun-n-Sand. Through the interview, Deepika did most of the talking. Ranveer was unusually quiet. When someone like Ranveer dials it down, the silence is deafening. After the interview, I asked him, 'What are you thinking?' He smiled and said, '*Jaan lagaa di hai picture mein. Chalegi na* [I have given the film my all. It will work, right]?' I smiled back and reassured him that of course it would.

I watched the film the next day and was wowed by Ranveer's performance. I didn't see the actor in the role at all—I only saw the character. Behind the lavish costumes, Ranveer Singh had vanished and left us with Bajirao for three hours.

> The country was changing. Perhaps even for the man, who for all practical purposes was the most famous Indian in the world and the most loved man in the country. Recognizing that there were things beyond his control, Shah Rukh, who had his ear to the ground, knew he had to do a film that was novel, innovative, sharp and shocking all at once.

Dilwale's press screening was next door and for the first time in my life, I delayed watching a Shah Rukh film. For, in *Bajirao Mastani*, Bhansali gave us a sweeping love saga that you wanted to savour a bit longer.

I watched *Dilwale* at a packed theatre that weekend. I enjoyed it. The music was great; Shah Rukh–Kajol as always were great. But that box office clash was truly about who made the better film. The answer to that was resoundingly clear to anyone who watched both the films that same weekend.

Bhansali's historical epic performed strongly in domestic markets, thanks to positive word-of-mouth reviews, eventually outperforming *Dilwale*. This had never happened before. Shah Rukh had never lost in a clash. This was a first.

But his star power helped *Dilwale* conquer the overseas market and its international reach secured its victory in the global box office war.

Critics weren't happy with *Dilwale*, and the audience watched it regardless—but one could feel that the love for Shah Rukh was diminishing. The audience can only forgive that much and, over the next few films—*Fan, Raees, Jab Harry Met Sejal*—the cracks that appeared with this film began to show.

There was another reason why *Dilwale* suffered at the box office. The issue of merit aside, Shah Rukh made a bold statement about the state of affairs in India. 'There is intolerance, there is extreme intolerance. It is stupid to be intolerant and this is our biggest issue. Religious intolerance and not being secular in this country is the worst kind of crime that you can do as a patriot.' He also said that 'people put words into the air even before thinking', adding that India 'will never be a superpower if we are not going to believe that all religions are equal'.[22]

This led to a dip in the film's earnings, as right-wing outfits opposed screenings in Rajasthan and Bihar, and protests were held in Ghaziabad, Pune, Jabalpur and Varanasi, among other cities. However, Shah Rukh stood by his statement. 'I have not said anything that I should apologise (for). I will fall in my own eyes if I do that.'[23] Acknowledging the impact of the protests, he said that he had seen messages on WhatsApp and social media, and heard about the screenings being disrupted, which he knew had affected the film's box office performance.

He expressed his disappointment that his words had been misinterpreted and hoped that those interested in watching the film would not be misled by those who misconstrued his statements. Shah Rukh felt saddened by the situation, apologizing to anyone who had been upset, and encouraged audiences to see the film for what it was—a work made with love by the entire cast and crew. He found it disheartening that something intended to bring joy could become controversial or misunderstood.

The country was changing. Perhaps even for the man, who for all practical purposes was the most famous Indian in the world and the most loved man in the country. Recognizing that there were things beyond his control, Shah Rukh, who had his ear to the ground, knew he had to do a film that was novel, innovative, sharp and shocking all at once. He didn't miss the brewing discontent, and tried to make up for it with *Fan*.

A psychological thriller directed by Maneesh Sharma, the film starred him in a dual role. '*Connection bhi na kamaal ki cheez hai, bas ho gaya toh ho gaya. Wi-fi, Bluetooth se bhi zyada strong hai apna connection. Woh sirf star nahin hai, duniya hai meri* [Connections are truly amazing; once they are made, they are made. It's stronger than Wi-Fi and Bluetooth, our connection. He's not just a star; he's my whole world],' said Shah Rukh as his doppelganger fan in the film.

The story revolves around Gaurav Chandna, a young and obsessive fan of Aryan Khanna, a Bollywood superstar. Gaurav's admiration for Aryan is boundless and he dedicates his life to imitating and idolizing him. However, when Gaurav's attempts to meet Aryan in person are unsuccessful and he feels slighted by his idol, his obsession takes a turn for the dark. Gaurav embarks on a mission to prove his loyalty to Aryan. His actions escalate into a dangerous game of cat and mouse, where the line between admiration and obsession blurs, leading to unforeseen consequences for both Gaurav and Aryan.

The film looks at celebrity worship in India and the psychological complexities of fandom. Shah Rukh was perfect in the film and satisfied critics, both as the superstar Aryan Khanna and his obsessive fan Gaurav Chandna. He brought depth and nuance to this story of hero-worship in show business.

The reviews were great. *The Indian Express* said, '*Fan* is a triumph. Shah Rukh Khan is played to all his strengths, and he plays it just right, gliding in and out of the star and the fan, creating distinct identities and outlines in one scene, and blurring the lines just so in the next. It is a wonderful, grasping, knowing performance, the actor and the star all rolled in one, all at our service, even as they service Shah Rukh Khan's stratospheric stardom,' the critic wrote.[24]

The international reviews joined in the praise. 'Shah Rukh Khan outdoes himself twice in this dual-role psychological thriller,' noted a *Guardian* review.[25]

But this time again the numbers fell short. Despite the superstardom, the film missed the mark at the box office. The worldwide gross was approximately $27 million. This included earnings from the Indian market. In India, it didn't win the mass love it was expected to. *Fan* was not a typical commercial film and did not appeal to everyone. The film's nuanced approach contrasted with the typical entertainment-oriented fare preferred by many Indian audiences.

In 2021 *Masala!* magazine explained what went wrong with the film. 'First of all, calling *Fan* (released on April 14, 2016) one of Shah Rukh Khan's biggest flops is a bit of a misnomer. When King Khan himself has such box-office failures like *Jab Harry Met Sejal* and most recently *Zero*, *Fan* doesn't seem like the worst choice in the world,' it said.[26] Instead of the typical larger-than-life portrayal of Shah Rukh, the film presented a psychological thriller that did something unexpected—it suggested that Shah Rukh was human. This unconventional approach contributed to the film's lack of success. *Fan* struggled to find its footing, wavering too much between genres to appeal to all audiences. It didn't offer enough action and thrills for the mainstream masala movie fans, nor was it deep enough in its psychological exploration to attract indie film enthusiasts. However, the film deserves recognition for its ambition—its attempt to depict one of Bollywood's most powerful figures not just as a star but as a man.

The same year he starred in a crowd-pleaser, but he never claims it to be his film. *Dear Zindagi* belongs to Alia Bhatt, but would it be what it is without Shah Rukh as Jug?

The film was a coming-of-age drama directed by Gauri Shinde, released in 2016. Alia Bhatt played Kaira, a young cinematographer in Mumbai. Dissatisfied with her relationships and struggling with emotional turmoil, Kaira seeks guidance through therapy sessions with Dr Jehangir Khan, played by Shah Rukh. As Kaira delves into her past and confronts her insecurities, Dr Khan helps her navigate the various aspects of her life, offering unconventional yet insightful advice. Through their sessions, Kaira begins to understand the importance of self-acceptance and forgiveness, and learns to embrace life's imperfections.

The film was among the first to explore themes of mental health, self-discovery and the complexities of modern relationships.

In a chat with Film Companion, Shinde recalled that when she narrated the part to Shah Rukh, he said, 'Okay, what do I have to do?' 'And that was it.' Shinde said. 'He got it.' He tapped into the details of the script. 'This is this person. Light, humorous, kind of what Shah Rukh is in real life where you sort of trust him, you just believe him. I can't think of anyone else who could have played Jehangir Khan. Because of him people have taken therapy a bit seriously. Because I needed a mainstream actor and a star. Apart from him being awesome and a great actor, when he says words, you want to listen.'[27]

Alisha Cariappa, a fan who now lives in Melbourne, tells me, 'I needed that film to nudge me into therapy. All my life I knew I was different. But until *Dear Zindagi* came around, I didn't know how much I needed to see a therapist. The scene where Jug takes Kaira for a walk on the beach and makes her call her parents and talk for a minute, I realized I needed to tackle the ghosts of my past if I had to have any hope of stability in the future. I don't think I would be half as convinced if there wasn't Shah Rukh playing Jug. He has a way of speaking to you and convincing you without being coercive.'

Were we imagining it, or was Shah Rukh's stardom really on the decline? Even as someone covering the industry, I couldn't tell. There were constant murmurs that the era of the stars was over. More and more actors were choosing stories that went beyond the usual masala fare. In 2015 Salman Khan, possibly the most 'masala star' there is in Bollywood, starred in *Bajrangi Bhaijaan*, which follows the heart-warming journey of a devout Hanuman devotee, Pawan, who embarks on a mission to reunite a mute Pakistani girl, Munni, with her family across the border. The star, known to ditch his shirt in the climax of every film he does, held on to his shirt for the entire run-time of this film. In fact, his only shirtless shot was when he got beaten up by cops in Pakistan. In 2014, the film that led the domestic box office was *PK* by Aamir Khan. Seen through the eyes of an alien, played by Aamir, it took a sharp look at religious dogmatism in India.

Stars were no longer taking their stardom lightly. They were marrying content with commerce. Stardom could now pull you to the theatres, but it was the film that would make you stay. There were box office report cards drawn out every year, and Shah Rukh was no longer topping like before.

But Shah Rukh isn't a man who knows how to give up. So he tried again. He realized that investing in talented directors was important. His next was with Rahul Dholakia, a National-Award–winning director who had made the heartbreaking *Parzania* in 2007 about a Parsi boy named Parzan who goes missing during the 2002 Gujarat riots, and his family's desperate search for him amid the chaos and violence.

Raees was set in the dry state of Gujarat in the 1980s and the 1990s. Shah Rukh played Raees, a cunning young man who navigates the world of illegal liquor trade. As Raees builds his bootlegging empire, he clashes with a rival gangster and a police officer determined to take him down. Despite his criminal activities, Raees wins the respect of his community through his philanthropic acts, but a fateful encounter with a crime boss leads to tragedy, forcing Raees to confront the dark side to his ambition. The film leaves the audience with a lingering question: Is Raees a Robin Hood-esque figure or simply a ruthless criminal caught in the pursuit of power?

The film was based on the life of gangster Abdul Latif. It was gorgeously mounted. In one of the scenes, Shah Rukh, seen in one of his most menacing avatars, his eyes deeply lined with kohl, walks out of smoke and fire from a trailer. It became the talk of the town. There was swagger, oomph, action and a Sunny Leone item number thrown in. Shah Rukh had a fair amount of action to do in the film. It had the epic gangster–cop face-off, which is a proven crowd-pleaser. This was bound to work.

But like the famous industry adage goes, success is all about timing and luck. This film fell prey to the country's social unrest. Its timing couldn't have been worse. The film saw Pakistani actress Mahira Khan make her Bollywood debut.

Pakistani shows had become a rage in India after the launch of Zee's Zindagi channel in 2014. The most famous was *Humsafar* starring Mahira opposite heart-throb Fawad Khan. The two were overnight successes in India. Fawad debuted with *Khoobsurat* opposite Sonam Kapoor in 2014. And with *Raees* it was Mahira's turn. She said in a 2021 interview that she received the film offer unexpectedly. She talked about how she had travelled to Mumbai for the promotions of *Humsafar*, which was airing three years after its original release. During her visit, she received multiple phone calls that she initially ignored, until she got a message saying it was about a 'big film'. Intrigued, she decided to take the call. When she learnt it was an Excel Entertainment production—a company known for acclaimed films such as *Dil Chahta Hai*—she became interested. She was then asked to meet the director the next day. In an early-morning meeting she was briefed on the story. 'Shah Rukh Khan remained a secret. I auditioned for them the next day and later got a call saying "you have got the part". I asked them what part it was and I was told "you are the lead opposite Shah Rukh Khan".'[28]

It was all going well. The film was to be released in January 2017. But a few months before its release, the Uri attack on an Indian Army base in Kashmir led to an industry-wide ban on Pakistani actors working in India. Fawad, who was starring in Karan Johar's *Ae Dil Hai Mushkil* (released on Diwali 2016) faced the ire of fringe groups. His scenes were eventually reduced in the film as the new norm was established. Mahira, too, was banned from promoting the film. In fact, there were reports of Shah Rukh and Mahira having to sneak out to the UAE to shoot the song *Zaalima*.[29]

The optics of promoting a film without a leading lady are not great. For a Shah Rukh film, it's worse. Mahira was devastated. She told *Dawn*, 'I also want to be in an interview with Shah Rukh Khan talking about it. Why not? Why is it I get told that that's asking for too much? It isn't! It is my right. This was also my film.'[30]

Mahira was diagnosed with bipolar disorder soon after, and spoke about how the aftermath of *Raees* triggered it.[31] She spoke about how she would constantly receive threats. 'Constant tweets, constant. In fact, I would get calls and very scary ones. The only thing I wanted was, okay fine, I can't go to India to promote it, I can't enjoy this, but I hope it releases in my country. Because I knew that people would rush to the cinemas to watch it, he (Shah Rukh Khan) is really loved here. That was heart-breaking. It brought on an anxiety that I've always had inside me, the depression, it came to the surface,' she said.[32]

Back in India, Shah Rukh had his own firefighting to do to take the film to the finishing line. There were threats for him if the film were to release. The Maharashtra Navnirman Sena's (MNS's) demand that film producers who worked with Pakistani actors had to contribute Rs 5 crore to the Army Welfare Fund faced widespread criticism, with many equating it with extortion. Farhan Akhtar, co-producer of *Raees*, refused to comply with the MNS's demand. In retaliation, the MNS threatened the makers with dire consequences. Farhan was quoted as saying, 'No question of giving Rs 5 crore to the Army as they have refused to take it. We are law abiding tax payers and the state should take care of us.' Responding to his remark, the MNS cine wing president Ameya Khopkar told *Mid-Day*, '*Release nazdik aane do phir dekh lenge* (Let the film's release come closer, we will talk then).'[33]

Shah Rukh stepped in and met MNS chief Raj Thackeray to sort out the matter.

The controversy became the talking point of the film, not the film itself. No one discussed the story or Shah Rukh's character of the bootlegger mafioso or Nawazuddin Siddiqui's robust cop Majmudar. One of Shah Rukh's peers, whom I wouldn't wish to name, believes the film didn't work because director Rahul Dholakia decided to kill off the character in the end. 'Shah Rukh Khan is larger than life ... you don't bump him off! And like that, on the side of the road. You don't do that to your hero or even to your anti-hero.'

Raees collected Rs 281.44 crore at the worldwide box office, with Rs 137.51 crore from India, but it remains one of Shah Rukh's least discussed films. It is a classic example of when politics overshadows art.

That year showed Bollywood that even the mightiest of monarchs can face setbacks. Small was the new big. The film that made the most money that year was the small-budget *Secret Superstar*, which had a cameo by Aamir Khan, who produced it. The most talked-about film that year was Irrfan Khan's *Hindi Medium*. Tentpole films, be it Salman Khan's *Tubelight* or Shah Rukh's *Raees*, underperformed at the box office. The trend continued for the next two years. In a 2018 article in ThePrint, the new box office trends were explained. 'Bollywood this year was ruled by the likes of Vicky Kaushal, Rajkummar Rao and Ayushmann Khurrana, with films like *Raazi*, *Badhaai Ho* and *Stree* crossing box office goals. The Khans have almost disappeared from the limelight except for their respective annual films.'[34]

Despite grand trailers, star outings fell flat when it came to storytelling. Audiences grew weary of the repetitive roles—Salman's action-packed stunts, Shah Rukh's outdated lover-boy persona and Aamir's increasingly disconnected film choices. There was a desire for fresh narratives and more relatable characters.

The years 2017 and 2018 witnessed a dip in Shah Rukh's box office dominance with the release of *Jab Harry Met Sejal* (*JHMS*) and *Zero*.

JHMS was the first film that Shah Rukh did with Imtiaz Ali, whose projects were translating love for a whole new generation. High expectations were set. There were murmurs about the choice of genre. Everyone was gravitating towards heartland stories, simple tales and medium-budget films. Was this the time for this film? Shah Rukh said in an interview to me, 'No one can ever have enough of love. There are way too many facets of love, and Imtiaz always has a fresh perspective on romance. There's always a new way to present love stories. Imtiaz has his own language. I have never been a lover like I play in this film, and only Imtiaz could've thought of something like this.'

However, even this film didn't land. Critics found the chemistry between Shah Rukh and Anushka Sharma lacking, and the plot, which revolved around a lost ring in Europe, felt uninspired. While the film wasn't a complete flop, its domestic gross of Rs 130 crore fell short of the Rs 200 crore mark, a benchmark for Shah Rukh-starrers at the time.

The film's humour, heavily reliant on stereotypical portrayals of Europeans, didn't resonate with audiences. The central conflict—the lost ring—felt flimsy compared to the weightier themes in Imtiaz's earlier films. Additionally, the film's pacing was criticized for being sluggish, and the climax left many viewers unsatisfied.

JHMS released amid immense hype. Considering Shah Rukh's past successes with the genre and the proven track record of both the director and the actor, a Rs 200 crore+ domestic haul seemed achievable. However, the film's flaws hampered its commercial prospects.

Shah Rukh had immense faith in the project and expected it to be a major comeback vehicle after a string of films that hadn't quite lived up to expectations. In a later interview he admitted he was bruised by *JHMS*'s failure. 'I let people down with *Jab Harry Met Sejal*, which was an utter flop. But I didn't want to let anyone down; I just liked the fact that *koi story nahin thi, sirf ek ring ke chakkar mein* the two people *kheechey chale jaate hain* [There was no story; it was just a ring that kept drawing two people together] … it was a very organic, slice-of-life film. The other day I met a director who mentioned the term "slice-of-life" and I said, "*Nahin, poora pumpkin do mujhe iss baar* [This time give me the whole pumpkin]."'³⁵

As a senior journalist I spoke to told me, 'It was almost like whatever he touched was failing. Was he choosing incorrectly? I don't think so. *Jab Harry Met Sejal* was a bad film.

Despite grand trailers, star outings fell flat when it came to storytelling. Audiences grew weary of the repetitive roles—Salman Khan's action-packed stunts, Shah Rukh Khan's outdated lover-boy persona and Aamir Khan's increasingly disconnected film choices. There was a desire for fresh narratives and more relatable characters.

The chemistry didn't sit right. It felt half-baked. But with Shah Rukh, for whatever reason, he wasn't doing the sort of movies as before. He was being advised incorrectly, he was unable to read the audience or the market. Sometimes, when you are that big a star, you are in your bubble and what happens on the ground stops reaching you. People are just too eager to praise you and they stop telling you the truth. The truth was Shah Rukh was making hasty, bad decisions. He had to reinterpret what Shah Rukh means in the new world to the new-age audience who is growing up on OTT content. Something innovative, something out of the ordinary and yet rooted.'

That was the idea with *Zero*, directed by Aanand L. Rai, an ambitious sci-fi fantasy film featuring Shah Rukh as a vertically challenged man in love with a celebrated actress (played by Katrina Kaif). The film boasted high production values and a unique concept. The film didn't start with Shah Rukh. As Katrina Kaif told me in an interview, 'Initially, I was supposed to play myself in *Zero*. The film was titled "Katrina Meri Jaan".

There was a different cast on board and Shah Rukh sir wasn't part of it. Now, it's a satirical take on an actress.'

But the story changed and it eventually became the film it did. Shah Rukh chose to do it because he fundamentally agreed with it. He said to *Filmfare*, 'We spend most of our life thinking, "I wish I could be happier." Or "I wish I was like this". There are also many people telling us how we should be. Each one of us has a little bit of something missing. Nobody's perfect. (Smiles)... We should accept that as soon as possible and not waste time trying to be someone else while life passes us by … We've shown three kinds of incompleteness in the film. One is a physically challenged person, one is a mentally challenged person, who's actually a genius but has cerebral palsy. And then you have the most beautiful girl in the world, who's not complete emotionally. The faster we accept our shortcomings, the better. Aanand L. Rai has tried not to win sympathy or empathy for any of these three characters—be it from the audience or the characters themselves.'[36]

Shah Rukh believed that *Zero* was a perspective that the world needed to see. He sees himself as an incomplete artiste, driven by a constant restlessness and a desire to explore new possibilities in his roles as both actor and producer. For him, being complete would equate stagnation—it was the ongoing journey that mattered. He views achievements merely as milestones rather than end goals and doesn't approach his career with calculated targets for earnings, awards or box office success. Having spent over twenty-five years in the industry, the specifics of film success have become less significant to him because predicting a film's business outcome is beyond anyone's expertise. 'After twenty-five years of working, I feel the only reason you should work is for the happiness of your art.'[37]

With the VFX included, *Zero* was made over 200 days, unlike the customary 140. Shah Rukh was trying to push the envelope, remould himself. The journalists who attended the press screening saw the film's fate on his face even before it bombed at the box office. A senior journalist who was at the screening told me, 'Shah Rukh wanted to meet after the film and I didn't know how to escape. I didn't have the heart to tell him it was a bad film. And he was so jittery and looked so worried that it seemed he knew it was bad.' By then enough focus group screenings had happened and the verdict from them wasn't very different either.

Zero's critical and commercial drubbing undoubtedly affected Shah Rukh. He took a brief hiatus and rumours swirled about a potential career decline. The problem with *Zero* again was the same as with *Raees*—you don't cut a star to size.

This time it wasn't just another film and just another flop. It got personal. 'Shah Rukh is down to zero' was the common theme of conversations around the film. Reviewers who lauded *Fan* as gutsy thought of *Zero* as preposterous. An *Indian Express* review said, '*Zero* fails spectacularly at giving us anything we can believe in, and we go from start to finish, with disbelief growing with each passing frame.'38

After *Zero*'s failure, Shah Rukh announced a break from films at the Indian Film Festival in Melbourne (IFFM). He said, 'I just finished the last film I made and to put it lightly, it was a disaster. I said to myself that let me enjoy a little bit of un-success as I had success for so long. So I have taken some time off for the next four or five months. As a matter of fact, I'm on these breaks ... Coming here (Melbourne) and meeting people, realizing and discovering new stories, doing intellectual speaking.'39

> 'I had massive flops, and they did very, very badly. I was licking my wounds. But you know what I did? I learnt to make the best pizza in the world. I stopped listening to stories, I stopped wanting to tell stories, I made myself a little kitchen, and I started learning how to make pizzas. I learnt perseverance. Because to make the perfect round pizza, you have to first make a million square ones.'

It wasn't an ending in any way, and he had made that clear. It was merely a pause, to re-understand and re-strategize. 'What drives me to do a film is the people around me who make such great cinema ... And I think I have a huge amount of capacity to do some really good cinema. I have 20-25 years of good cinema left in me,' he said.40

Breaks aren't unheard of in Bollywood, especially with stars who are growing legs to be more and do more. After the debacle of *Laal Singh*

Chaddha (2022), Aamir Khan took a year-long break too. People close to him told me that he would read a new script every day. He didn't want to limit himself to being a star—he wanted to be bigger than that.

'What did Shah Rukh do in that time?' his fans have often asked.

When he attended the IFFM in 2019, where he received an honorary doctorate, he did an interview with Rajeev Masand in which he said he was restlessly peaceful. 'I have huge patience, huge peace and huge restlessness. I am not hyper. I have a relaxed energy. My energy evokes happiness,' he said. Shah Rukh created a lot of writers' rooms that year and busied himself as a producer, commissioning and greenlighting projects. Bobby Deol's *Class of '83* and Alia Bhatt's *Darlings* were both born in that time. In that interview, Shah Rukh admitted that he wanted to do an action film. 'I want to kick some ass; do some boxing. Say dialogues like "*Rishtein mein toh hum tumhare baap lagtey hai* [from Amitabh Bachchan's *Shahenshah*] ... But no one writes an action film for me.'[41] He also dropped his X handle in that interview, requesting film-makers to reach out to him with an action-film script.

Right after the Covid-19 years, he told everyone about the time in between. 'I had massive flops, and they did very, very badly. I was licking my wounds. But you know what I did? I learnt to make the best pizza in the world. I stopped listening to stories, I stopped wanting to tell stories, I made myself a little kitchen, and I started learning how to make pizzas. I learnt perseverance. Because to make the perfect round pizza, you have to first make a million square ones.'[42]

Destiny had something else in mind for him and the world. Covid-19 took over our lives the next year. There was a good chance none of us would ever enter a film theatre again.

I, for one, will not forget the panic of returning to the cinemas. I didn't want to be anywhere except on my couch. The first film I watched was Christopher Nolan's *Tenet*. I was the only person in an empty theatre and went with an entire bottle of sanitizer to make sure I was safe. I had Dimple Kapadia's interview scheduled for the next day, and Mr Nolan and his studio wanted us to experience the film on the big screen before we did any cast interviews.

Fear overshadowed my experience and, frankly, it didn't feel worth it. Those were the days when theatres were directed to operate at 50 per cent capacity and leave every alternate seat empty. Film-makers who could afford to hold their films did so, and others went the OTT way, selling their ready projects for large amounts to OTT platforms.

Over the Covid-19 years, 'Netflix and chill' became a lifestyle. The convenience of watching films at home gradually replaced the effort and appeal of going out to theatres. This phase marked a fundamental change in our viewing habits, one that the Hindi film industry continues to grapple with.

The impact on the stars was far-reaching. After three decades of having audiences go gaga over them, they now faced the daunting challenge of proving they could still pull crowds to the theatre. At a time when cinema owners and trade analysts were counting on them to revive the industry, the pressure was at its peak.

Aamir's big flick, *Laal Singh Chaddha*, didn't do well. Salman starred in *Radhe*, and *Antim*, too, underperformed. Shah Rukh had been shooting for two films and had disappeared from the public eye.

He had drowned himself in work. It seemed that something had changed in him while he was gone. He spoke about it at an event: '*Main thoda sa apne aap se door ho gaya. Actor ko apne kareeb rahna bahut zaroori hai* [I had distanced myself from my true self. It is very important for an actor to stay connected to their own self].'[43]

Reflecting on his time away from the spotlight, Shah Rukh explained that he never truly intended to take a four-year break. Initially, he felt somewhat disconnected from himself as an actor. The grand scale of film-making can sometimes cause one to lose focus, not in a negative way, but rather due to the sheer magnitude of it all. Known for being selective and unhurried in choosing films, he found comfort in simply resting. What began as a year-long hiatus extended unexpectedly due to the pandemic. 'In that time I watched a lot of films—all types and kinds of films. I rarely get the time to do that.'

Somewhere between the long hours of TV viewing and panic attacks during Covid-19, we all bounced back. And so did the film industry.

In 2023, Shah Rukh put all the learnings from his solitude into a film that marked his comeback on the 70-mm screen. I opened this book with scenes of celebration and revelry because maybe, beyond everything else, Shah Rukh is a celebration of old-school cinema—those days when one would wait with bated breath for a film to hit the screens, with its big, glossy posters all over the city, and get friends and family along to see it in a theatre. In those three hours inside the darkened hall, with the big screen in front playing out a new story starring our favourite actor, we all left our worries behind for glorious escapism. Often, those hours were enough to ensure we slept peacefully that night, full of hope and happiness. For what are films but gateways to wondrous stories and characters that remain with us our whole lives?

And who better to heal our hearts than someone who has had it for more than three decades—Shah Rukh Khan.

EPILOGUE

For the past two years I have wondered about the legacy of Shah Rukh Khan. In every interview I have done in 2023, every director, writer and actor has said, 'You can't compare anyone to Shah Rukh sir. He is a phenomenon. He is no longer just an actor or a star.'

Over the course of this year, he received the prestigious Pardo alla carriera Ascona-Locarno Tourism, or the Career Leopard, for his contribution to cinema. He joked that in English it means 'the leopard award for being the most awesome in the world and in the history of mankind'. A few weeks later, he made his debut on the 2024 Hurun India Rich List with a net worth of Rs 7,300 crore.

Are these awards his legacy? Is his wealth the legacy? Or the box office figures?

The answer came to me just a week before this book was going to press. It had been lying in front of me all along. I only needed someone to remind me of it.

At a dinner party that week, I bumped into an old friend. He is now a well-known director and writer. He and I had met in 2013 when I was a cub reporter on the field and he an aspiring actor. The two of us had bonded over common woes, obnoxiously high rents and the lack of good butter chicken in Mumbai.

That night, we got talking about his slew of rejections before he landed his big break.

Back in 2013, I was always on duty to drop him to his auditions because auto fares would have thrown off his monthly budget. Fair to say, I have seen his struggle. In 2015 he faced a brutal rejection. He was replaced by a star kid in a big-budget production after being told that he had the part. Of course, as the common story in Bollywood goes, he was told that 'they loved him so much' that they ended up offering him a supporting role. 'Screen time is not important. You need someone to take a punt on you. We are doing that,' they told him. He passed on the film.

It felt like the end of the road for him. His phone didn't ring for nine months after that. It was clear that he wasn't going to make it as an actor. He told himself that if nothing worked out in a year, he would go back to Delhi.

A bunch of us took turns to take him to our favourite Versova watering hole every day. Nothing fixes a broken heart like vodka. When the place would shut down, we would take an auto to Mannat. He would stare at the bungalow for hours. Some nights silently and on other nights, he'd play the song *'Chand Taare Tod Laoon'* on full volume. Every time he was angry, he'd say, *'Kisi ke baap ki industry nahi hai!'* One day mid-rant, in a dramatic moment, he dashed towards the sea and shouted, 'If Shah Rukh can, I can too!'

And he did. By the time it was 2020, his days of struggle were gone. Last week after dinner, he drove us around the city in his new car, and we crossed Mannat again that night, playing the same song.

It can be said that when you become an idea, or a metaphor, for people, that is when you have truly made a difference. And Shah Rukh Khan has become just that.

Every year, thousands of hopefuls arrive in Mumbai, driven by the dream of making it in Bollywood. And many inevitably end up in front of the star's home—a shrine to hope, success, dreams and faith.

Yet, for most, the industry remains an elusive finishing line, with only a rare few breaking into the spotlight. Everyone here is trying to sell a dream, and that is the magic of movies. But beneath the magic are a thousand untold stories of people living in the hope that it will all work out one day. Every outsider in Mumbai who is dreaming big turns to

Shah Rukh's story to remind themselves: 'Study hard. Work hard. Play harder. Don't be bound by rules, don't hurt anybody, and never, ever live somebody else's dream.' It's what makes them get up after every failed audition and try again. It's what drives them to put in that extra effort to rise a notch above the ordinary.

Everyone caught in the rush of this vast city and constantly grappling with making ends meet holds fast to the belief that if a middle-class boy from Delhi could rise to rule a city he didn't belong to and win the hearts of people he didn't know, perhaps they, too, would be just fine.

'Luck is a misnomer. Either you believe in hard work or God. In between, the excuse is luck ...'

—*Shah Rukh Khan*

A TRIBUTE

Pradeep Bandekar. This name had great value to me growing up, but I didn't realize just how much until three months ago.

Since my father's demise, I have realized the legacy he has left behind. Everything I know about the Hindi film industry, and of my own work as a photographer, comes from him. I am incredibly privileged to have had both a father and a teacher in the same person. But, more than anything else, his legacy is that of love.

Over the past few months, many have messaged and called to tell me how he made people feel. He was someone everyone in the industry sought guidance from. And that's the legacy I hope to take forward.

As I grew up to walk in the footsteps of my father, choosing to go into the same profession, he shared many learnings with me. One of the most important was: Actors are our colleagues who you should treat with respect and dignity. As someone who worked with stars every day, he insisted that it was important to keep the right expectations from them.

I never fully understood my father's enduring love for Shah Rukh Khan. I would often joke: 'You have more pictures of him than you have of me!' It was only after his death that I was able to make sense of his bond with Shah Rukh when the actor spoke at my father's prayer meet: 'Pradeep was one of my first friends in the film industry. When he took my first photograph, I felt like a star ...'

Over the course of this book, we went through all of my father's old work. It was only when I was rifling through the stacks of boxes at home, which stored the many photographs my father took over his long career, that I realized how phenomenal his life, and work, had been. His photographs captured the essence of the film industry like no one else could. My father would spend hours reminiscing about the good times on set, often regaling us with stories from the films we watched together during lockdown. He always had fascinating trivia to share about the songs, locations and actors, and I could see in his eyes a wistfulness for the times gone by.

The overwhelming sense of emptiness he has left cannot be filled. He won't be here to scan the papers, looking for my name and the photos I take. But like Shah Rukh said, he is up there in heaven, clicking pictures of those who have departed and making them look good.

—Prathamesh Bandekar

ACKNOWLEDGEMENTS

Every '90s kid has, at some point in their lives, been in love with Shah Rukh Khan. Now that you have read the book, you know I'm quoting my friend Prerona Sanyal.

It's only right that I begin by thanking him: Thank you, Shah Rukh Khan. You have made my entire generation believe in goodness. Without you, we might have been lost.

I have had the good fortune of being raised by Shah Rukh fans. Starting with my mother, my late father, aunts, uncles, cousins, my life has always been filled with them. Perhaps I attract them (just like this book). Thank you to my family, especially my mother Ellora Basu, for pushing me to work hard and for standing by my side.

When I moved to Mumbai, one of the first friends I made was Pratishtha Malhotra, another die-hard Shah Rukh fan (maybe I do attract them). We spent many of our early evenings in the city talking about life and him at the Starbucks under the Red Chillies office in Khar. It used to be our happy place. In some ways, every time we felt lonely, we had him and his movies by our side. Thank you, Pratishtha, for those evenings and for making my life in this city infinitely better with your warmth.

This book belongs to my wonderful editor, Bushra Ahmed. The past four years of working with her have been one of the most fulfilling experiences of my work life. Thank you for trusting me with this project and your incredible patience with me. Thank you to the wonderful team at HarperCollins India—Ananth Padmanabhan, Poulomi Chatterjee, Ujjaini Dasgupta, Shabnam Srivastava, Rahul Dixit, Gunjan Suyal, Anita Sharma, the team at Ashima Obhan & Associates and everyone else who has worked on this.

A big thank you to my work family at *Mid-Day*—Mayank Shekhar, Eepsita Guha, Aastha Atray Banan, Krishna Padmanabhan and Tinaz Nooshian. If I hadn't met you all, I would have never known what loving work feels like. I am who I am because of you all. Thank you to my ex-colleagues Sonil Dedhia and Uma Ramasubramanian, whom I miss very dearly.

Writing is a heartbreaking job. Everything goes wrong a thousand times before anything good comes of it. I would have given up if it weren't for my friends Shamik Bose, Debanjana Moitra, Rudrani Chattoraj, Purvaja Sawant, Garvita Sharma, Devki Pande, Tushar Joshi and Ebrahim Contractor. Thank you for holding my hand through thick and thin.

Thank you to my tribe of writers: Abhishek Thukral, Kashyap Kapoor, Raghav Raj Kakkar, Syed Shadan and Siddhi Dutta.

Over the course of writing this book, a lot happened. The best part was getting to spend time with my friend, Prathamesh Bandekar, and his family. Just like me, he, too, is surrounded by fans of Shah Rukh—from his wife, Samhita, to his father, the late Pradeep Bandekar. Bollywood remembers him as one of the most-loved press photographers of all time. My favourite memory from the writing of the book is of an afternoon spent with Pradeep Dada, as we fondly called him. We were going through over 10,000 pictures for the book, laughing and listening to stories about Shah Rukh Khan. In Dada's words, *'Yaaro ka yaar hai Shah Rukh!'* My generation will never know love like that between a journalist and a star. Words cannot capture the grief of losing Dada so suddenly while we were in the middle of this project. I am grateful that his last project was with me, and we had a wonderful time working on it. I wish he were here to see this book come to life.

After 93,000 words, I'm not sure my editor will be pleased if I add more to the word count. But I have to say this: I truly believe anyone can write a book about Shah Rukh Khan, and each book will have something new to say about this man who has the unique ability to bind this diverse country and its people together, cutting through everything that divides us.

Acknowledgements

This book contains stories of people from around the world—those who bared their hearts to me, sharing their joys and heartbreaks. I have cried with them, laughed with them and, over time, we have become a tribe that believes in love, even in a world that often makes it feel impossible. This book exists because of them, and to remind everyone who picks it up of love.

NOTES

Scan this QR code to access the detailed notes.

Here's to some of Shah Rukh Khan's most popular songs!

ABOUT THE AUTHOR

Mohar Basu is Chief Correspondent (Entertainment) at *Mid-Day*. She previously worked as a film critic at Koimoi.com and later reviewed movies for *The Times of India*. Her work focuses on the dynamics of the Hindi film industry. Her stories include in-depth coverage of censorship in films and OTT platforms, the 2016 ban on Pakistani actors in India and their eventual return with the rebirth of the Zindagi channel in 2020, and the systemic culture of sexual harassment in Bollywood, among others. Basu's reporting has contributed to industry changes, such as the creation of safe spaces at casting agencies and talent-management companies. In 2024, she was recognized by the Indian Achiever's Club in their '40 under 40' list for her piece on the toxic nature of Indian paparazzi and the rising tide of vitriol on social media.

HarperCollins *Publishers* India

At HarperCollins India, we believe in telling the best stories and finding the widest readership for our books in every format possible. We started publishing in 1992; a great deal has changed since then, but what has remained constant is the passion with which our authors write their books, the love with which readers receive them, and the sheer joy and excitement that we as publishers feel in being a part of the publishing process.

Over the years, we've had the pleasure of publishing some of the finest writing from the subcontinent and around the world, including several award-winning titles and some of the biggest bestsellers in India's publishing history. But nothing has meant more to us than the fact that millions of people have read the books we published, and that somewhere, a book of ours might have made a difference.

As we look to the future, we go back to that one word—a word which has been a driving force for us all these years.

Read.

   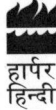